IN SEARCH OF GHOSTS

IN SEARCH OF GHOSTS

HANS HOLZER

FALL RIVER PRESS

Book Design by Lundquist Design, New York

Fall River Press
122 Fifth Avenue
New York, NY 10011

ISBN-13: 978-1-4351-0421-1
ISBN-10: 1-4351-0421-8

Printed and bound in the United States of America

10 9 8 7 6 5 4 3 2 1

CONTENTS

FOREWORD

$\mathcal{I}$ ought to explain what ghosts are, even if you have read my previous books or even if you have a ghost of your own. In my view, ghosts are the surviving emotional memories of people who have died tragically and are unaware of their own passing. A ghost is a split-off part of personality remaining behind in the atmosphere of their previous existence, whether a home or place of work, but closely tied to the spot where their death occurred.

Ghosts generally do not travel, do not follow people around, and they rarely leave the immediate vicinity of their own tragedy. Once in a while, ghosts roam a house from top to bottom, or may be observed in the garden or adjacent field. But they do not take buses and appear at the other end of town: those are free spirits, able to reason for themselves and to attempt communication with the living.

In the mind of the casual observer, of course, ghosts and spirits are the same thing. Not so to the trained parapsychologist: ghosts are similar to psychotic human beings, incapable of reasoning for themselves or taking much action. Spirits, on the other hand, are the surviving personalities of all of us who pass through the door of death in a reasonably normal fashion. A spirit is capable of continuing a full existence in the next dimension, to think, to reason, to feel, and to act, while his unfortunate colleague, the ghost, can do none of these things. All he can do is repeat the final moments of his passing, the unfinished business, as it were, over and over until it becomes an obsession. In this benighted state he is incapable of much action and ghosts are therefore nearly always harmless. In the handful of cases where ghosts seem to have caused people to suffer, there was a relationship between the person and the ghost. In one case, someone slept in a bed in which someone else had been murdered and was mistaken, by the ghost of the murderer, for the same individual. In another case, the murderer returned to the scene of his crime and was attacked by the person he had killed. But by and large ghosts do not attack people and there is little danger in observing them or having contact with them, if one is able to.

The majority of ghostly manifestations draw upon energy from the living to be able to penetrate our three-dimensional world. Other manifestations are subjective, especially where the receiver is psychic. In that case, the psychic person hears or sees the departed individual in his mind's eye only, while others cannot do so.

Where an objective manifestation takes place, and everyone present is capable of hearing or seeing it, energy drawn from the living is used by the entity to cause certain phenomena, such as an apparition, a voice phenomenon, or perhaps the movement of objects, the recreation of footsteps or doors opening by themselves, and other signs of a presence. When the manifestations become physical in nature and are capable of being observed by several individuals or recorded by machines, they are called poltergeist phenomena, or noisy phenomena. Not every ghostly manifestation leads to that stage, but many do. Frequently, the presence in the household of young children below the age of puberty or of mentally handicapped older people lends itself to physical manifestations of this kind, since the unused or untapped sexual energies are free to be used for that purpose.

It should be kept in mind that the sexual energies and the

glands producing the sexual fluids are identical with the psychic centers, and when physical energies are not used in one fashion, they are available for other uses. The so-called ectoplasm which has been observed under test conditions especially in séances with physical mediums, is nothing more than a temporary emanation from the glandular system of the medium, which must be returned to the body—otherwise serious harm will result. Ghosts, that is individuals unaware of their own passing or those incapable of accepting the transition because of unfinished business, will make themselves known to living people at infrequent intervals. There is no sure way of knowing when or why some individuals make a post-mortem appearance and others do not. It seems to depend on the intensity of feeling and the residue of unresolved problems, which they have within their system at the time of death. Consequently, not everyone dying a violent death becomes a ghost—far from it. If it were otherwise, our battlefields and such horror-laden places as concentration camps or prisons would be teeming with ghosts, but they are not. It depends on the individual attitude of the person at the time of death, whether the passing is accepted and the individual proceeds to die next stage of existence, or whether he is incapable of realizing that a change is taking place and consequently clings to the physical environment with which he is familiar, the earth sphere.

A common misconception concerning ghosts is that they appear only at midnight, or, at any rate, only at night; or that they eventually fade away as time goes on. To begin with, ghosts are split-off parts of personality incapable of realizing the difference between day and night. They are always in residence, so to speak, and can be contacted by properly equipped mediums at all times. They may put in an appearance only at certain hours of the day or night, depending on the atmosphere; for, the fewer physical disturbances there are, the easier it is for them to communicate themselves to the outer world. They are dimly aware that there is something out there different from themselves, but their diminished reality does not permit them to fully grasp the situation. Consequently, a quiet moment, such as is more likely to be found at night than in the daytime, is the period when the majority of sightings are reported.

Some manifestations occur on the exact moment of the anniversary of the death, because at that time the memory of the unhappy event is strongest. But that does not mean that the presence is absent at other times, merely less capable of manifestations. Since ghosts are not only expressions of human personality left behind in the physical atmosphere but no longer part of it, but are in terms of physical science electromagnetic fields uniquely impressed by the personality and memories of the departed one, they represent a certain energy imprint in the atmosphere and, as such, cannot simply fade into nothingness. Professor Albert Einstein has demonstrated that energy can never dissipate, only transmute into other forms. Ghosts do not fade away over the centuries; they are present for all eternity, so to say, unless someone makes contact with them through a trance medium and brings reality to them, allowing them to understand their predicament and thus free themselves from their self-imposed prison. The moment the mirror of truth is held up to a ghost, and he or she realizes that the problems they feel are insoluble are no longer important, they will be able to leave.

Frequently, the rescuer has to explain that the only way they can leave is by calling out to someone who was close in life—a loved one, or a friend, who will then come and take them away with them into the next stage of existence, where they should have gone long before. This is called rescue circle and is a rather delicate operation calling for the services of a trained psychical researcher and a good trance medium. Amateurs are warned not to attempt it, especially when they're alone.

THE DEMONS
OF TYLER

I am frequently asked to comment on poltergeists, or noisy ghosts, a term derived from the German that somehow conjures up the image of violent physical activity beyond the pale of ordinary understanding. Poltergeists have been generally considered the work of youngsters in a house, youngsters below the age of puberty, when their physical energies have not yet been channeled either sexually or occupationally and are therefore free to play pranks on others in the household. The majority of parapsychologists consider poltergeists the unconscious expression of such repressed feelings, attention getters on the part of young people, and do not connect them to supernormal beings such as spirit entities or any other form of outside influence. I have investigated dozens of cases involving poltergeists where physical objects have been moved by their own volition and found that another explanation might be the true one. In each case, to be sure, there were young people in the household, or sometimes mentally handicapped adults. I discovered, for instance, that a mentally handicapped adult often has the same kind of suppressed kinetic energy as the unused energy of youngsters—energy that is capable of being tapped by outside forces to perform the physical phenomena. I also discovered that in each and every case with which I came in contact personally there had been some form of unfinished business in the house or on the grounds on which the house stood. Sometimes this involved a previous building on the same spot. At other times it involved the same building in which the activities took place. But in each instance there was some form of psychic entity present, and it is my conviction that the entity from beyond the physical world was responsible for the happenings, rising, of course, the physical energy in the young people or in the mentally handicapped adult. Thus, to me, poltergeists are the physical activities of ghosts expressed through the psychic powers within young people or mentally handicapped older people, but directed solely by outside entities no longer in the flesh. This link between the physical energies of living persons and the usually demented minds of dead persons produces the physical phenomena known as poltergeist activities which can be very destructive, sometimes threatening, and sometimes baffling to those who do not understand the underlying causes.

The purpose of these physical activities is always to get the attention of living persons or perhaps to annoy them for personal reasons. The mentality behind this phenomenon is somewhere between the psychotic and the infantile, but at all times far from emotionally and mentally normal. But it can still be dealt with on the same basis as I deal with ordinary hauntings. That is to say, the cause of the activities must be understood before a cure for them can be found. Making contact with the troubled entity in the nonphysical world is, of course, the best way. When that is not possible, a shielding device has to be created for the living to protect them from the unwanted poltergeist activities. In the well-publicized Seaford, Long Island case years ago, a young boy in the household was held responsible for the movement of objects in plain daylight. Even so astute an investigator as Dr. Karlis Osis of the American Society of Psychical Research, who was then working for the Parapsychology Foundation of New York City, could not discern the link between the boy's unconscious thought and the unseen, but very real, psychic entities beyond the world of the flesh. In his report he intimates that the activities were due to the unconscious desires of the youngster to be noticed and to get the sort of attention his unconscious self craved. I was not involved in the Seaford case personally although I was familiar with it, having discussed the matter with Mr. Herman, the boy's father. I did not enter the case, and, at any rate, others in my field had already entered the case. I saw no reason to crowd the scene, but, with the help of medium Ethel Johnson Meyers, I did go into the background of the house independently of the investigation conducted by Dr. Osis. For what it may be worth at this late date, my sitting with Mrs. Meyers disclosed that an Indian burial ground had existed on the very site of the Seaford house and that the disturbances were due to the fact that the house had been erected on that spot. They had not occurred earlier since no physical medium lived in the house. When the young man reached the age of puberty, or nearly so, his energies were available to those wishing to manifest, and it was then that the well-publicized movement of objects occurred.

Similarly, years ago a case attracted public attention in the city of Rosenheim, Bavaria. A young lady working for an attorney in that city was somehow able to move solid objects by her very presence. Reputable witnesses, including the attorney himself, recorded a long list of paranormal phenomena. Eventually Dr. Hans Bender of the University of Freiburg entered the case and after an investigation pronounced it a classical poltergeist situation. He too did not link the activity with any outside entity that might have been present on the premises from either this house or a previous one standing on the spot. It seems to me that at the time great haste was taken to make sure that a physical or temporal solution could be put forward, making it unnecessary to link the phenomena with any kind of spirit activity.

But perhaps the most famous of all poltergeist cases, the classical American case, is the so-called Bell Witch of Tennessee. This case goes back to the 1820s and even so illustrious a witness as Andrew Jackson figures in the proceedings. Much has been written and published about the Bell Witch of Tennessee. Sufficient to say here that it involved a certain woman and a farmer named John Bell. This relationship resulted in a postmortem campaign of hatred and destructiveness ultimately costing the lives of two people. In the Bell Witch case the entire range of physical phenomena usually associated with poltergeist activities were observed.

Included were such astounding happenings as the appearance or disappearance of solid objects into and out of thin air; strange smells and fires of unknown origin; slow, deliberate movement of objects in plain sight without a seeming physical source; and voices heard out of the air when no one present was speaking. Anyone studying the proceedings of this case would notice that the phenomena were clearly the work of a demented individual. Even though a certain degree of cunning and cleverness is necessary to produce them, the reasoning behind, or rather, the lack of reasoning, clearly indicates a disturbed mind. All poltergeist activities must therefore be related to the psychotic, or, at the very least, schizophrenic state of mind of the one causing them. As yet we do not clearly understand the relationship between insanity and free energies capable of performing acts seemingly in contradiction to physical laws, but there seems to be a very close relationship between these two aspects of the human personality. When insanity exists certain energies become free and are, at times, capable of roaming at will and of performing feats in contradiction to physical laws. When the state of insanity in the mind under discussion is reduced to normalcy these powers cease abruptly.

I have, on occasion, reported cases of hauntings and ghostly activities bordering upon or including poltergeist activities. Generally we speak of them as physical phenomena. A case in point was the haunted house belonging to Mr. and Mrs. John Smythe of Rye, New York. The phenomena in this house included such physical activities as doors opening by themselves, footsteps, the sound of chains rattling, ashtrays flying off the table by themselves, and, most frightening of all, a carving knife taking off by itself on a Sunday morning in full view of two adult, sane people and flinging itself at their feet, not to hurt them but to call attention to an existing unseen entity in the house. These are, of course, the kind of activities present in poltergeist cases, but they are merely a fringe activity underlying the need for communication. They are not the entire case, nor are they as disorganized and wanton as the true poltergeist cases. In the case of Rye, New York, the physical activities followed long mental activities such as apparitions and impressions of a presence. The physical phenomena were primarily used here to make the message more urgent. Not so with the true poltergeist case, where there was no possibility of mental communication simply because the causing person was incapable of actual thinking. In such a case all energies are channeled toward destructive physical activity and there is neither the will nor the ability to give mental impressions to those capable of receiving them, since the prime mover of these activities is so filled with hatred and the desire to manifest in the physical world that he or she will not bother with so rational an activity as a thought message.

It is therefore difficult to cope with cases of this kind since there is no access to reasoning, as there is in true ghost cases when a trance medium can frequently make contact with the disturbed and disturbing entity in the house and slowly, but surely, bring it back to the realm of reason. With the true poltergeist case nothing of the sort can be established and other means to solve it have to be found. It is therefore quite natural that anyone who becomes the victim of such activities and is not familiar with them or with what causes them will be in a state of panic, even to the point of wanting to abandon his property and run for his life.

On September 1, 1968 I was contacted by a gentleman by the name of L.H. Beaird. He wrote to me from Tyler, Texas, requesting that I help him understand some of the extraordinary happenings that had made his life hell on earth during the period between 1965 and 1968. Through his daughter who lived in Austin he learned of my work with ghosts and finally concluded that only someone as familiar with the subject as I could shed light on the mysterious happenings in his home. He had purchased the home in 1964, but after three years of living with a poltergeist and fighting a losing battle for survival he decided that his sanity and survival were more important, and in 1968 he sold it again, losing everything he had put into it. The move, however, was a fortunate one, for the new home turned out to be quiet and peaceful. Once Mr. Beaird got his bearings again and learned to relax once more he decided to investigate what had occurred during the previous three years and find some sort of answer to this extraordinary problem.

I wasn't familiar with Tyler and decided to look it up on the map. It turned out to be a city of about 60,000 inhabitants also known as the "rose capital" because of the large number of horticultural activities in the area. Tyler was connected with Dallas and Houston by a local airline and was located about halfway between Dallas and Shreveport, Louisiana. It had only one television station, one newspaper, and many pleasant ordinary citizens going about their various businesses. The people of Tyler whom I got to know a little after my visit later on were not concerned with such things as the occult. In fact, anyone trying to lecture on the subject would do so in empty halls.

Howard Beaird worked in a nearby hospital and also ran a rubber stamp shop in which he had the company of his wife and more orders than he could possibly fill. Their son, Andy, was enrolled in barber school at the time of my visit and presumably later went on to cut people's hair, to everyone's satisfaction somewhere in Texas. The big local hotel was called the Blackstone and it was about the same as other big hotels in small towns. Everything was very quiet in Tyler, Texas, and you could really sleep at night. There was a spirit of not wanting to change things in Tyler, of letting sleeping dogs lie, pervading the town, and I had the distinct impression that cases such as the poltergeist case were not exactly welcome subjects for discussion over a meal at a local eatery.

It must be held to Mr. Beaird's credit that despite the indications of small town life, he felt compelled to make inquiries into the extraordinary happenings in his life, to look into them without fear and with great compassion for those involved—his wife and son. Others in his position might have buried the matter and tried to forget it. This is particularly important since Mr. Beaird was reasonably prosperous, did business with his neighbors, and had no intention of leaving Tyler. To ask me for an investigation was tantamount to stirring things up, but Beaird took this calculated risk because he could not live with the knowledge of what he had observed without knowing what had caused it.

At the time of our correspondence in September 1968 the phenomena had already ended as abruptly as they had come. This too is typical of genuine poltergeist activities, since they depend solely on the available free energies of living people. As will be seen in the course of my investigation, that energy became no longer available when the principals were removed from the house. There are other factors involved of course. It is not as simple as plugging in on a power line, but in essence poltergeist activities depend not only on the desire of the disturbing entity to manifest but also on the physical condition of the unconscious part of those whom they wish to use as power supplies.

The house, which the Beairds had to leave under pressure from their poltergeists, was on Elizabeth Street. It was a one-story ranch-type dwelling, pleasant enough to look at and then about fourteen or fifteen years old. The new owners were not particularly keen on the history of their house, and it was for that reason that I am keeping confidential the actual location, but the house had not been altered in any way after it was sold to Mr. M. and his family. One entered the house through a porch that was located somewhat above the road. There was a garage and a steep driveway to the right of the porch. Once inside the house one was in the living room, with a den to the left and a dining area to the right. Beyond the living room were the kitchen and a rather long room leading directly to a breakfast room. On the extreme left were two bedrooms. To the right of the house behind the garage was the workshop, which, in the period when Mr. Beaird owned the house, was used as such. There was also a concrete slab separating the shop from the garage proper, and the garage contained a ladder leading up to the attic.

Howard Beaird, then sixty-five years of age, was a pleasant man with a soft Texas accent, polite, firm, and obliging in his manner. He was overjoyed when I expressed an interest in his case and promised to cooperate in every way. In order to get a better understanding of the extraordinary happenings at Tyler I asked that he dictate in his own words the story of these three years in the house that had come to be three years of unrelenting terror. The principals in this true account besides Howard Beaird were his wife Johnnie, whom he has always called John; a daughter named Amy who lived in another city and was in no way involved in the strange experiences at Tyler; and a son, Andy, then nineteen, who shared all of the unspeakable horror of the experiences between 1965 and the early part of 1968 with his parents. Most of the others mentioned in his account had been dead for several years.

A few were still alive, and there were some names in this account Mr. Beaird had never heard of. Here then is his own account of what occurred in the little house on Elizabeth Street in Tyler, Texas:

"My story begins late in 1962, which marked the end of nearly thirty-nine years of employment with the same company. During the last twenty years of that time John worked in the same office with me; in fact her desk was only a few feet from mine. We both retired during September of 1962.

"John had always been an excellent employee, but devoted much more time to her work than the company required for any one person. She would never take a vacation, and was rarely away from her job for more than an occasional half-day at a time, mainly, I think, because she would trust no one with her work. I cannot say when her mind began to show signs of being disturbed, although as I think back on it today, she had acted a little strangely for several years prior to the time of our retirement. This, however, did not affect her work in any way; in fact she was even more precise in it than ever, and I suppose I just could not bring myself to admit that there was anything wrong with her mind. At any rate, during the next twelve months she began to act more abnormally than ever, especially when at home, until finally it was necessary that she enter a mental institution. Although the doctors there were reluctant to release her, they did not seem to be having any success in whatever treatment they were giving her, so I asked for her release after about three months. Being of modest means I naturally had to obtain employment as soon as possible, but after working about three months in another city I felt that it was most urgent that I move my family from Grand Saline, Texas, to some other place, believing that the mere change of environment would play a big part in helping John to get well. So about the middle of 1964 we moved to Tyler,

Texas, a place where John had always said she would like to live. We bought a house, and after about a month I obtained employment that, in addition to a sideline business I had begun a few years before, gave us a satisfactory, if not affluent living. For almost a year John did seem to be better; she would go places with Andy and me, to the Little League baseball games in which Andy played, to the movies occasionally, sometimes to bowling alleys and a miniature golf course, but all of a sudden she stopped.

"She had not actually kept house since we made the move and had not cooked a single meal for Andy or me. About this time she started walking to a drugstore in a nearby shopping center for breakfast, and then in the late afternoon just before I would get home she would walk to a restaurant a few blocks away for the evening meal, usually by herself. A little later she began calling a taxi nearly every morning to go to a different place for breakfast: once to a downtown hotel; once way out on the other side of town to a roadside restaurant on the Mineola Highway, and to many other places within the course of a few weeks. Always in the evenings though she would go to the restaurant near our home. She would come home usually just after I arrived, and would change clothes and stay in her room from then on. She would get up very early in the morning, about five o'clock, something she had never done during our entire married life. For the next few years she insisted that people were spying on her, and finally, when I did not agree with her, she accused me of being at the head of this group set out to torment her, and even said that I had television cameras set up in the house to spy on her.

"John smoked almost incessantly, every kind of cigarette made, but later began to smoke little cigars the size of a cigarette, and still later started on the big regular ones that men smoke. Once she bought a small can of snuff. She had never used snuff before. This was a little while after she had begun to lay cigarettes down just anywhere, although there were plenty of ashtrays throughout the house. She also began putting lit cigarettes on table tops, the arms of a divan, or even on the bed, and if Andy or I had not been there to put them out, no doubt the house would have been burned down. She did burn holes in several sheets and in the mattress on her bed. When that happened I told her that she simply could not smoke any more. She did not protest. Andy and I searched the house and found cigarettes and matches everywhere. John had hidden them everywhere, inside a little table radio by removing the back, inside a flashlight where the batteries were supposed to be, in those little shoe pockets she had hanging in her closet, in a little opening at the end of the bathtub where a trap door in the closet exposes the pipes for repairs, under the mattress, inside pillow covers, and even in the dog house outdoors. We gathered up cigarettes, matches, and cigarette lighters every day when I got home and there is no telling how many we finally found and destroyed. Of course she would get more every day at the shopping center, and once we even found one of those little automatic rollers that a person can use to make his own cigarettes.

"Exactly what part John played in the frightening events that took place at our house I cannot say. I am convinced though, as is Amy, that there was some connection. The three years from late 1962 to the summer of 1965 preceded the most awesome, fantastic chain of events that the human mind can imagine. In fact, as these unbelievable episodes began to unfold before us I was beginning to doubt my own sanity. Andy, who was 13 at the time this began, shared with me every one of the horrible experiences, which started in midsummer of 1965 and lasted without interruption until the end of 1966, when we were 'told' that they were over with, only to find that during the next fifteen months we were in for even worse things. If Andy had not been with me to substantiate these awful experiences I would have indeed considered myself hopelessly insane.

"The frightening events began to take place near the middle of 1965, about the time John quit going places with Andy and me. When at home she would stay in her bedroom and close the door and leave it closed after she went to bed. Andy and I shared a bed in another room.

"During our first year at this house we were not bothered by the usual summertime insects, so I did not bother to repair the screens needing fixing at that time. However, during July of 1965, Andy and I would go to bed, and as soon as we turned out the light we were plagued by hordes of June bugs of all sizes, which would hit us on our heads and faces, some glancing off on the floor, others landing on the bed, and some missing us entirely and smashing themselves against the metal window blinds. Night after night we fought these bugs in the dark, grabbing those that landed on the bed and throwing them against the blinds as hard as we could.

"Then we discovered that at least half of the bugs that hit us were already dead, in fact had been dead so long that they were crisp and would crumble between our fingers when we picked them up! I would get up and turn on the lights, and the raids would cease immediately; we could see no sign of them in the air…only those hundreds that littered the floor and bed The instant I turned off the light, though, the air would be filled with bugs again, just as if someone were standing there ready to throw handfuls at us as soon as it was dark. One night I got up and swept and vacuumed the entire room, moved every piece of furniture away from the walls, dusted the backs of the dresser, chest and tables and vacuumed the floor again. When I was through, I could swear that there was not a living creature in that room other than Andy and me. I got some rags and stuffed them in the cracks beneath the closet door and the one leading from the room into the hall. The windows were closed. The room was absolutely clean. Andy was in bed, awake. I turned off the light. At that exact instant hundreds of bugs hit us!

"About this time John began to act more strangely than ever, doing things she would not dream of doing under ordinary circumstances. For example I might look in my closet to get a shirt or a pair of trousers, and there wouldn't be any there. I do not know what prompted me to do it, but I would go to John's closet and there would be my clothes hanging alongside some of hers.

"At this time I had a rubber stamp shop in a room behind the garage, which was a part of the house, and I worked out there every night. There was no direct connection from the house. One had to go out the kitchen door into the garage and then through another door into the shop. On many occasions I would hear the kitchen door being opened, and would rush to the shop door to see who it was. No matter how hard I tried though, I could never get there fast enough to see anybody...only my clothes, suits, shirts, etc., on hangers just as they landed in the middle of the garage floor.

"It was during the hottest part of summer while we had the air conditioners running that other strange things took place for which we assumed John was responsible. Andy or I would suddenly find the bathroom wall heater lit and the flames running out the top, with the door closed. The room would be hot enough to burst into flames. John insisted that she had not lit the heater...that one of us had. After this had happened several times, I removed the handle that turns on the gas. A short time later, while I was out in the shop, Andy came running out and called me in. There was a bunch of paper towels stuffed into the heater where the burners were and they were on fire, some of them on the floor, burning. I then decided to turn off all the pilot lights in the house. This was on the weekend before Labor Day, and I did not know how

I could possibly go to work on Tuesday following the holiday and leave John at home alone, since Andy would be in school. I had talked with Dr. Bankhead, a psychiatrist, and asked if I might put her in the hospital until I could determine what I would be able to do with her, but the psychiatric wards were already running over and he did not want to admit her as a patient. I decided to tell John that if she did 'any of those things' again I would have to put her in jail. Monday night she started waving a pistol around, so I called the police station and told them the predicament I was in. They said they would keep her until things could be settled and told me to bring her on down. She went without protest. When my lawyer returned he made appointments for her to be examined by two psychiatrists, after which I thought there would be no further question about the need for commitment, and she stayed at home that week. However, on the Monday following Labor Day she called her sister-in-law Mack in Daingerfield, Texas, about a hundred miles from Tyler, and asked if she could come visit her at once. I was at work and knew nothing of this until Mack got to Tyler and asked if it would be all right for John to go with her. I objected, but my lawyer advised me that I should let her go, as she could be brought back for the commitment hearing, so they left that day for Daingerfield.

"A few days later John's lawyer had her examined by a psychiatrist again, and he finally said that she might benefit from getting a job, although she would have to undergo psychiatric treatment at various times in the future. It would be almost impossible to have her committed involuntarily, so we decided to just let things stand as they were. For the record, John's attorney insisted that the same doctors who had examined her also examine me. The reports on me were favorable.

"Shortly after John had gone off to stay with Mack, Andy and I were lying in bed with the lights off, talking about the terrible things we had gone through. Suddenly I heard a voice calling my name—a high-pitched, falsetto voice that seemed to he coming from out in space. The voice said it was John, and although it sounded nothing at all like her, I am convinced it was, since she talked about several things that only she and I knew of. One was about some disagreeable words she had had with one of my sisters at the time of my father's death in 1950. She said that although my other sister had insulted her, she was good, and that she had forgiven her. Andy did not hear any part of this conversation. Apparently John, or the voice, could talk to either of us without the other hearing. I even suspected that Andy was doing the talking, and I held my fingers to his lips while listening to the voice. I knew then that it could not have been coming from his lips.

"One night while I was lying on the bed and Andy was in the bathroom I heard his voice say 'goodbye,' though, just before he came to bed, and he told me he had been talking with his mother. During the following weeks we heard six other voices from right out of nowhere, all from people who had been dead for some time. I knew all but one of them while they were living. Two of them had always been friendly toward me, and both were old enough to be my mother. Andy also knew these two women and one of the men named George Swinney. This latter person was killed in an accident some time *after* he visited us 'by voice.' The other two women were mothers of friends of mine and both had died some time before we moved to Tyler. One was Mrs. Snow and the other was Mrs. Elliott, and theirs were the next two voices we heard after John had left, and they came to us about the time the visits by Henry Anglin started. He was the only one of the lot who gave us trouble to start with; in fact I am convinced that he is the one responsible for the bug raids and other awful things that happened to us.

"One of the work benches in my shop was against the wall dividing the shop and the kitchen, and at the bottom of the wall was an opening with a grill over it to handle the return air from the central heating system. For some reason the grill on the shop side had been removed, and by stooping down near the floor under the bench I could see much of what was going on in the kitchen. I worked in the shop every night, and when these 'ghosts' first began visiting us they would call my name, the voices seeming to come from the opening into the kitchen. I would stoop down and answer. At that time I would carry on lengthy conversations with all of them. Mrs. Snow and Mrs. Elliott were very friendly and seemed to want to give me all kinds of good advice. Henry Anglin was just the opposite. He was extremely mean and demanded that I do all sorts of things I would not do. When I refused, he would be very nasty. Once he got a can of insect spray we kept on the kitchen cabinet top and held it down at the opening to my shop. He would start spraying through the hole. He used a whole can of spray and in that little room and I nearly suffocated. One cannot imagine what a feeling it is to see a can of insect spray suspended in midair with apparently nothing holding it and to have it sprayed right in one's face! When I went inside I would see the dents made by the edge of the can where he had banged it against the wall.

"About the middle of September, 1965, the nightly bug raids began to taper off. We thought that we were going to get a few nights' sleep without fear. However, when we went to bed we would feel something moving on an arm or in our hair—*after* we had turned off the lights. We jumped up and found one or several slugs somewhere on us or on the bed. They are the ugliest, slimiest wormlike creatures that can be imagined, big at the head and tapering to a point toward their rear end. They have whiskers on each side of the head, and although they have eyes, they are not supposed to see very well, according to Andy, who, strangely enough, was studying them at school at that time. The large ones are as big as a Vienna sausage, about three inches long, and leave a silvery looking trail wherever they crawl. When the first few of these creatures appeared Andy thought they had clung to his shoes while he was playing in the yard and had gotten into the house that way. However, night after night the number of slugs increased, and we went through the same torture as with the bugs, only much worse. One cannot imagine how awful it is to wake up in the middle of the night and find oneself surrounded by a horde of slimy, ugly worms! Andy said that salt would dissolve the slugs. So we sprinkled salt all around the baseboard, around the bed legs, but still the slug came as soon as the lights were out. A few nights later we were again bombarded with bugs…not June bugs this time, but the wood louse, the little bug about the size of a black-eyed pea. They have lots of tiny legs, which roll up onto a round ball when touched, and are generally called pill bugs. I knew they could not fly, yet there they came, hitting us just as if they were shot out of a gun, at the exact moment we turned out the lights! Mixed in with these were some bugs I had never seen anywhere before, like a doodle bug, but brown in color. I knew doodle bugs couldn't fly, and these things no more had wings than I did. Yet there they came, shooting through the air, and, just as the June bugs had done, they started out one or two at a time, until finally dozens began hitting us at once the moment the lights were out. I also found little pieces of clear material that looked like pieces of broken glass. I finally discovered that these pieces were making the loud noise against the blinds…some of them landed on the bed along with the peculiar bugs. I then washed off a piece about the size of a pea and tasted it; it was pure rock salt! I had not the slightest idea where it came from, as we certainly had had no use for any here. As baffling as the idea of bugs flying without wings was, it was no more so than rock salt sailing through the air with apparently nothing to propel it. There was absolutely no human being in the house except Andy and me.

"A day or two after John had left I cleaned up her room thoroughly, moved every piece of furniture, swept, vacuumed, dusted, and made up the bed, putting on a spread that came nearly to the floor. A few days after the second series of bug raids, Andy called me into John's room. He raised up the spread, and there under the bed was a conglomeration of objects, among which was a ten-pound sack of rock salt, most of which had been poured in a pile on the carpet under the bed. There was an old hair net mixed with it, some burned matches, an unwrapped cake of 'hotel' soap, and on top of the pile was a note, printed the way a six-year-old child would do it, 'Evil spirit go away.'

"In the next few days we began looking through things in John's room and found lots of notes written in longhand, most of which were like those of a child just learning to write, although a few words were unmistakably John's handwriting. They were mainly of people's names, a date that might be the birth date, and then another date some time in the future...some up past 1977. There were many names contained in the notes. One name was of a man I am sure John could not have known: he was Henry Anglin, a pitifully ignorant old man who used to farm just west of Grand Saline, and, like all farmers in the adjoining territory back in 1918, would come to town each Saturday to buy groceries and other supplies foe the following week. When I was about fourteen years old I worked in a department store that also handled groceries. My job was to keep track of the farmer's stacks of groceries so that when they were ready to leave in the evening I could show them where their purchases were and help load their wagons. Henry Anglin was among the people I regularly waited on. He seemed old to me then and that was about fifty years ago. I have no doubt that he has long since died. I cannot imagine how his name entered John's mind. There were also some typewritten sheets in John's room that contained the same items as the notes we had found. One mentioned a certain 'Tink' Byford. There was a date that was probably his birth date, then a date in 1964. We had moved to Tyler in July of 1964, and several months after that I read in the paper that 'Tink' Byford had been killed in an auto accident while returning to Grand Saline from Dallas. Another name was 'Bill' Robertson, a friend of both of us. There was an early date, then 'Hosp. 1965, death 1967.' There were many other names, some now dead, but most still living, *always with two dates!* One day when I got home from work Andy and I found in the living room between the divan and the fable a new bar of soap that had been crumbled up and scattered over a two to three foot area. Andy found a potato masher in John's room with soap on it, so we assumed it was used in the living room where the soap was scattered. We did not clean it up right away. That night, after we went to bed, several piece of soap about the size of a quarter hit our blinds like bullets, although the door to the living room was closed and the den and hallway were between the living room and our bedroom.

"I had had to wash some clothes that night, and it was after dark when I hung them on the line. While I was doing that, Andy came to the door and advised me that bugs and slugs were flying all over the house. I told him I thought I had heard something thud against the dog house near the clothesline. He checked and picked up a little leather wallet about the size of a billfold, which we had seen earlier in John's room, filled with loose tobacco. I told him to put it into the garbage can at the end of the house. The can had a lid on it. When I got through, it was time to take a bath and go to bed. While I was in the tub and Andy was in the den, I heard something that sounded like a shotgun just outside the bathroom window. I called to Andy to run out and see what he could find; he had heard the noise, too. Just beneath the window he picked up the same leather purse he had put into the garbage can just an hour earlier! It had hit the house flat, I suppose near the bathroom window, to cause such a loud noise.

"During the preceding days we found several other notes, all written or printed in the same peculiar way, as a little child might write. I had no idea what they meant, if anything, but some examples are:

Johnnie Beaird   Joe Bailey-1972   Amy Beaird
                                            Reid Lesser-1966   The End
1913 Murder   TiNK Byford-1964
Bill Robenson-1967
The dog-leave 1965
Die 1972

"In a little notebook we found:

Allie L. Lewis (This woman worked for the same company we did).

Luther Anderson (He owns a truck line that hauls salt).
Die 1980

Jeraldine Fail (This woman used to be a good friend of John's).
Die 1977

Louise Beaird (This is my sister, who would be 118 years of age in 2018).
Die. 2018.

"One day we found an old wooden box where John had kept her canceled checks. She had burned something in it, as the ashes were still in the box. The only thing left was one half of a calling card saying, 'burn spirit burn.' On just a scratch of paper were the words, 'Johnnie Beaird-Death 1991.'

"There were many more. Note the peculiar use of capital letters. All of those notes were printed:

JoHN is goIn To Die	Be NIce IN FROnt OF OLD FOOL- ish MACK	There IS A Hertz in Mt PleaSant SnEak AWAY From There (I checked, and there is not a Hertz in Mt. Pleasant).	I pOisOned little FOOLS White kittEn ShALL i poisOn The Jap Cat (Andy did have a white kitten which had died for some reason, and at this time he still had a Siamese cat).

"On a Canton bank blank check was written in the 'pay to' line: Johnnie B. Walker $1,000,000; in the 'for' line Bill is NUTTY, and on the 'signature' line: ha ha.

"The ghastly events continued through October and into November, when they seemed to be letting up a little. One day early in the month when I got home from work Andy took me into John's room. Lined up under the edge of her bed but behind the spread were some pictures in little frames of various kinds. There was one of Amy, of John and Andy, of me, of Thelma Lowrie, who had been John's best friend and who had died in 1951, and several others. I don't know what significance they were supposed to have, but I left them right there. I assumed that John had been to the house that day. Bugs, dead and alive, continued to bombard us every night; even the slugs started flying through the air, gnashing against the blinds and walls, making an awful mess wherever they hit.

"I decided to clean up both bedrooms as soon as I could, and to start by taking up the carpets. While I was doing that Andy found a note in John's room saying: 'Bugs will end for Thursday, Nov. 23.' I think the 23rd was the day I cleaned up our room, and the bugs were worse than ever that night, so we decided that maybe it was meant that the 23rd would be the last night. The next night, strangely enough, was pretty quiet.

"On the 24th I took up the carpet in John's room. While doing that, I was hit by hundreds of bugs, slugs, and even some of the nails I pulled out of the floor simply flew through the air and hit against the blinds. Finally I was able to completely clean the room, paint the walls and woodwork, put up curtains, and the room looked very nice when I was finished.

"On November 26th I cleaned the house thoroughly, and no unusual activity took place that night. On the 27th bugs were everywhere. Just before dark I was taking a bath, and when I was through, standing up in the tub, I saw something hit the screen but could not tell what it was. I called Andy from the den and told him to go out to see what it was. It turned out to be one of John's rubber gloves I had put out beside the garbage can to be hauled off.

"On Thanksgiving day I took all of our outside locks and had Andy take them to a locksmith in town the next morning to have them changed and get new keys, as I was convinced that John had been somehow coming from Daingerfield and using her keys to get in. I put the locks in place on Saturday. On Wednesday, December 1, 1965, somebody (I supposed it was John) punched a hole in the back screen door near the hook and unhooked the door. If it was John, though, her key would not fit.

"December 4th was the worst. It was Saturday, and we went to bed about 10:30. Something that sounded exactly like fingers drummed lightly on the bed. Although we were under the covers we could feel whatever it was tugging at the sheets, actually trying to jerk the covers off us! We would turn on the light and the tugging would stop. There were no bugs that night, but when the lights were off both Andy and I could feel something on our arms that seemed like small flying bugs bouncing up and down, sort of like gnats might do. We would slap at them, but there was absolutely nothing there. We sprayed the air everywhere with insect spray but it did no good. It felt exactly like someone lightly grabbing the hair on your arms with the thumb and forefinger, not actually pulling very hard at first, but later jerking the hair hard enough to hurt.

"While we were lying in bed with the light on, my shoes, weighing possibly two pounds each, flew right over our heads and landed on the other side of the bed. Andy's house shoes got up from the floor and flung themselves against the blinds. My clothes, which were hanging in the closet with the door closed, got out of there somehow without the door being opened and landed across the room. Finally we turned off the lights and heard a strange sound we could not identify. It was under the bed, and sounded like bed rollers being turned rapidly with the fingers; but the bed was not on rollers! Suddenly something hit the blind like a bullet. We turned on the light and found that the handle from the gas jet under the bed had unscrewed itself, and both the bolt and the handle had flung themselves against the blind. Then the bed started moving away from the wall. We would roll it back again only to have it do the same thing over and over. That was about all we could stand, and as it was 2 a.m. Sunday, I told Andy to put on his clothes. We went to a motel to spend the rest of the night.

"As we were walking down the driveway, after closing and locking the door, a handkerchief still folded hit me on the back of the neck. Just as we got in the car another handkerchief I had left on the bedside table hit me on the back after I had closed the car doors.

"We were so weary that we were asleep almost by the time we were in bed at the motel, and nothing happened to us while we were there. We came home about 9:30 the next morning. Some of John's clothes were in my closet, and most of mine were in hers. All sorts of weird notes were flying all about the house. I cleaned the house, and just as I was through, a big cigar hit the back of my neck from out of nowhere. I put it in the kitchen wastebasket. Andy wanted some soup, so I started to a Cabell grocery store a few blocks away. Just as I left the house Andy saw the cigar jump out of the wastebasket and land on the floor. He put it back in the basket. When he came to the door to tell me about it I was getting into the car parked at the foot of the driveway, and when I turned toward him I saw the cigar come sailing over his head and land at the side of the car, about sixty feet from the house. When I came back and stepped in the door from the garage to the kitchen I saw a clean shirt of mine come flying from the den and land near the back door of the kitchen.

"By this time I had decided that it did absolutely no good to change the locks on the doors, although John had not broken in, if, indeed, this was John. Apparently whoever it was did not need a door, nor did he need to break in. Andy and I were standing in the kitchen watching things fly through the air, when all of a sudden his cap, which had been resting on the refrigerator, hit me in the back of the head. A roll of paper towels flew through the air; a can of soup on the cabinet top jumped off onto the floor several times after Andy picked it up and put it back.

"All of a sudden we heard a click. The toaster had been turned on, and the click meant it had turned itself off. There was a piece of soup in it, melted! A note nearby read 'clean toaster.' I felt something like a slight brush on my shoulder and heard Andy shout 'Look out!' He saw the faint outline of a hand that looked like his mother's vanish near my head.

"Later, while in the den, I began to ask questions aloud, such as: John, tell me where we stayed last night?' A few seconds later a note came floating down in front of us, reading 'Motel on T.B. Road. Couldn't get in.' 'Got to go, you've ruined me.' We did spend the night before at a motel on the road to the Tuberculosis Hospital where I work. I then said aloud, trying to sound funny in a totally unfunny situation: 'With all that power, why don't you just drop $5,000 on us?' Almost immediately a check with nothing but $5,000 written on the face dropped from out of nowhere. I said, 'John, why don't you appear here before us right this minute?' In about five seconds a note came down saying: 'Can't come ToDay haPPy YuLeTide.' I then asked, 'Are you going to be able to sleep tonight?' This answer came down to us: 'CaN't maKE aNyTHing happen tONighT you BROKE MY POWER Call HOUsTon.'

"Previously she told me to call Houston police and ask them about a witch who had solved the murder of a man named Gonzales. I felt like a fool, but I did call the Houston police department. I told them they could think I was drunk, crazy, or anything they wished to, but I just wanted a yes or no answer, and asked if they had any record of a witch ever helping the Houston police solve a murder of a man named Gonzales. The man I talked to did not appear surprised and simply asked me to wait a moment, and a few seconds later said that he could find no record of any such event.

"John had also given us directions for breaking her power. It was to 'break an egg, mix with a little water and a dash of salt and then throw it out in the back yard.'

"I have never been superstitious before, and this sounded awfully silly to me, but I think I would have done absolutely anything I was told if it meant a chance to put an end to these uncanny events, so I told Andy to go ahead and follow the directions. That night we had a few bugs and a note came floating down reading, 'power will end at 10 o'clock give or take an hour.'

"For several days we received what seemed like hundreds of notes from right out of nowhere, simply materializing in midair, some folding themselves us they came toward us. Some time after he had seen the hand vanish near my head, Andy was sitting in the den facing the outside windows. For a few fleeting seconds he saw the outline of John in front of the windows. Her back was to him as she looked out the windows, and Andy heard a faint 'goodbye' just as the figure melted in the air.

"We heard other voices after talking with John. All seemed very strained, especially the female speakers, and they would often say that they had a 'mist' in their throat and could not continue talking to me, although they could always talk to Andy and he would hear them. I have dozens of notes that fell down to us from somewhere above, and most of them are from the same two people who stayed with us for the longest period of time. One of these was Mrs. Elliott who had been dead for three or four years when all this began to happen. The other was from a Mr. Gree, of whom I had never heard, but who seemed eager to help Andy and me with advice, especially concerning the care of Andy's cats and dogs. We were 'visited' by a great variety of 'people,' some long since dead, some still living, most of whom we know, or knew, but also some well-known public figures whose names were often in the news. I dated the notes from then on, but at times so many descended on us at once that I did not try to record the exact order in which we received them.

"It was Henry Anglin who tormented us from the very beginning, and who caused us to move out of the house. One night Anglin came to our room after we had gone to bed and his voice asked if he could cook himself an egg. We heard nothing eke from him that night, but the next morning when I went to the kitchen to prepare breakfast, there in a teflon-lined skillet on the stove burner turned down low was an egg burned to a crisp!

"Another night Anglin came to our room and insisted that I call Houston. This was about the time he was beginning to be so terribly mean. I told him that I had already made one silly call to the Houston police, and that I had no intention of doing it again. He countered that I had not questioned them enough, and for me to phone them again. I refused, and he tormented us relentlessly. Finally he said he would leave us alone if we would drive around the loop, which was a distance of a little over twenty miles around the city of Tyler. Andy and I put on our clothes and did just that. We drove completely around the town, and sure enough, when we got home we were able to sleep the rest of the night without further trouble.

'A few nights after this, both Mrs. Elliott and Mrs. Snow told me verbally, while I was working in my shop, that they had taken Henry Anglin 'back to his grave,' and had driven a stake, prepared by Mr. Gree, through Anglin's heart. They promised that he would not bother us again.

"About this time we received notes allegedly from people who were still living, and also some from persons other than those previously mentioned who had been dead for several years. Among those still living were Mrs. W.H. Jarvis, and Odell Young, who lives in Grand Saline at this time, I also had one note from Mr. W.H. Quinn, who had been dead for several years. He used to be a railroad agent in Grand Saline.

"For a number of years I had occasion to have him sign numerous shipping papers, so I had become familiar with his handwriting. The note I got from him was written in the same backhand fashion. I believe that this note was written by him:

Dear Howard and Andy,
    I pay tribute to you. You have put up with a lot from old man Anglin. It is all over now. Friday I am going to my grave to join my wife, whom I love. I am going to Marion's house to see him once more. He is my favorite child I have always liked

you, John, and the boy and hope someday you will be together again.

Hiram Quinn

P.S. I enjoyed hearing about John going with Marion to get new teeth.

"The P.S. about his son's false teeth refers to the time about thirty years ago when John and I went to see Marion just after he had received his first set of dentures. At that time we lived just across the street from Marion and his wife and were friendly with them.

"We also got notes allegedly from Marilyn Monroe, Dorothy Kilgallen, and former Governor Tim Allred, who sympathized with us for what Henry Anglin was doing to us and also about John's condition. Mrs. Snow and Mrs. Elliott had previously told us that Anglin had caused many deaths, some by auto accident, and some by switching a person's pills, as they said he had done in the case of Dorothy Kilgallen. The note we received with her name also said that was the cause of her death. I am not certain, but I believe they also said Anglin caused Marilyn Monroe's death.

"None of the people still living, except John, ever spoke to me; they just dropped their notes from the air. Mrs. Jarvis actually spoke to Andy, though, and had him tell me to answer aloud each of the questions she put in her note to me. Mr. Quinn's note was stuck in the grate between the kitchen and my shop.

"For the first few weeks in January 1966 only Mrs. Elliott and Mr. Jack Gree 'visited' us. She and I had lots of conversations, but she gradually got so she could barely talk to me, although Andy could still hear her. The notes were written either on some note paper Andy kept in the kitchen or on some Canton, Texas, bank deposit slips in John's room. If I was working in my shop she would stick the notes in the grill and bang on the wall to attract my attention, and then I would stoop down under the work bench and retrieve the note. Mr. Gree, who told us we had never heard of him, had a very low, deep, gruff voice. Most of his communications to me were in the form of notes, however, but he and Andy carried on lengthy conversations nearly every day. He also used the grill 'post office' for depositing his notes, and then banged on the wall to let me know they were there.

"At times, when Andy and I were in the car, Mrs. Elliott or Mr. Gree would be with us. They would ride along for a while and then suddenly say they were going to Canada, Russia, Minnesota, or some other far-off place, saying it took only two or three minutes for them to travel those distances, and then we might not hear anything eke from them until the next day or night. Early in January of 1966 Andy came out to my shop and said Mr. Gree wanted to know if it was OK for him to use the telephone, and of course I told him it was. I did not know what control I would have over the situation anyway. That first time he said it was something personal and asked Andy if he would mind leaving the room. I could hear the phone being dialed, and stooped down near the floor so I could look through the grilled opening, but of course I could not see anyone there and could not quite see the phone itself. After that he used the phone many times, while I was working and while Andy was studying at the kitchen table in full view of the telephone. It was really spooky to see the receiver stand up on end by itself, and then after a while put itself back down where it belonged, but always upside down. Some nights he would dial many times after we had gone to bed, and we could hear the sound plainly in our bedroom. The next morning I would find the receiver on the phone upside down. One night while Andy was taking a bath Mr. Gree called somebody and I heard him say in a low, deep voice, 'I'm weird…I'm unusual.' I thought to myself, 'You can say that again.' He repeated it several times and then all I could hear would be a series of low grunts, from which I could not make out any real words. One evening while we were in the car coming home from the post office I asked Andy whom he supposed Mr. Gree called on the phone. Without a moment's hesitation Mrs. Elliott, who we did not know was with us, spoke up and said he was calling her. We did not ask her where she was when she received the call!

"Both Mr. Gree and Mrs. Elliott certainly had Andy's welfare in mind. Practically every day for the whole month of January there was a note from one of them stuck in the screen door. It appeared to be Mrs. Elliott's job to help John home and to take care of Andy. She said if she could do that she would probably go back to her grave early.

"After John had left home, I felt very sorry for Andy. He was lonely being at home alone so much of the time. He indicated a desire for a cat, and a little later for a dog. At the insistence and complete direction of Mrs. Elliott I spent quite a sum of money for such pets. Mr. Gree then took over completely the directions for our taking care of these dogs and cats.

"On January 29, 1966, while I was writing a letter, there was a pounding on the kitchen wall, indicating that there was a note in our 'post office.' It was from Mrs. Elliott. 'I love that beagle. Sorry the pets have been sick. I feel responsible. Andy worries. He loves them so much. If something happens to one don't let it worry you. Andy understands that one dog is a good companion and easier.. If something does happen I only hope it isn't the beagle. The beagle will be a better companion. Andy would give up one if you asked him too. Not that he wants to. But he would understand. He loves dogs. He understands. El. Reply to this note. Reply to every line I wrote.'

"The other dog she referred to was a brown dachshund, which did not look very healthy when we bought it. It never did gain weight and after we had given away the black dachshund the brown one continued to get worse. During the next few days and nights some of the most unbelievable things happened in connection with this brown dachshund. I would be working in my shop and suddenly hear a slight noise on the roof of the house. It would be utterly impossible for the dog to jump up there from the ground, and there was nothing else around for him to get on in order to jump up on the house. Yet there he was clear up on the peak walking from one end to the other! We would get a ladder and finally coax him down into the eave where we could get hold of him and put him on the ground. This happened time after time. We finally decided to leave him up there and go to bed. The next night Mrs. Elliott told us she knew about the dog. We asked her how it was possible and said we would like to see how the dog got up there. She said we could not see it...that it was just a case of 'now he's down here...now he's up there.' She said that even if we were watching him, he would just simply vanish from his spot on the ground at the same instant be on the roof. Later that night Mrs. Elliott called Andy and me and said the dog was trying to commit suicide and for us to go to the back door and look in the flower bed on the south side of the back steps. Sure enough we looked, and the ground had been freshly dug and it had been loosely put back in place. We could see the dirt moving, and I told Andy to go and get the shovel from the garage. Mrs. Elliott said it was not in the garage, but for us to wait just a few seconds and we would find it in the front yard under the tree, where it would be when it got back from 'Heaven.' Andy did go and found the shovel just where she said it would be and brought it to me. I dug down beside where the dirt was moving and pulled the dog out by his tail. He was barely breathing and looked very pitiful, but after a few seconds was able to feebly walk a little. Mrs. Elliott told us that we had better put it out of its misery that night. I told her I did not have anything to put it to sleep with, but she finally told me to just go ahead and kill it, using a hammer, a brick or anything that would put it to death. It was a sickening experience, but I did kill the dog with a brick, as I was certain that it was in pain and would be better off dead. We buried the dog where it had apparently dug its own grave! I cannot say that the dog actually dug this hole, crawled into it and covered itself up with dirt, as I find it hard to see how it could possibly have dragged the dirt in on top of it...I have only Mrs. Elliott's word for that. I am merely stating what she told us, although I did find the dog in the hole, covered with loose dirt and barely breathing when I pulled it out.

"While John was away in Daingerfield, I had bought a little plastic toilet bowl cleaner on which a disposable pad is used. The handle had come apart the first time I tried to use it. It only cost a few cents, and ordinarily I would have just bought another and forgotten about it. However, I decided to write the manufacturer, and some time later I received a letter from them, advising me that they were sending me another handle. Eventually I received a notice that there was a package at the post office. I would have had to drive about ten miles from the place where I work to the post office and back during the noon hour to pick it up, and since it was of no importance I intended to just wait until Saturday to call for the package. That evening, though, when I went to my shop to start work there was a package on my workbench. The shop had been locked all day and was still locked when I started to work. I asked Andy if he knew anything about it and he assured me that he did not know about the package being in the post office. At that moment Mrs. Elliott spoke up and admitted she had gotten it out of the post office and brought it home to me!

"Not long after John had gone to Daingerfield another mystifying thing happened. In one of the kitchen drawers where we kept some silverware in one of those little compartments made for that purpose, there was a space five or six inches behind that section clear across the drawer. In there I kept a few tools such as a screwdriver, pliers, and tack hammer—where they would be conveniently available when I needed them. I had not had occasion to look in there for some time, and when I finally did I noticed a pistol. It was a .22 cal. and looked very real, and only when I picked it up did I discover that it was just a blank pistol. I asked Andy where it came from, but he knew nothing whatever about it. Mrs. Elliott spoke up and said she had brought it from Daingerfield She told us that John had ordered it from some magazine ad and had paid $12 for it. She said it was awfully hard for her to bring it to our house and that it had taken her several hours to do so. She did not say why she did it but intimated that she just wanted us to know about it. Later, when we were moving away from that house, the pistol was gone, and I have not seen it since.

"For many years I had owned a .25 cal. Colt automatic pistol. I always kept it in good condition but it had not been fired in thirty years at the time we moved to Tyler. John's mother also had had a pistol exactly like mine except for the handles, as I bought a pair of white, carved bone handles for mine. When she died we brought that pistol to our house, although we never had occasion to shoot it either. We still had them both when we moved to Tyler. With so many mysterious events taking place, I decided to keep a pistol out in my shop, so I brought the one that had belonged to John's mother and left it on top of my workbench. It stayed there for several weeks. One night it was missing. My shop was always locked and I had the only key. I had wrapped my own gun in a polyethylene bag after cleaning it thoroughly, and put it in a little compartment between the two drawers in a chest in my room. One of the drawers had to be removed completely to get the gun, and even then one had to look closely to find it. I had told no one about the hiding place. When the gun in my shop suddenly disappeared I decided to get mine that I had hidden in the chest. However, when I looked in the hiding place my pistol was not there, but in its place was the one that had been in my shop! I did not take it to my shop then, but some time later when I decided to, that gun was also gone, and we have seen neither of them since that time.

"Occasionally during all this time I would write to John, saying that I wished she would come home so that we might be able to get her well and be happy together again. She never replied to any of my letters, although she wrote Andy a note now and then when he would write her first. I talked to her on the phone a short while later. I do not remember whether I called her on the phone or whether she was the one who called, but she finally said she would be home on a given date in February 1967, and that Mack would bring her. When she got to Tyler she called me at work. She had taken a room in a private home for a few days before coming back to our house. Andy and I talked her into coming home that night, though, and during the remainder of 1967 things seemed to be more normal for us than they had been in many years.

"During March of 1967 I moved my shop to a building downtown. It was getting too crowded in the little room I had been using at the house, and when I got things all set up at the new location I thought that it would be good for John to run the shop during the day, or at least part of each day, which she agreed to do. Things went along very well throughout the rest of the year. Our daughter Amy came for a few days' visit at Christmas time. A little while before this, though, John had begun to throw cigarettes all over the house again, and there were burned places everywhere. John, of course, insisted that she had not thrown them there.

"Some time in late 1967 Mrs. Elliott reappeared and began giving us more advice about how to handle John. By this time I believe Andy was about to go to pieces. One of the officials of the school Andy attended called me and asked why Andy had not been to school. Mrs. Elliott had said for him not to go to school anymore, that he could take a correspondence course and get his high school diploma that way. But, I tried to convince him to return to school. The last note I received from her read as follows:

Howard,
You might wish I wouldn't come back but I did. You can do whatever you want to with John. I won't ask Jr. if he wants to come with me, though he might kill himself. Taking John away will only make him worry more. You don't care. THERE IS ONE THING YOU CARE ABOUT AND THAT IS YOU. I wish you would leave Jr. alone. He can get a course to finish school and get a diploma and leave you. If you cause any trouble I'll take him or he'll kill himself. I could help him to go to California but that wouldn't be good, he'd be better off dead, which probably he will be. There's not going to be a world in 15 years so he doesn't care. He just wants to have some enjoyment. You are real silly. John's going to get violent. That's the silliest riling I ever heard. Now you are really going to hurt things when you send John away. All I asked was one week. You don't want John well you just want rid of her, so you cause trouble and get her mad. John doesn't cost you all that much money you selfish fool. I can't make John love you but I could get her to clean house and if you had any sense (which you don't) you would leave her at Trumark. Now when you send her away and start giving Jr. trouble you are going to be sorrier than you have been or will ever be. I don't know Jr. is good at music and would be excellent and be able to make 3 times your money. Maybe he will be better off gone. You silly old selfish idiot. You can holler and anything else but it will be of no avail. When you see the nut doctor, tell him about me, maybe they'll put you away.

"During the last part of February and early March the most ghastly things yet began to happen at the house. Henry Anglin came back. I could not hear him, but Andy said he talked very little and what few words he did speak were barely understandable. Andy could hear his evil laughter. He began by putting an egg under the mattress about where my head would be. We would not have known at the time, of course, but he would tell Andy to have me look in certain places. There was an egg, broken, in one of my house shoes, one in a pocket of my robe, one in the shade of the ceiling light, one broken in the corner of the room where it was running down the wall, and one broken against the chest of drawers. There was even one inside my pillow case. Andy said that Anglin would just give a sort of insane-sounding laugh each time we would find another egg. We cleaned up the mess, and that was the end of the egg episode.

"A few days later when I got home from work, Andy called me into our room and there in the middle of the bed was our dresser. It was not very heavy, and I was able to lift it down by myself. The next day the chest of drawers was on the bed. This was very heavy, and it took both Andy and me to set it on the floor again. The following day, when I got home, Andy was not there. I noticed that the door to the room he and I shared was closed. That was not unusual, though, as we often kept it closed during the day. However, when I started to open it, it simply came off the hinges in my hands. I could see that the pins had been removed from the hinges, so I just leaned the door against the wall. The next day I found the closet door wrenched from the opening, bringing most of the door facing with it. These were hollow doors and both of them had holes knocked in them about the size of a fist. The next night, about nine o'clock, while I was working at the shop, Andy telephoned me and said the refrigerator was in our room. He had heard a noise while he and John were watching television, and he got up to see what it was. To reach the bedroom the refrigerator had to go through the length of the breakfast room, the den, and a hallway before reaching our room. I knew he could not move it back that night so I told Andy to just leave it alone and we would decide what to do the next day. However, a little later he called and said the washing machine, which was located in the kitchen, had been pulled away from the wall and the faucets behind it were leaking and water was running all over the floor.

"I told him to cut off the hydrants which he did. I then called the police and asked them to meet me at the house. When we got there the holes in the two doors in the bedroom had increased to about fifteen or twenty and some of them were through both sides of the doors and big enough to put one's head through.

"Pretty soon, the house was swarming with policemen and detectives. That is when I decided to tell them as briefly as I could what we had been going through. Some of them, I am certain; thought the whole thing was a hoax, and came right out and said they thought I was being hoodwinked by John, who had enlisted Andy's help. That was absolutely ridiculous, though, as practically all of the strange happenings occurred while Andy and I were together, and while John was staying with Mack about a hundred miles away. One of the chief detectives talked a long time with John, and later told me that she talked sensibly, but that he was amazed at her lack of concern about the strange things that had happened. I too had noticed that she was wholly indifferent to the entire 'show.'

"About the middle of February 1968 things got so bad that I made John give me her key to the shop, and told her that I was going to have to do one of three things. I was going to try and have her committed to a state hospital as I was not financially able to have her take psychiatric treatments, or she could take them and pay for them herself, or I was going to get a divorce. A divorce at my age I thought was ridiculous, but I felt as if I could not stand to go on as things were. Andy was going to move with me as soon as I found a suitable place. John did not seem perturbed one way or the other, and probably did not believe I would really do any of those things. However, on February 24th, I did move out of the house, and had my attorney begin divorce proceedings, since he again stated that he did not think I would have a chance in trying to have her committed. I think that when the papers were served on John it was the first time she actually realized what was happening. I got an apartment only a few blocks from my shop. I told Andy to call me every night to let me know how things were at home. I met him at a nearby shopping center each Saturday and gave him enough money to buy food for himself and John during the following week.

"For several weeks we went on this way. One night Andy called me and said that the dining table was up in the attic. The only opening to the attic was a rectangular hole in the garage ceiling about 16 by 25 inches, through which it was absolutely impossible for the table to go. The next night the table was back in the house again. This happened several times. Other things also 'went' to the attic, such as a small table, an ottoman and another kidney-shaped end table. Finally, the dining table came down and Andy found it in the garage; after considerable work he was able to get it inside the house, where it belonged.

'Eventually, John was beginning to believe that the strange things we had been talking about were really happening. Previously she had just made fun of us whenever we would mention them. Several weeks after I had left, Andy was sitting in the den, playing his guitar, when the lights went out. At first he thought that a bulb had burned out, but when he looked at the switch he could see that it had been turned off. This happened several times. Once when John was going through the den the light went out and she saw that the switch had been turned; Andy was not anywhere near it, and there was nobody else who could have done it.

"It was well into the second month after I left home. I had just finished work in the shop. The telephone rang. It was John and she sounded almost hysterical. She said she was very sick and begged me to come home. I got there a few minutes later, and she could hardly talk. She continued to beg me to come home, but I told her I could never spend another night in that house. Finally I got her calmed down enough to talk seriously. I finally told her that I would come back, but that first we would have to find another place to live. I demanded that she never smoke again. Finally, on April 15, 1968, we moved out of the house of horrors, and I have not been there since.

"John has not smoked since that time. It has now been over three months since we left the house, and John does the normal things about the house except cook. She is again at my rubber stamp shop and seems to enjoy it."

In retrospect, as I read over these words, I realized how difficult it must have been for Mr. Beaird to report on his experiences, especially to a stranger. What had appeared completely impossible to him would, of course, have been even more unbelievable to someone who was not present when it happened, and he doubted his own sanity at times, which was not surprising.

Having met Howard Beaird I was sure that he was completely sane, in fact, so sane he could not even be called neurotic. Had I not heard of parallel cases before, perhaps I too would have wondered about it. None of the phenomena reported by Mr. Beaird were, however, impossible in the light of parapsychological research. We were dealing here with forces that seemed to be in contradiction of ordinary or orthodox physical laws, but the more we learn of the nature of matter and the structure of the atom the more it seems likely that poltergeist activities connect with physics in such a way as to make seeming de-materialization and re-materialization of solid objects possible practically without time loss. But the case was a question of studying not so much the techniques involved in the phenomena as the reasons behind them and those causing them.

I informed Mr. Beaird that I was eager to enter the case, especially as I wanted to make sure that the poltergeist activities had really ceased once and for all and would never recur at his new location. In cases of this kind there was always the possibility that the phenomena are attached to one or the other person in the household rather than to a location. Moving to another house seemed to have stopped the activities, but as there had been pauses before that culminated in renewed and even stronger physical activities, I wanted to be sure that this would not be the case in this new location. I explained that I would have to interview all those concerned, even the police detectives who had come to the house on that fateful night. Mr. Beaird assured me that he would make all the necessary arrangements, and, after discussing my plans with his wife and son, they too agreed to talk to me. Mack, her sister-in-law, who had been hostess to Mrs. Beaird while most of the phenomena took place at the house, was unable to meet me in Tyler, but I was assured that Mrs. Beaird had never left her care during all that time. For a while Howard Beaird had thought that his wife had returned without his knowledge and had done some of the things about the house that had startled him. This, of course, turned out to be a false impression. At no time did Mrs. Beaird leave her sister-in-law's house in Daingerfield, 75 miles away. Whether or not her astral self visited the house was another matter and would be subject to my investigation and verification, as far as possible.

Mr. Beaird also went back to his former home to talk to the present owners. Somewhat suspicious of him, for no apparent reason, they were willing to see me if I came to Tyler. Mr. M.

worked for a local bakery and returned home at 5:30 p.m., and since his wife would not entertain strange visitors in the absence of her husband, my visit would have to be at such an hour as was convenient to the M's. Perhaps the somewhat battered condition of the house when the M's had bought it from Mr. Beaird might be the reason for their reluctance to discuss my visit. At any rate it was agreed that I could call briefly on them and talk to them about the matter at hand. Howard Beaird's daughter, who had become Mrs. Wilson, lived in Austin, Texas. She had had some interest in the occult and mind development and had suggested that someone from the Silva Mind Center in Laredo should come up to Tyler to investigate the case. That was prior to my entering the situation, however, and now Mrs. Wilson wanted very much to come up to Tyler herself and be present during my investigation. Unfortunately, it turned out that she was unable to keep the date due to prior commitments. Thorough man that he was, Howard Beaird also talked to Detective Weaver at the police station to make sure I could see him and question him about his own investigation of the house. I was assured of the welcome mat at the police station, so I decided to set the time when I could go down to Tyler and look for myself into what appeared to be one of the most unusual cases of psychic phenomena.

On February 5, 1969, I arrived at the Tyler airport. It was 5:42 in the afternoon, and Howard Beaird was there to welcome me. We had made exact plans beforehand so he whisked me away to the Blackstone Hotel, allowed me to check in quickly, and then went on with me to see Detective Weaver at the police station.

As we passed through town I had the opportunity to observe what Tyler, Texas, was all about. Clean shops, quiet streets, a few tree-lined avenues, small houses, many of them very old—well, old anyway in terms of the United States—and people quietly going about their business seemed to be characteristic of this small town. We passed by Howard Beaird's shop, a neat, tidy little shop, the company name Trumark plainly written on the window pane. As in many American small towns, the telephone wires were all above ground, strung in a lazy haphazard fashion from street to street. The police station turned out to be a modern concrete building set back a little from the street. Detective Weaver readily agreed to talk to me. Howard Beaird left us for the moment in a fine sense of propriety just in case the detective wanted to say something not destined for his ears. As it turned out there wasn't anything he could not have said in front of him. Was there anything in the detective's opinion indicating participation by either the boy or Mrs. Beaird in the strange phenomena? The detective shrugged. There was nothing he could pinpoint along these lines. He then went to the files and extricated a manila envelope inscribed "pictures and letter, reference mysterious call at—Elizabeth, February 19, 1968, 11:00 p.m., case number 67273. Officer B. Rosenstein and Officer M. Garrett." Inside the envelope there were two pictures, photographs taken at the time by the police photographer named George Bain. One picture was of the door, clearly showing the extreme violence with which a hole had been punched into it. The entire rim of the hole was splintered as if extremely strong methods had been employed to punch this hole through the door.

The other picture showed a heavy chest of drawers of dark wood sitting squarely upon a bed. Quite clearly the description given to me by Howard Beaird had been correct. What exactly did the two police officers find when they arrived at the house on Elizabeth Street? The house was in disorder, the detective explained, and furniture was in places where it wasn't supposed to be. On the whole he bore out the description of events given by Howard Beaird.

Somehow he made me understand that the police did not accept the supernatural origin of the phenomena even though

46

they could not come up with anything better in the way of a solution. Almost reluctantly, the officer wondered whether perhaps Andy wasn't in some way responsible for the phenomena although he did not say so in direct words. I decided to discuss the practical theories concerning poltergeists with him and found him amazingly interested. "Would you like to have the photographs?" the detective asked and handed me the folder. Surprised by his generosity, I took the folder and I still have it in my files. It isn't very often that a researcher such as I is given the original folder from the files of a police department. But then the mystery on Elizabeth Street was no longer an active situation—or was it?

After we had thanked Detective Weaver for his courtesies, we decided to pay a visit to the house itself. After a moment of hesitation, the officer suggested that he come along since it might make things easier for us. How right he was. When we arrived at the house on Elizabeth Street and cautiously approached the entrance, with me staying behind at first, there was something less than a cordial reception awaiting us. Mr. M. was fully aware of my purpose, of course, so that we were hardly surprising him with all this.

After a moment of low-key discussion at the door between Howard Beaird and Detective Weaver on one hand and Mr. M. on the other, I was permitted to enter the house and look around for myself. The M. family had come to see me, if not to greet me, and looked at me with curious eyes. I explained politely and briefly that I wanted to take some photographs for the record and I was permitted to do so. I took black and white pictures with a high sensitivity film in various areas of the house, especially the kitchen area where it connects with the garage and the living room, both places where many of the phenomena have been reported in Mrs. Beaird's testimony.

On developing these, under laboratory conditions, we found there was nothing unusual except perhaps certain bright light formations in the kitchen area where there should be none since no reflective surfaces existed. Then I returned to the living room to talk briefly with Mr. M. and his family.

Was there anything unusual about the house that he had noticed since he had moved in? Almost too fast he replied, "Nothing whatsoever. Everything was just fine." When Mr. M. explained how splendid things were with the house he shot an anxious look at his wife, and I had the distinct impression they were trying to be as pleasant and as superficial as possible and to get rid of me as fast as possible. Did they have any interest in occult phenomena such as ghosts? Mr. M. shook his head. Their religion did not allow them such considerations, he explained somewhat sternly. Then I knew the time had come to make my departure.

I made inquiries with real estate people in the area and discovered a few things about the house neither Mr. Beaird nor Mr. M. had told me. The house was thirteen years old and had been built by a certain Terry Graham. There had been two tenants before the Beairds. Prior to 1835 the area had been Native American territory and was used as a cow pasture by the Cherokee.

I also discovered that Mrs. M. had complained to the authorities about footsteps in the house when there was no one walking, of doors opening by themselves, and the uncanny feeling of being watched by someone she could not see. That was shortly after the Ms had moved into the house. The Ms also had young children. It was conceivable that the entities who caused such problems to the Beaird family might have been able to manifest through them also. Be that as it may, the matter was not followed up. Perhaps their religious upbringing and beliefs did not permit them to discuss such matters and they preferred to ignore them, or perhaps the activities died of their own volition. At any rate, it seemed pretty certain to me that the poltergeist activities did not entirely cease with the removal of the Beairds from the house. But did these activities continue in the new house the Beairds had chosen for their own? That was a far more important question. I asked Howard Beaird to send me a report of further activities if and when they occurred at the new house. On February 23rd he communicated with me by letter. I had asked him to send me samples of John's and Andy's handwriting so that I could compare them with the notes he had let me have for further study. In order to arrive at a satisfactory explanation of the phenomena it was, of course, necessary to consider all ordinary sources for them. Among the explanations one would have to take into account was the possibility of either conscious or unconscious fraud, that is to say, the writing of the notes by either John or Andy and their somehow manipulating them so that they would seem to appear out of nowhere in front of Mr. Beaird For that purpose I needed examples of the two handwritings to compare them with some of the handwritings on the notes.

There were a number of noises in the new home that could be attributed to natural causes. But there were two separate incidents that, in the opinion of Howard Beaird, could not be explained. Shortly before I arrived in Tyler a minor incident occurred which made Howard wonder whether the entities from beyond the veil were still with him in the new house. One evening he had peeled two hard-boiled eggs in order to have them for lunch the following day. He had placed them in the refrigerator on a paper towel. The following morning he discovered that both eggs were frozen solid even though they were still on the lower shelf of the refrigerator. This could only have been accomplished if they had spent considerable time in the freezer compartment during the night. Questioning his wife and son as to whether they had put the eggs in the freezer, he discovered that neither of them had done so. He decided to test the occurrence by repeating the process. He found that the two new eggs that he had placed in the refrigerator that night were still only chilled but not frozen the next day. What had made the first pair of eggs as hard as stone he was unable to understand, but he was satisfied that the occurrence may be of non-psychic origin.

Then there was the matter of a clock playing a certain tune as part of its alarm clock device. For no apparent reason this clock went off several times, even though no one had been near it. Even though it had not been wound for a long time and had only a 24-hour movement, it played this tune several times from deep inside a chest of drawers. Eventually the clock was removed, and in retrospect Mr. Beaird does not think that a supernatural situation could have been responsible for it. But the two separate incidents did frighten the Beairds somewhat. They were afraid that the change of address had not been sufficient to free them from the influences of the past. As it turned out, the move was successful and the separation complete.

I had to work with two kinds of evidence. There was, first of all, the massive evidence of mysterious notes which had fallen out of the sky and which showed handwriting of various kinds. Perhaps I could make something out of that by comparing them with the handwritings of living people. Then there was the question of talking personally and in depth with the main participants, the Beairds, and, finally, to see what others who knew them had to say about them. Howard Beaird's daughter, Amy, now Mrs. Howard C. Wilson, thought that the real victim of what she thought "a circus of horrors" was her brother Andy. "If you had known Andy when he was small, up to the time Mother began to show real signs of her illness, it would be impossible for you to recognize him as the same person now. He was, typically for a little boy, simply brimming over with mischievous humor. He would do anything to make people laugh and would run simply hooting with joy through the house when he had done something devilish." That was not the Andy I met when I came to Tyler. The boy I talked to was quiet, withdrawn, painfully shy, and showed definite signs of being disturbed.

The following morning I went to see the Beairds at their new home. The home itself was pleasant and small and stood in a quiet, tree-lined street. As prearranged, Mr. Beaird left me alone with each of the two other members of his family so that I could speak to them in complete confidence. Andy, a lanky boy, seemed ill at ease at first when we sat down. In order to gain his confidence, I talked about songs and the records popular at the time, since I had seen a number of record albums in his room. Somehow this helped open him up; he spoke more freely after that. Then sixteen, he was studying at a local barber college. When I wondered how a young man, in this day and age, would choose this somewhat unusual profession, he assured me that the money was good in this line of work and that he really liked it. He felt he could put his heart and soul into it. After some discussion of the future as far as Andy was concerned, I brought the conversation around to the matter at hand.

"When these peculiar events took place you and your father lived alone in the other house. Did you ever see anyone?" "Well, I had seen a vision of my mother this one time. It looked like her but nobody was there really...kind of like a shadow, or a form." "Have you ever seen the notes?" "Yes." "Did you ever actually see anyone writing them?" "No." "Did you ever hear any voices?" "Yeah. I talked to them." "How did they sound?" "Well, the women that were here all sounded alike...real high voices. The men were dead, you know...the spirit is, or whatever you want to call them. They had real deep voices. They were hard to understand." "Did they talk to you in the room?" "From out of nowhere. No matter where I might be." "You didn't see them anywhere?" "Never saw them." "Was your father with you at the time you heard the voices or were you alone?" "He was with me at times and not at others." "These voices...are they in the daytime or are they at night?" "At night...mostly at night, or afternoon, when I'd get home from school." "Did it start right after you moved in?" "No...it was two or three months after..." "Did you see the insects?" "Oh yes." "Where did they come from?" "It seemed like just out of the ceiling." "Could they have come in any other way?" "They couldn't have come in...not that many." "Whose voices did you hear?" "First of all my mother's." "The time she was away at Daingerfield?" "Yes." "What did the voice sound like?" "The same high voice. It sounded a little like her." "What did she say?" "She started to talk about my grandfather's funeral and about someone being mean to her."

Clearly the boy was not at his best. Whether it was my presence and the pressure the questioning was putting on him or whether he genuinely did not remember, he was somewhat uncertain about a lot of the things his father had told me about. But he was quite sure that he had heard his mother's voice at a time when she was away at Daingerfield. He was equally sure that none of the insects could have gotten into the house by ordinary means and that the notes came down, somehow of their own volition, from the ceiling. I did not wish to frighten him and thanked him for his testimony, short though it was. I then asked that John, Mrs. Beaird that is, be asked to join me in the front room so we could talk quietly. Mrs. Beaird seemed quite at ease with me and belied the rather turbulent history I knew she had had. Evidently the stay at her sister-in-law's house and the prior psychiatric treatment had done some good.

Her behavior was not at all unusual; in fact, it was deceivingly normal. Having seen one of her earlier photographs I realized that she had aged tremendously. Of course I realized that her husband would have discussed many of the things with her so that she would have gained secondhand knowledge of the phenomena. Nevertheless, I felt it important to probe into them because sometimes a person thinks she was covering up while, in fact, she was giving evidence.

"Now we are going to discuss the other house," I said pleasantly. "Do you remember some of the events that happened in the other house?" "Well, I wasn't there when they took place. They told me about it...and actually, you will learn more from my son than from me because I don't know anything." "You were away all that time?" "Yes." "Before you went, did anything unusual happen?" "Nothing." "After you came back did anything happen?" "Well, I don't know...I don't remember anything." "Before you bought the house, did you ever have any unusual experience involving extrasensory perception at any time?" "Never. I know nothing whatever about it." "You were living some where else for awhile?" "I was with my sister-in-law." "How would you describe that period of your life? Was it an unhappy one? A confusing one? What would you say that period was?" "I have never been unhappy. I have never been confused." "Why did you go?" "I felt I needed to go for personal reasons." "During that time did you have contact with your husband and son? Did you telephone or did you come back from time to time?" "I did not come back, but I had some letters from them and I believe that I talked some..." "Did your husband ever tell you some of the things that had happened in your absence?" "Yes. He told me." "What did you make of it?" "I didn't understand it. If I had seen it, I'd have gotten to the bottom of it somehow." "The people who are mentioned in some of these notes, are you familiar with them? Were there any of them that you had a personal difficulty with or grudge against?" "None whatever. They were friends." "Now, you are familiar with this lady, Mrs. Elliott, who has, apparently, sent some notes?" "Oh yes. She was a very good friend of mine. Of course, she is much older. She had a daughter my age and we were very good friends." "Did you have any difficulties?" "I have no difficulties," she replied and her eyes filled with tears. "No? You had at the time you left here." "Not real difficulties. For several reasons, I needed a change. I didn't intend to stay so long. She was living alone and she worked during the day. And we sort of got into a most enjoyable relationship whereby I took care of certain household chores while she was gone…" "What made you stay so long?" "I just really can't tell you what it is." "You still have no answer to the puzzle as to what happened?" "None. I have no idea." "Do you remember having any treatments?" "I'm just getting old. That is the difficulty."

It was clear that her mind had blocked out all memory of the unpleasant occurrences in her life. As often happens with people who have undergone psychiatric treatment, there remains a void afterwards, even if electric shock therapy has not been used. Partially this is, of course, due to the treatment, but sometimes it was self-induced deliberately by the patient in order to avoid discussing the unpleasant. Mrs. Beaird had returned to her husband and son to resume life and try to make the best of it. To go back over the past would have served no purpose from her point of view. This was not a matter of refusing to discuss these things with me. She did not remember them quite consciously and no amount of probing would have helped, except perhaps in-depth hypnosis, and I was not prepared to undertake this. Clearly then I could not get any additional material from the principal. I decided to re-examine the evidence and talk again with the one man who seemed, after all, the most reliable witness in the entire case, Mr. Beaird himself.

In particular, I wanted to reexamine his own personal observations of certain phenomena, for it is one thing to make a report alone, quietly, filled with the memory of what one has experienced, and another to report on phenomena while being interrogated by an experienced investigator. Quite possibly some new aspects might be unearthed in this fashion. At the very least it would solidify some of the incredible things that had happened in the Beaird household.

On the morning of February 6, 1969, I met with Howard Beaird at my hotel and we sat down, quietly, to go over the fantastic events of the past three years. In order to arrive at some sort of conclusion, which I wanted very much to do, I had to be sure that Mr. Beaird's powers of observation had been completely reliable. In going over some of his statements once again I wasn't trying to be repetitive but rather to observe his reaction to my questions and to better determine in my own mind whether or not he had observed correctly. In retrospect I can only say that Howard Beaird was completely unshaken and repeated, in essence, exactly what he had reported to me earlier. I feel that he had been telling the truth all along, neither embellishing it nor diminishing it. Our conversation started on a calm unemotional note which was now much more possible than at the time when he first made his report to me, when he was still under the influence of recent events. Things had been quiet at the house and seemed to continue to remain quiet, so he was able to gather his thoughts more clearly and speak of the past without that emotional involvement which would have made it somewhat more difficult for me to judge his veracity.

"Now we had better start at the beginning. I am interested in discussing whatever you yourself observed. Your wife was still in the house when the first thing happened?" "Yes." "Were those real bugs?" "Yes." "When you turned the light on?" "You could see thousands of bugs on the floor." "How did you get rid of them?" "We had a vacuum cleaner." "Did they come from the direction of the windows or the door?" "The door." "Now, after the bugs, what was the next thing that you personally observed?" "I heard my wife's voice. After my son and I had gone to bed we were lying there talking about these things that had happened. That was after she had left Tyler." "Did it sound like her voice?" "No. It didn't sound like her voice to me but it was her..." "Well, how did you know it was her?" "She told me it was and was talking about my sister having insulted her. Nobody eke knew that except my wife and I." "Where did the voice seem to come from? Was it in the room?" "Yes." "What happened after that?" "Several nights after that, she appeared to Andy. I heard him talking in the bathroom. He talked for two or three minutes and then I heard him say, 'Well, goodbye.'" "Didn't it make you feel peculiar? His mother was obviously not there and he was talking to her?" "Well, I had already had my encounter with her." "Did you call your wife in Daingerfield?" "No." "Why not?" "Well, she wouldn't have believed me. I had thought about writing her sister-in-law and telling her that you've got to keep my wife in Daingerfield. I don't want her here. Yet, I thought, that's a foolish thing to do, because all she'll say is, she wasn't here. She wasn't in person. Her body wasn't here." "After the voice, what came next?" "Well, it was shortly after that we started hearing those other voices." "Did you hear those voices?" "All of them, yes. All four." "Did they sound alike or did they sound different?' "The men had deep, rough voices, but I could tell them apart. And the ladies were all subtle voices and I couldn't tell *them* apart, except when they told me." "Did you ever hear two voices at the same time?" "I don't believe so. However, Mrs. Snow and Mrs. Elliott were there at the same time. That is, they said they were. That was when Henry Anglin was giving us so much trouble and they had to carry him back to his grave." "Let's talk about anything that you have actually seen move." "I saw these notes that were folded. Sometimes as many as ten or fifteen notes a day." "From an enclosed room?" "Well, the doors weren't closed between the rooms, but I'd be sitting at the table eating something, and all of a sudden, I'd see one fall. I'd look up toward the ceiling and there'd be one up there." "Most of these notes were signed 'Mrs. Elliott'?" "Yes. Later she signed them Elie and then El. Now after my wife came back from Daingerfield she, too, would send me notes through Andy. I was working in my shop and Andy would bring me a note written with numbers, in code. 1 was A, 2 was B, and so forth. I hated to take the time to decipher those things, but I would sit down and find out what they said. In one note she asked me if I didn't 'lose' some weight." "Did your wife ever write you a note in longhand or in block letters?" "No." "Was there any similarity in the writing of your wife's notes and those notes that later came down from the ceiling?" "I can't say, but Mrs. Elliott had been after me to lose weight. I thought it was peculiar that my wife came from Daingerfield and asked about my losing weight also." "Mrs. Elliott was a contemporary of your wife?" "She died in 1963. About a year before we moved here." "Were those two women very close in life?" "Not particularly. They were neighbors." "What about Mrs. Snow?" "She was peculiar." "What objects did you see move in person?" "I saw a heavy pair of shoes lift themselves off the floor and fly right over my bed and land on the opposite side of the bed." "Did they land fast or did they land slowly?" "It was just as if I'd picked them up and thrown them. Andy's house shoes came the same way. I've watched the cat being lifted up about a foot from where he was sitting and just be suspended for several seconds and it didn't fall on the floor. I saw a can of insect spray which was sitting on the cabinet come over and suspend itself right over that opening, and spray into that little room, and I was nearly suffocated. I had to open the doors or the insect spray would have got me." "You weren't holding the can?" "No." "I am particularly interested in anything where you were actually present when movement occurred, or voices were heard." "I've seen my clothes fly through the air as I was coming home." "Did these things occur whether your wife was physically in the house or not?" "Yes." "Did anything ever happen while neither your son nor your wife were at home but you were alone?" "I believe so." "Your wife had some personal shock in 1951, I believe. When her best friend died suddenly. Do you feel her mental state changed as a result?" "Very gradually, yes. She was very happy, though, when she found out she was going to have another child, because she thought this would make up for the loss of her friend. She was just crazy about him." "Now, when was the first time you noticed there was something wrong with her mentally?" "In 1960 my wife took over our daughter's room. She stopped up all the windows with newspapers scotch-taped against the wall and hung a blanket in each window of the bedroom." "Why did she do that?" "She felt someone was *spying on her*. At the office, she took the telephone apart, and adding machines and typewriters, looking for microphones to see who was spying on her." "But the phenomena themselves did not start until you moved into this house?" "That's right."

I thanked Mr. Beaird for his honest testimony, for he had not claimed anything beyond or different from his original report to me. I took the voluminous handwritten notes and the letters pertaining to the case and went back to New York to study them. This would take some time since I planned to compare the hand writing in the notes with samples of actual ordinary handwriting by both Mrs. Beaird and Andy. I didn't, for a moment, think that the notes had been written consciously by either one of them and simply thrown at Mr. Beaird in the ordinary way. Quite obviously Mr. Beaird was no fool, and any such clumsy attempt to fake phenomena would not have gone unnoticed, but there were other possibilities that could account for the presence of either Mrs. Beaird's or Andy's handwriting in the notes, if indeed there was that similarity.

There were already, clearly visible to me, certain parallels between this case and the Bell Witch case of Tennessee. Vengeance was being wrought on Howard Beaird by some entity or entities for alleged wrongs, in this case his failure to execute minor orders given him. But there were other elements differing greatly from the classic case. In the Bell Witch situation there was not present, in the household, anyone who could be classed as psychotic. In Tyler we have two individuals capable of supplying unused psychic energies. One definitely psychotic, the other on the borderline, or at least psychoneurotic.

I then decided to examine the notes written in this peculiar longhand style, almost always in block letters but upper case letters in the middle of words where they do not belong. It became immediately clear to me that this was a crude way of disguising the handwriting and was not used for any other reason. It is of course a fact that no one can effectively disguise his handwriting to fool the expert. He may think so, but an expert graphologist can always trace the peculiarities of a person's handwriting back to the original writer provided samples were available to compare the two handwritings letter by letter, word for word. Some of the notes were outright infantile. For instance, on December 6, 1965, a note read, "My power is decreasing, I'm going back to Mack. I must hurry. I would like to come home but I don't guess I will. I love you. Please give me a Yule gift. I can't restore my power. I am allowed only three a year. Phone police." What the cryptic remark, "I am allowed only three a year," was supposed to mean was not explained.

Sometimes Howard Beaird played right into the hands of the unknown writer. The Sunday morning after he and Andy had spent the night at a motel because of the goings-on in the house, he received a notice of a package at the post office. He knew that he couldn't get it except by noon on a weekday, so he asked aloud, "Is this notice about anything important, as I don't want to come in from the hospital if it doesn't amount to anything?" A few seconds later a note fluttered down from the ceiling reading only "something." That of course not a satisfactory answer such as an adult or reasonable person would give. It sounded more like a petulant child having a game. On December 6, 1965, a note materialized equally mys-teriously, reading, "I don't want to admit to Mack that I'm nutty." Another note dated December 6, 1965, simply read, "Howard got jilted." Another note read, "My powers were restored by the Houston witch. Call the police and ask about her." There doesn't seem to be any great difference between the notes signed by Henry Anglin or by Mrs. Elliott or not signed at all by someone intimating that they were the work of Mrs. Beaird. The letters and the formation of the words were simi-lar. A note dated December 8, 1965, read, "Dear Howard, I love you. I have been wrong. I want to come home but I don't want stupid Mack to know I am unusual. I am really two people. If things end I won't remember nothin. I can be in three places in one. I love you and Junior. Please dear."

The note signed "Dorothy Kilgallen," mentioned previ-ously and received by Howard Beaird December 22, 1965, reads, "Dear Mr. Beaird: Mrs. Elliott told me about what all has happened to your family and what Henry Anglin is responsible for. It is very tragic. He is the reason I am dead because he changed my pills. Good night and good luck." Having been personally acquainted with the late Hearst columnist Dorothy Kilgallen, I am quite certain that she would not have expressed herself in this matter, dead or alive.

A note signed Pont Thornton dated December 23, 1965, reads, "Dear Howard P.S. an Andy: I no you well. I no you good. I don't drinck much do you haf had hardships. Anglin is a mean man. I am smarter than Henry Lee. I am a distant kin of Abe Lincoln and Lewis Armstrong and Sam Davis Junior and Jon F. Kenede." Not only was the note atrociously mis-spelled but also it listed several improbable relationships. When writing as Mrs. Elliott the personality was much more concise and logical than when the writer was supposed to be Henry Anglin or Mrs. Beaird. But despite the difference in style the letters were very similar. Of course since the notes came down for almost three years it was to be expected that there were some differences in both style and appearance between them.

On September 17, 1967, Howard Beaird observed, "About 9 or 10 p.m. Andy heard Mrs. Elliott call. She told him he could talk to her and that mother could not hear so he did and apparently mother knew nothing of it. Just as I was getting ready for bed I heard Mrs. Elliott calling me. The sound seemed to come toward the kitchen and as Andy and Johnny were watching TV in her bedroom I went to the kitchen. Mrs. Elliott called me several more times and the sound then seemed to be coming from my room. She said that Johnny couldn't hear me so I tried to talk to her but Andy said she told him she never could hear me. Anyway before going to bed I found a very small piece of paper folded so small on the floor in the hall and also a South Side Bank deposit slip folded near it. The small note said 'Be very generous. Say hi to me. Mrs. Snow.' The larger note said, 'Don't be stingy Sam be a generous Joe. George Swiney.' After I had gone to bed I heard Mrs. Elliott calling me several times but could never make her hear me answer. Just as I was about to go to sleep, Andy came in and said Mrs. Elliott told him she had left me a note on the floor. Just as I got up to look for it a note dropped in the chair next to my bed. I took it to the kitchen to get my glasses and it said, 'Howard, I hope there won't be any more slugs. Try to be generous, you have a lot of money. There's so much you could get you, John and Andy.' "This was followed by a list of objects, clothing primarily, which he could get for his family on her suggestion. Howard Beaird tried to talk to Mrs. Elliott to ask her where all that alleged money was but he could never get an answer to that.

On September 29, 1967, Howard Beaird noticed that Mrs. Elliott came to visit him around 7:30p.m. He can't understand how she can make him hear her when she calls him by name and then make it impossible for him to hear the rest of her. Apparently the rest of the conversation has to be relayed through Andy. On the other hand, if he speaks loudly enough she can hear him. That night Mrs. Elliott informed him that a Mr. Quinn had been by earlier. A little later Mr. Quinn himself came back and Howard Beaird actually heard him call, but he could hear nothing else, and again Andy had to be the interpreter. Andy said that Mr. Quinn sounded like a robot talking, and that, of course, made sense to Mr. Beaird, since he knew that Quinn, who had lost his voice due to cancer prior to his death, used an instrument held to his throat to enable him to talk. The late Mr. Quinn apparently wanted to know how some of the people back in Grand Saline were, including a Mrs. Drake, Mr. and Mrs. Watkins, and the McMullens. This information, of course could not have been known to Andy, who had been much too young at the time the Beairds knew these people in the town where they formerly lived.

Mrs. Elliott also explained the reason she and the other spirits were able to be with Mr. Beaird that evening was that they had been given time off for the holidays—because of Halloween, although that was a little early for All Hallow's Eve. Mrs. Beaird thought it peculiar that spirits get furloughs from whatever place they are in.

On September 30, 1967, Beaird had heard nothing at all from Mrs. Elliott during the day. Andy had been out pretty late that night and Mr. Beaird was asleep when he came in. Sometime after, Andy woke him and said that Mrs. Elliott had left him a note. They found it on his bed. It read, "Howard, think about what I said. Are you going to do it Monday. Elliott." Just below it was a note reading, "John wants a vacuum cleaner and a purse, Junior wants a coat for school and some banjo strings. Hiram." Now the remarkable thing about this note was that the first part was definitely in the handwriting of Mrs. Beaird, while the second part was a crude note put together with a lot of capital letters where they did not belong and generally disorganized. Hiram Quinn, the alleged writer, was of course a very sick man for some time prior to his passing. When Howard Beaird confronted the alleged Mrs. Elliott with the fact that her note was written in the handwriting of his wife, she shrugged it off by explaining that she could write like anybody she wished.

On October 2, 1967, Mr. Beaird noted, "About 7:30 p.m. Mrs. Snow called my name. I was in the kitchen and the voice seemed to come from the back part of the house where Andy had to tell me what she said. She just wanted to tell me about my stamp business and how John had been. She barely could hear me and told Andy to turn off the attic fan and for me to go into my room and close the door so she could hear. She couldn't explain how I could hear her call my name and then hear nothing more and said it was some kind of 'law.'"

The notes signed by Mrs. Elliott from that period onward frequently looked as if Mrs. Beaird had written them. The handwriting was unquestionably hers. That is to say it looks like hers. Howard Beaird does not doubt that the notes were genuinely materialized in a psychic sense. On October 23rd, he had dozed off to sleep several times and on one occasion was awakened by the rustling of papers on the floor beside his bed. He was alone in the room at the time. He turned the light on and found a sort of pornographic magazine folded up on the floor. Andy came in at that point and explained that Mrs. Elliott had told him she had found this magazine in Mrs. Beaird's room. She said that Mrs. Beaird had gotten it at the beauty shop and the piece of paper was torn from it. On the note was printed, "Somebody loves you," signed underneath, El.

On November 12, 1967, a Sunday, Howard Beaird heard Mrs. Elliott talk to him. She advised him that he should go to Mrs. Beaird's room and look for some nude pictures and also some hand drawn pictures of naked men and women. Mr.

Beaird found all these things but his wife denied any knowledge of them. The following night, November 13, 1967, was particularly remarkable in the kind of phenomena experienced by Howard Beaird. "Mrs. Elliott came by before I left for the shop and told me to look for some more lewd pictures. I found some and destroyed them. Mrs. Elliott told me to be sure and tear them up in front of John and maybe she would quit drawing them, and also quit buying the nudist magazine pictures. Later that night, about 9:15, Mrs. Elliott called me on the telephone. That's the first time I ever talked to a ghost on the telephone. I could understand what she said to me on the phone, yet I could never hear anything except her calling my name when I was at home. I then talked to Andy and he said she wanted me to come home right then and get some more drawings and nudist magazines from John's hiding places. I did go home and got the pictures and went back to the shop after I had destroyed them."

Some of the notes showed the underlying conflict, imagined or real, between the young boy and his father, which was of much concern to "guardian angel" Mrs. Elliott. On January 11, 1968, a note read, "Howard, I need to write you notes. Junior has had to worry so much. Why do you mind him coming with me? He would be happy. It would be right for him not to worry. I agree he must get an education but at seventeen he could get a course and then to college. In the meantime I will help John and him. He could play music and he would be great at seventeen. He would also like to take care of the house. John would get so much better. You would be better financially and Junior could get better. This is the only thing I will allow or I will take him with me if he wants to...He said he would tell me to go and wouldn't go but that wouldn't change him from wanting to. You had better pay attention cause he wants to come. I have all the divine right to take him. El." This threat by the spirit of Mrs. Elliott to take the young boy with her

64

into the spirit world did not sit lightly with his father, of course. Analyzed on its face value, it had the ring of a petulant threat a mentally handicapped youngster would make against his parents if he didn't get his way. If Mrs. Elliott was the spirit of a mature and rational person then this kind of threat didn't seem, to me, to be in character with the personality of the alleged Mrs. Elliott.

The following night, January 12, 1968, the communicator wrote, "Howard, I have the divine right. I will prove it by taking Junior and I take him tonight. You don't love him at all. You don't care about anyone." Mrs. Elliott had not taken Andy by January 15, but she let Howard know that she might do so any time now. In fact, her notes sounded more and more like a spokesman for Andy if he wanted to complain about life at home but didn't have the courage to say so consciously and openly. On January 18th, Mrs. Elliott decided she wasn't going to take the boy after all. She had promised several times before that she would not come back any longer and that her appearance was the last one. But she always broke this pledge.

By now any orthodox psychologist or even parapsychologist would assume that the young man was materially involved not only in the composition of the notes, but in actually writing them. I don't like to jump to conclusions needlessly, especially not when a prejudice concerning the method of communication would clearly be involved in assuming that the young man did the actual writing. But I decided to continue examining each and every word and to see whether the letters of the words themselves gave me any clue as to what human hand had actually written them, if any. It appeared clear to me by now that some if not all of the notes purporting to be the work of Mrs. Elliott were in the hand of Mrs. Beaird. But it was not a very good copy of her handwriting. Rather did it seem to me that someone had attempted to write in Mrs. Beaird's hand who wasn't actually Mrs. Beaird. As for the other notes, those signed by Henry Anglin, Hiram Quinn, and those unsigned but seemingly the work of Mrs. Beaird herself, they had certain common denominators among them. I had asked Mr. Beaird to supply me with adequate examples of the handwriting of both Andy and Mrs. Beaird That is to say handwritten notes not connected in any way with the psychic phenomena at the house. I then studied these examples and compared them with the notes which allegedly came from nowhere or which materialized by falling from the ceiling in front of a very astonished Mr. Beaird.

I signed out the following letters as being characteristic of the writer, whoever he or she may be. The capital letter *T*, the lower case *e*, lower case *p, g, y, r,* and capital *B, C, L,* and the figure *9*. All of these appeared in a number of notes. They also appear in the sample of Andy's handwriting, in this case a list of song titles which he liked and which he was apparently going to learn on his guitar. There is no doubt in my mind that the letters in the psychic notes and the letters on Andy's song list were identical. That is to say that they were written by the same hand. By that I do not mean to say, necessarily, that Andy wrote the notes. I do say, however, that the hand used to create the psychic notes is the same hand used consciously by Andy Beaird when writing notes of his own. I was less sure, but suspected, that even the notes seemingly in the handwriting of his mother were also done in the same fashion and also traceable to Andy Beaird.

On December 7, 1965, one of the few drawings in the stack of notes appeared. It showed a man in a barber chair and read, among other annotations, "Aren't the barbers sweet, ha ha." It should be remembered that Andy's great ambition in life was to become a barber. In fact, when I met and interviewed him he was going to barber school.

What then is the meaning of all this? Let us not jump to conclusions and say Andy Beaird wrote the notes somehow unobserved, and then made them fall from the ceiling seemingly by their own volition, somehow without Mr. Beaird noticing this. In a number of reported instances this is a possibility, but in the majority of cases it simply couldn't have happened in this manner, not unless Howard Beaird was not a rational individual and was, in fact, telling me lies. I had no doubt that Mr. Beaird was telling me the truth and that he was a keen and rational observer. Consequently the burden of truth for the validity of the phenomena does not rest on his gift of observation, but on the possibility of producing such paranormal occurrences despite their seeming improbability, yet reconciling this with the ominous fact that they show strong indications of being Andy Beaird's handwriting.

We must recognize the tension existing for many years in the Beaird household, the unhappy condition in which young Andy found himself as he grew up, and the fact that for a number of years he was an introspected and suppressed human being unable to relate properly to the outside world and forced to find stimulation where he could. Under such conditions certain forces within a young person can be exteriorized and become almost independent of the person himself. Since these forces are part of the unconscious in the person and therefore not subject to the logical controls of the conscious mind, they are, in fact, childish and frequently irrational. They are easily angered and easily appeased and, in general, behave in an infantile fashion. By the same token these split-off parts of personality are capable of performing physical feats, moving objects, materializing things out of nowhere and. in general, contravening the ordinary laws of science. This we know already because cases of poltergeists have occurred with reasonable frequency in many parts of the world. In the case of the Beaird family, however, we have two other circumstances that must be taken into account. The first was the presence in the house of not one but two emotionally unstable individuals.

Mrs. Beaird's increasing divorce from reality, leading to a state of schizophrenia, must have freed some powerful forces within her. Her seemingly unconscious preoccupation in some aspects of sex indicates a degree of frustration on her part yet an inability to do anything about it at the conscious level. We have long recognized that the power supply used to perform psychic phenomena is the same power inherent in the life force or the sexual drive in man, and when this force is not used in the ordinary way it can be diverted to the supernormal expression, which in this case took the form of poltergeist phenomena. We have, therefore, in the Beaird case, a tremendous reservoir of untapped psychic energy subject to very little conscious control on the part of the two individuals in whose bodies these energies were stored and developed.

Were the entities purporting to use these facilities to express themselves beyond the grave actually the people who had once lived and died in the community? Were they, in fact, who they claimed to be, or were they 'simply being reenacted unconsciously perhaps by the split-off part of the personalities of both Andy and Mrs. Beaird? Since Howard Beaird had examined the signature of one of those entities, at least, and found it to be closely similar, if not identical, with the signature of the person while alive, and since, in that particular case, access to the signature was not possible to either Andy or Mrs. Beaird, I'm inclined to believe that actual nonphysical entities were, in fact, using the untapped energies of these two unfortunate individuals to express themselves in the physical world. Additional evidence, I think, would be the fact that in several cases the names and certain details concerning the personalities of several individuals whom Howard Beaird knew in their former residence in Grand Saline were not known or accessible to either his wife or the young man. I was not fully satisfied that there could not have been some form of collusion between Andy and these so-called spirit entities in creating the phenomena, but if there was such collusion it was on the unconscious level. It is my view that Andy's unexpressed frustrations and desires were picked up by some of these discarnate entities and mingled with their own desire to continue involving themselves in earth conditions and thus became the driving force in making the manifestations possible.

What about the fact that Andy Beaird's handwriting appears in the majority of the notes? If Andy did not physically write these notes himself, could they have been produced in some other manner? There is no doubt in my mind that in at least a large percentage of the notes Andy could not have written them physically and dropped them in front of his father without Mr. Beaird noticing it. Yet, these very same notes also bear unmistakable signs that they were the work of Andy Beaird's hand. Therefore the only plausible solution is to assume that a spiritual part of Andy's body was used to create the notes in the same way in which seemingly solid objects have, at times, been materialized and dematerialized. This is known as a "physical" phenomenon and it is not entirely restricted to poltergeist cases but has on occasion, been observed with solid objects which were moved from one place to another, or which appeared at a place seemingly out of nowhere, or disappeared from a place without leaving any trace. The phenomenon is not unique or particularly new. What was unique, or nearly so in the case of the Beaird family of Tyler, Texas, was the fact that here the obvious was not the most likely explanation; I do not think Andy Beaird wrote those notes consciously. I do believe that his writing ability was used by the entities expressing themselves through him. I believe that Andy was telling the truth when he said he was surprised by the appearance of the notes and at no time did he have knowledge of their contents except when one of the other spirit entities informed him about them. The same applies, of course, to Mrs. Beaird. In the phenomena known as automatic writing, the hand of a living person, normally a full, rational and conscious individual, is used to express the views, memories and frequently the style of writing of a dead individual. The notes that fluttered down from the ceiling at the Beaird home were not of the same kind. Here the paper had first to be taken from one place and impressed with pencil writing in the hand of another person before the note itself could be materialized in plain view of witnesses. This is far more complex than merely impressing the muscular apparatus of a human being to write certain words in a certain way.

Why then did the phenomena cease when the Beairds moved from one home to another if the entities expressing themselves through Andy and Mrs. Beaird had not found satisfaction? There was no need for them to simply leave off just because the Beairds moved from one house to the other. There must have been something in the atmosphere of the first house that in combination with the untapped psychic energies of Andy and Mrs. Beaird provided a fertile ground for the phenomena.

Apparently some disturbances continued in the former Beaird home, while none were reported by them in their new house. The new owners of the old Beaird home, however, refused to discuss such matters as psychic phenomena in the house. They were fully convinced that their fundamentalist religion would allow them to take care of these occurrences. To them psychic phenomena are all the work of the devil.

And so the devil in Tyler, Texas, may yet erupt once again to engulf a family, if not a community, with the strange and frightening goings-on which, for three years, plagued the Beaird family to the point of emotional and physical exhaustion. The Beairds themselves were out of danger. Andy has grown up and his untapped powers will unquestionably be used in more constructive channels as the years go by. Mrs. Beaird assumed her former position in her husband's house and closed the door on her unhappy past. Howard Beaird, the main victim of all the terrible goings-on between 1965 and 1968, was satisfied that they were nothing but memories. He had no desire to bring them back. His sole interest in my publishing an account of these incredible happenings was to inform the public and to help those who might have similar experiences.

THE PHANTOM COURIER

*S*py drops, or secret meeting places where spies may meet and more or less freely exchange information—for which of course they are highly paid—must exist in quite a number in Washington, D.C. But how many of them are ghostly spy drops? I wager, not one of them—except, of course, possibly the one in Arlington that I know about.

It all started when Ruth Montgomery, a journalist for the Hearst syndicate who was then still officially a skeptic in matters psychic, called my attention to a friend's plight. Would I please help and look into the matter of a haunting in suburban Arlington? This particular friend was a rather important man and a little nervous about the wrong kind of publicity.

Now I can be the soul of discretion when properly asked, and I assured Ruth that I would do everything in my power to prevent information about the investigation to leak to the press, at least in such a manner that it would hurt anyone's standing in a community.

The gentleman in question was Bob Gray, who was then an official with a large advertising agency and working out of Washington, D.C. Shortly before, he had been in government. In fact, he was Secretary to the Cabinet in the Eisenhower administration. I was somewhat surprised by a column in which Ruth Montgomery heralded my coming to Washington to look into the matter of Bob Gray's haunted house. I am quite sure that Sybil Leek, my English friend, who had then just begun to work with me as a medium, had never read that particular column. For one thing, newly arrived in this country, she was not aware of the identity of Ruth Montgomery, nor was she in the habit of picking up local newspapers and reading gossip columns.

Later I questioned Sybil about it, even showed her the column in question, and was assured that she had never seen it or been told about it. I have no reason to doubt Sybil's honesty and, under the circumstances, am confident that the little that Ruth Montgomery did publish about the case never reached Sybil Leek's ears or knowledge.

Here is Ruth Montgomery's own summation of what had happened until May 1965 that had caused Bob Gray to seek my help:

"Bob bought the rambling house on a wooded hillside three years so, from a foreign official who seemed so reluctant to give possession that it took Gray six months to get him out. Almost immediately afterwards, neighbors began calling to tell him that the house was haunted, and to report rumors of a secret panel within.

"Gray, a leader in the Eisenhower 'Great Crusade,' merely scoffed, but while doing some yard work he discovered a mysterious tunnel leading from the hillside to a bedroom on the ground floor. It divided into two passageways, and several empty cement sacks were found inside.

"When the new owner got around to painting the walls of the bedroom he says he distinctly heard his name called twice, but no earthly visitors were present. Fearing that his driveway might cave into the tunnels, he prosaically had them filled in with cement.

"Shortly afterwards he agreed to keep a big dog belonging

to the widow of Chicago Tribune publisher, Robert R. McCormick, while she went abroad. To his chagrin, Gray was awakened every 4 a.m. by the barking of the dog in a corner of the library.

"The dog eventually returned home, and gave up his 4 am. barking. Eerie happenings continued, however, at Gray's residence. In the middle of the night he heard music coming from the living room, and on going downstairs to investigate discovered that the player piano had turned itself on.

"He mentioned it a few evenings later; and immediately after a guest proclaimed that he did not believe in ghosts "a 30-mile-an-hour wind whooshed through the closed room," according to Gray and his friends.

"At a recent dinner party Bob again spoke of the alleged haunting, the mysterious panel which had not come to light, and the dog's nocturnal barking in the same spot each night. One of the women slipped into the library, and in a few minutes excitedly shouted that she had found it.

"The other guests sprinted into the room, and there it was. By removing books and pushing on a panel that looked like all the others, an aperture to a closet appeared. Behind it was a five-foot-high block of cement to bar whatever lay on the other side. An architect who came to inspect the secret closet said the cement had obviously been spread by an amateur."

As no one was paying us to come down and look into the matter, I had to wait until I was sent to Washington to publicize one of my books. That is when a publisher covers your expenses in return for appearing, for free, on radio and television and talking about your newest book. The date was June 15, 1965, and Sybil and I had rooms at the Washington Hilton Hotel. Even if Sybil Leek had no knowledge of this column, apparently the Washington newspaper fraternity did. During our stay, we learned to our surprise that everyone in

Washington knew about our coming to look into a haunted house. Fortunately, I was always present when the question "Where are you going to go to look for a ghost?" was asked. In one or two cases, I was able to prevent the name of Bob Gray being mentioned in front of Sybil. This was not as difficult as it seems since I never left her side during the interviews.

When the newspapermen had left, I breathed a little easier. Sybil was still in the dark about the whole thing. She knew we had come down to look into a haunted house, but she knew nothing further. For that matter, neither did the newspapermen, except for what Ruth Montgomery had prematurely disclosed in her column.

Immediately after our arrival I had telephoned Ruth and received exact instructions on how to get to the house in Arlington. That very evening we drove out in a taxicab, almost got lost en route, and when we finally arrived at the house, realized why it was so difficult to find. Situated in the most expensive section of Arlington, the house was located on a secluded hillside and was surrounded by trees and bushes. The nearest house was visible, but there must have been considerable privacy for those in the Gray's house at all times. The house itself was a building perhaps forty or fifty years old on first inspection, and seemed solid and somewhat imitative of European country houses.

Apparently we were the last ones to arrive, for I noticed several cars parked about the front and back entrances to the house. At the door we were greeted by Bob Gray and Ruth Montgomery, and after an exchange of polite greetings, we were led into the living room on the ground floor of the house. There we met another five or six people including Arthur Ford, who had come as an observer and not in his capacity as a renowned medium. He and Ruth Montgomery had been friends for years, and she had invited him to witness the investigation.

I decided first to let Sybil look around the place and to stay close to her, at the same time requesting that no one talk to her or say anything about the experiences they might have had in the house. Afterward, we returned to the living room, and Sybil sat down in a comfortable large chair in the middle of the room, with me in a chair next to her and the others loosely grouped around. There was expectation in the air, for Ruth Montgomery had assured Bob Gray that Sybil Leek and I would surely get to the heart of the matter.

I knew from experience that Sybil would at first give me her clairvoyant impressions about the house before going into full trance. There was, incidentally, nothing about the house or the room we were in that was in the slightest bit disturbing or eerie. It seemed a pleasant, relaxed atmosphere, and if I had not known that there was something strange about the house, I would have taken it for just another suburban residence.

I tapped Sybil on the hand and looked at her expectantly. "Sybil, do you feel anything in the atmosphere of this downstairs room that seems out of the ordinary?"

"Not particularly in this room. I feel it much more in the region of the doorway as you come in the house—I think that must be the front door—and at the room on the right as you come in. That gives me a much stronger atmosphere."

'Is there any disturbed feeling in this room we are in now?"

"I am disturbed now, but I'm more disturbed since I went in the other room."

"What is it that seems to disturb you?"

"Something very restless, arid also very excited."

"Man or woman?"

"Well, I don't know. I just know there's something very

restless that has probably been here for some time. I don't really think it's too long. But something very, very restless, and inclined to be noisy."

"And you don't know what it wants?"

"No, I don't know what it wants."

"All right, let us try and see whether we can get it to make a contact directly."

"Who are you?" I said as soon as Sybil was entranced.

"Peter Ellis."

The voice, very masculine and not at all like Sybil's own, was very British.

"Is this your house?"

"No."

"Do you live here?"

"No."

"What are you doing here?"

"Hiding."

"Why are you hiding?"

"I have to get something. Something from the girl."

"Who is the girl? What's her name?"

"Marilyn."

"Marilyn what?"

"Wade."

"Marilyn Wade? Does she live here?"

In an almost indistinguishable voice, the entranced medium mentioned "some children living here." Evidently Marilyn had some working connection with those children.

"Whose children are they?"

"Wassir's."

"Does he live in the house?"

"Lives here."

"Who owns the house?"

"Devasser."

"Can I help you in any way?"

77

"Find the papers."

"Well if you don't tell me anything about them, how will I recognize them?"

"They're here. She said they were here."

"Who said? What has Marilyn got to do with the papers?"

"She wrote part of them."

"For whom?"

"For me."

"What is in the papers?"

"I don't know."

"Who gave you the papers?"

"Lord Case."

"Lord Keyes?" The British pronunciation of the name would sound as if spelled "Case," I realized.

"Case. Case. Case."

"Did you work for him?"

"Don't ask questions…"

"Did you work for Lord Keyes?"

"Yes."

"In what capacity?"

"I'm not answering questions."

"Is he alive?"

"No."

"What were the papers concerned with?"

"I don't know."

"What profession do you have?"

"I am a grayhound."

"You're a what?"

"Grayhound."

"Grayhound? What does that mean?"

"Find out."

"How long are you in this house now?"

"Three weeks."

"What day did you come here?"

"May twenty-six."

"What year?"

"Nineteen thirty-five."

'Nineteen thirty-five. Did anything happen to you in this house?"

"I—I got—I got lost."

"You got lost? In which way did you get lost?"

"I—I don't know. I got confused."

"Whom did you meet outside of Marilyn? Did you meet anyone else in this house?"

"Devasser."

"Would you spell that name for me?"

"D-E-V-A-S-S-E-R."

"Devasser?"

"Yes."

"What did you do with him? What was the reason for meeting this person?"

"I shan't tell you."

"You must tell me if I am to help you."

"Find the papers."

"If you will tell me why, I can help you; not any other way."

"She is not to be helped."

"Who are the papers for?"

"Everyham. "

"Who is he?"

"He was here."

"Repeat that name."

"Ev-ry-ham."

"Abraham?"

"No. I, not A."

"Ibraham? Ebrehem?"

"Ebreham."

"Where does he live?"

"I don't know."

"Did you meet him?"

"Yes."

"Here in this house?"

"Upstairs."

"And what happened during your meeting?"

"I—nearly—hit him."

"Why did you nearly hit him?"

"He was not a gentleman."

"In which way was he not a gentleman?"

"He lost his temper."

"Why did he lose his temper?"

"Because he asked questions, and I didn't answer."

"What did he want to know of you?"

"Questions like you."

"About the papers?"

"Yes."

"And why couldn't you tell him?"

"I'm a grayhound."

"You are a gray hound. For which government?"

"British."

"Did anyone hurt you in this house?"

"Yes."

"Who?"

"Ebreham."

"Who does he work for?"

"Why do you ask?"

"Because I'd like to help you. I'm on your side, remember? I've come a long way to help you. Now I'm here; that is proof enough that I'm on your side, is it not?"

"No."

"You're speaking to me and I'm listening. What would you like us to do?"

"Find the papers."

"Well, where would I find them?"

"Where the hell is Marilyn?"

"Are they in this house?"

"Yes."

"Are they hidden in this house?"

"Yes."

"Where are they hidden?"

"In the wall."

"In the wall?"

Suddenly the voice grew angry and desperate. "No…I'm not telling you."

"I'm on your side, my friend. I will help you carry out your plans. You have my word of honor."

"I'll get them myself."

"You cannot. You are not what you used to be. Something has happened to you."

"Go away!"

"Then you'll be alone again, and it will be many, many years before anyone will find you. Tell me, is there anything in the wall?"

"I'm not telling you if he kills me."

"No one is going to touch you. I will protect you."

"Oh? [A dog barks faintly in the background.] The dog."

"What about the dog?…What about the dog? Is there anything about the dog you want to tell me?"

"No—no—no." [Agitated breathing.]

"Tell me, why are you upset? Why are you upset? I'm here to help you. You've been hurt."

"Let me go outside."

"I'll help you. Do you want to stay in this house or do you wish to leave?"

"I want to go outside."

"What would you do outside?"

"Get some air."

"Is there an errand you wish to make outside?"

"Yes. Yes."

"Can I make it for you?"

"I want some—air."

"Why do you want some air? Has someone hurt
you?"

"Breathe."

"Tell me, what is there downstairs? What is downstairs in
this house?"

"He sleeps there."

"Who does sleep there?"

"Ebreham."

"Then why does he sleep there? What does he do in this
house?"

"Works and works and works."

"What is his profession, his work? What does he do?"

"Steals papers." The voice had a tinge of sarcasm now
mixed in with the anguish and bitterness.

"How did he get into this house?"

"Visited."

"Did you see him visit?"

"Yes."

"What were you doing here?"

"Watching.

"Watching what?"

"People lying—"

"Who were you watching?"

"Ebreham."

"What is in those papers?"

"Don't ask."

"I have to ask if I am to help you."

"I shan't tell you."

"Do you realize that this house is no longer in the same
hands? That time has gone on?"

"Time?"

"What year do you think this is?"

"Thirty-five."

"No. This is 'sixty-five."

"Sixty-five?"

 "Nineteen sixty-five."

"No."

"Yes. You have been asleep for a long time; you have been ill; something has happened to you. Do you understand? That is why you are confused."

"I'm confused." The voice sounded very tired now.

"Someone hurt you. Now you must tell us exactly who hurt you and what happened, and we will be able to help you. Do you understand? It is thirty years since nineteen thirty-five. You have—what is commonly called 'died.' You are no longer in the flesh. It is your mind that speaks to us. Do you understand that? There has been a change. It is your memory that keeps you in this house, but you are in no danger. No one can hurt you ever again. We are your friends. We have come to help you find peace. Now you must tell us what you want done."

"The papers."

"Whom do you wish to have them delivered to?"

"Keyes."

"Keyes? Is 'Keyes' a name, or do you mean the keys?"

"Lord Keyes."

"Lord Keyes. Is he your—employer?"

"Room one-two-one-six. "

"Room one-two-one-six—where?"

"In London."

"Where in London? Where?"

"Admiralty."

"Admiralty?"

"London. "

"London. You want the papers delivered in London? But

Lord Keyes is dead too. He's gone. You need not keep your secret any longer."

"Has he died?" Genuine surprise filled the voice now.

"You are free to divulge your secret now. Thirty years have gone on; you are free to speak."

"I'm a grayhound. You don't understand"

"Then how can we locate these papers if we don't know where to look?"

"I can't find them either. So I'll keep on looking."

"Tell me, what is this house like? Is there anything underneath this house that is unusual?"

"I could hide outside if you'll take me out."

"How would you get out from this house?"

"I won't tell you. I've been hidden and I want to go back. There's not much room."

"There's not much room where?

"Where are you hiding?"

"Outside."

"Where outside?"

"Why do you want to know?"

"So I can help you."

"How?"

"Protect you."

"Too late."

"Don't you want to be helped?"

'It's too late."

"Why is it too late?"

"Something's gone wrong."

"What has gone wrong?"

"I don't know."

"Can you guess what has gone wrong?"

"No."

"Did someone kill you?"

"What's 'kill you'?"

"Has someone killed you? Taken your life?"

"Yes. Hit me."

"Someone hit you. Who hit you?"

"Ebreham."

"Did he take the papers from you?"

"No. Some of them."

"Where did he hit you? What part of the house?"

'By the fire."

"Upstairs or downstairs?"

"Downstairs.' By the door."

"And then what did he do with you?"

"I fell asleep."

"Yes. You fell asleep. And then what happened?"

"Then I came back to find the papers."

"Did you find them?"

"I don't know. My head's bad."

"And then what happened?"

"She said she'd let me in."

"Who'd let you in?"

"Marilyn."

"What did she do in this house? What was her position?"

"She was looking after the children."

"Did she know you?"

"Yes."

"So she let you in. What did she do then?"

"No, she didn't let me in."

"Why didn't she let you in?"

"She wasn't faithful. She played."

"Did she see you?"

"She knew I was there. She played, and I knew it was wrong."

"What was wrong?"

"That she played. She wasn't safe."

"Why did she play?"

"She played 'Moonlight and Roses.'"

"On what instrument?"

"A piano."

"What happened after that?"

"She played, but I came in."

Evidently Marilyn's playing the song was a prearranged signal.

"Where did you go?"

"I went to his bedroom."

"Whose bedroom?"

"Ebreham."

"All right, you went to his bedroom. What happened then?"

"We talked. And then we came to the door and then we went to the fireplace. And then I made him angry."

"What did you make him angry with?"

"About half the papers."

"You mean you had half the papers? Or did he have them?"

"He had half."

'Who had the other half?"

"I did."

"And you didn't want to give him the other half?"

"No."

"Where was the other half?"

"Marilyn hid them."

"Where did she hide them?"

"In the house."

"Where in the house?"

"I don't know. She was going to tell me, and then I went to sleep."

"And she never told you? What did he do with his half of the papers?...Can you hear me? Can you hear my voice? Can you hear-my voice?"

But apparently the "grayhound" had slipped away. Still, I

needed more information. I decided to let Sybil look for it.

"Sybil," I suggested, "stay on your side of the veil and before you awaken, answer me. Is there anything about this house that involves violence of any kind?"

"Yes."

"Can you tell me what you feel?"

"Very confused. Two people—two people tried to come through."

"Who are they?"

"A man and a woman. I can see the man. I can't see the woman."

"Did he die in this house?"

"He was hurt. I think he died outside."

"Why was he hurt?"

"Let me look around…I don't like this place."

"Why don't you like this place?"

"It has got so many people coming and going."

"What is going on in this place that is unusual?"

"People come for a little while, and then they go away. They leave very bad vibrations."

"What sort of business is going on in this place?"

"Business?"

"What sort of business? What are they doing here, these people? What is their business in coming here?"

"I don't know. It's some exchange."

"Exchange of what?"

"Of—books, or something like that."

"Books. Is there anything underneath this house that needs explanation? Is there anything unusual about the structure of this house?"

"He hid there."

"You mean after he was killed?"

"No, before he was killed—and after."

"And whom did he hide from?"

"A man in the bedroom."

"Why did he hide from him?"

"I think he was watching him."

"Whom was he watching him for, and why?"

"I don't know."

"Do you know what is in those papers that he seems to have told me about?"

"He wants the papers, but I don't—"

'What is in the papers?"

"The papers are in the book room."

"The book room? Are they in a book?"

"Behind a book."

"Are they still there?"

"Deep down, though."

"Deep down?"

"Deep down; not where you'd put your hand on them. You have to—"

I had to change tapes at this moment and the entranced Sybil mentioned something about a wall.

"What do you mean a wall?" I continued my line of questioning.

"There're two walls."

"And what is in back of those two walls?"

"A cavity."

"What is in back of the cavity?"

"Another wall."

"What is the cavity for?"

"Books and papers, and that sort of thing. I can't see; hard…"

"Try."

"I can't get in very well."

"Try again."

"This is so dusty."

"But it is still there now, is it?"

"Still there, but it's dusty, and the dust comes into my throat."

"What sort of dust?"

"Thick dust, like flour."

"Is there anything behind those two walls?"

"Papers."

"Outside of the papers, what else is there?"

"I can't see because the wall goes on."

"Where does it lead to?"

"Wait a minute, don't rush me."

"All right, take your time."

"He came this way."

"He came this way? From where?"

"From the woods."

"Who came this way, the man who was killed?"

"Peter. This is where he hid. How can I prove he was not? I'm in the house; and now I'm out. What's in between? There's something in between."

"All right, let us say there's something in between that wasn't always there. But try to see what there is now, at this moment, behind the wall. Papers and what else?"

"Papers."

"Is there anything else there?"

"It's deep. I can only see papers. I don't like going outside. I'm not going outside."

"Is there a man or a woman behind there—?"

"I'm not going outside."

"Is there a body in there?"

"I'm not going outside." The voice sounded positively agitated now.

"Why don't you want to go outside? Why are you afraid?"

"I'm not afraid."

"Well, why is it that you don't like going outside? Is it you, or do you feel this man who doesn't wish to go outside?"

"He had to go outside, but I don't."

"Well then, stay inside and tell us what you see in the cavity. What you call the cavity ."

"He's still there."

"Who is?"

"That man."

"He is still there?"

"You said something about it. Don't leave him there."

"We have no intention of leaving him there. Is he there alone?"

"Yes. You shouldn't leave anyone there."

"Would you tell this man, Peter, that there's no reason for him to stay in this house; that his mission has been accomplished and he may leave."

"He's not in the house…"

"Where do you sense him?"

"He's outside."

"Is he free to go?"

"He comes in. Now, let me go."

"All right. Is there anything else you want to tell me?"

"I want to go. I don't like this room. I don't like that wall."

"What is in the papers. Look at the papers. What is in those papers? Quick, look."

"If I look you'll come?"

"Yes. You must look. What are the papers about?"

"Ships."

"Ships? What sort of ships?"

"I don't know."

"Go and look at the papers and report back to me what you see."

"I can't read the writing; they're handwritten, not typed, and it's very difficult to read."

"Can you read any of it? Can you read the signatures?"

"The signature is King KR…"

"King?"

"Royalty…R-O something…R-O-G."

"R-O-G?"

"Eight papers."

"What do they concern themselves with?"

"I can't see. The writing is big, and 1 can't read them very well."

"Is there anything printed on top of the pages that you can easily read?"

"It's written."

"Nothing official, no seal, no printing?"

"Seal."

"Whose seal is it?"

"R. K."

"What language are they in?"

"English."

"Look at the first line of some of the papers and see who they are addressed to."

"Just wait a minute…They're not letters."

"What are they?"

"Ah—bout some ship business."

"Specifically, what sort of ship business?"

"I think it's some naval thing. I can't read this writing."

"Can you make out any words at all? Try."

"Make out Devasser. D-E-V-A-S-S-E-R."

"Who is Devasser?"

"He is an Admiral."

"All right, I will call you back."

"I hate things in walls. Two walls. Who wants two walls?"

"What should we do with those walls?"

"I would take them away. But don't let him know."

"Don't let who know?"

"Peter."

"Peter? But he's not there anymore."

"Oh yes he is."

"If we open those walls, would we find his body?"

"Body. He's there."

"With those papers?"

"Not with the papers!"

"But you said they were there too."

"Papers in the house."

"Where in the house?"

"In there. Behind the books; behind the wall. Behind another wall. And then there's another wall. And he's outside."

"But his body is in that cavity, is it?"

"His body is outside."

"Where outside?"

"From the paper you go through the drains."

drains. And in there?"

"To the woods."

"To the woods?"

"Where he is hiding."

"Where will we find the body, exactly?"

"I'm not going to go down that drain."

"I don't want you to go down the drain, but look."

"I am not going down that drain. I'm in the place where the books are, and there's a big slope. A big slope. And then there's a straight piece to some trees; three trees and you dig in there."

"Near the trees?"

"In the trees!"

"You mean underneath?"

"There's a long tunnel."

"Long tunnel."

"It's a drain or something. I don't know."

"And that is where he is?"

"That's where he is, poor man."

"All right, Sybil. I want you to come away from this wall, Come back to your own body, to the present."

But Sybil was still fascinated by the past. "Who put the wall there? Why did he have three walls?"

"Never mind, don't worry about it. Come back."

And back she came, waking up, rubbing her eyes, and remembering absolutely nothing of the past hour. Everyone was very quiet, still under the impact of what they had heard. I decided to question Bob Gray about his experiences now.

"Would you bring me up to date on what you personally have experienced in this house that you might classify as unusual."

"Shortly after coming into the house," Bob Gray began, "I was fixing up one of the rooms, and thought I heard my name called. There was no one else around at that particular time. One other evening, in the middle of the night the player piano began to play. But it is electric and plays on a switch."

"What did it play. Did you recognize the tune?"

"Whatever the roll that was on the piano, it finished the roll and automatically shut itself off."

"Can the piano be played manually , too?"

"Oh yes."

"Go on."

"One evening a group of us were talking about ghosts and someone said they didn't believe in ghosts, and a wind went whistling though the room. We checked, and on the lowest level of the house a door which is never opened—it has an air conditioner in the door and a dehumidifier in front of it and a latch on it—was nevertheless fully open."

"By itself, somehow?"

"By itself."

"Is there anything unusual about the structure of the house?"

"Well, it roams all over the countryside a little. It's been added to and added to, that's the only thing that's unusual."

"Is there anything unusual about the library?"

"Well, there is this panel in the wall."

"Tell me about the panel, and how it was found."

"Well, it was found just very recently,"

"How long ago did you get the house?"

"Two and a half years."

"And when did you get to the panel?"

"I got to the panel just three months ago but had the idea shortly after I came to the house. A woman who had lived here at one time stopped by and wanted me to identify the location of the panel. She said she'd been told by the owner at the time of her tenancy here that there was a panel, but he didn't want to tell her where the panel was unless she bought the house. She was curious to know if there was one and where it was. I denied its existence, not having located it at that point. I was telling this story one night at a party some months ago. One of the couples went up to the library and the woman just went right to the wall and started pulling books away and discovered the panel."

"This woman—was she any way psychic or unusual?"

"Not to my knowledge, but she said later that she felt she knew right where it was."

"What did it look like?"

"It was wide enough to be a passage, and the passageway was blocked with a piece of concrete; maybe twenty-five inches wide and thirty inches long."

"Did you try to remove the cement?"

"No."

"Did you have any desire to see what was in back of that?"

"A curiosity that didn't match the desire to tear the wall apart."

"Is there anything underneath the house, or outside the

house that you found that was unusual for a dwelling of this kind?"

"Well—at the time we first came into the house, there was a passageway, or cave, tunnel, call it what you will, leading from one of the bedrooms out into the hillside. It went back about fifteen feet and then branched off in a T. It was shored up by four-by-fours on the side, but with very thin boards at the top. I was afraid to have anyone go in, and I simply had a man come with a claw digger and pull the dirt away and clear the top away and fill it in. It took a couple of loads before it stopped settling and that was the end of the tunnel."

"Were the tunnels high enough for a man to go through?"

"Yes, from the room side. It was only about four feet above the floor level, but if you stepped across down into the tunnel itself it was about seven feet tall. It was quite tall."

"So one could use it as an escape hatch?"

"One could. This was obviously—to my eye at least—a very recent construction, and the tenant—the colonel—a Canadian Air Force colonel, who had the house before me, had admitted later that he had built the tunnel. He said he did it because President Kennedy had told him to build an air raid shelter."

"How long had the colonel been in this house?"

"Around three years."

"Did any of the previous tenants, before the colonel, talk about the tunnels?"

"No. The only previous tenant I've ever talked to was the woman who stopped by and wanted to know where the passageway was, or the panel."

"You have no idea how old the house is, then?"

"No. It's thirty years or so."

"Can you recognize the spot described by Sybil in trance as the likely spot—the trees—where one might find the body?"

"No, the place is surrounded with trees, and I have no idea

where any group of trees is."

"At the end of the tunnel, I believe."

"Well, this particular tunnel I've described to you is one that went toward the drive rather than toward trees in any area. In fact, one of the reasons that prompted me to have it filled in so quickly was that I was afraid the drive would collapse."

"Are there other tunnels going in other directions?"

"There may be, but I don't know of any."

"Have you lived in Washington a long time?"

"Eight years."

A close associate of Bob Gray's, who had lived at the house for a long time also, then requested to be heard. "I heard some noises," the gentleman said gravely, "last winter."

"What exactly did you hear?"

"I heard something that could have passed as a knock or a rattling at the door. I went to the door and though there was fish snow outside there were no tracks."

"Was this the door upstairs, or downstairs?"

"Actually, I went to each of the doors, because I thought that it was someone at the door."

"Did anyone else outside yourself hear those noises?"

"Yes, one other in the house."

"Another gentleman in the house."

"Yes."

"You have a lovely dog. What is his name?"

"Well, his name is so distinctive I'd like to skip that."

"All right, all right. Doggie then. Did Doggie have any unusual experiences in this house?"

"Yes—as a matter of fact the dog is only here on loan; he's not mine. But the last time I had him here was for a matter of ten days or so, while his owner was away. Every night, at exactly the same time, around four o'clock in the morning, the dog would start barking. Really barking up quite a storm.

Always against the wall down here, just against the living room wall."

"In this room?"

"Yes. Rather than against, or at, a door. He would always be barking at the wall."

"Is the wall in any way connected with the panel?"

"It's on the other side of the panel area."

I thanked the young man, who preferred that his name be withheld for personal reasons.

Ruth Montgomery, the columnist for the Hearst papers who was then already interested in psychic research even though she had not yet written her best-selling books along these lines, looked up with a serious expression. I asked her who knew enough about Washington to be able to fill us in on the background of this house, and with her help, and that of others in the room, I was able to piece together a most unusual account.

The house had been built about thirty years earlier by a man named Smith who had been working with the OSS, the Office of Strategic Services. That agency was the forerunner of the CIA, a kind of secret super-spy agency of the United States Government. He was a man of taste, who collected artistic glass with a vengeance. Ostensibly to enrich his collection, he traveled around the world, although in reality he was gathering information for the OSS.

The song that had been the signal for the spy to come in out of the damp was still on the old player piano roll. With a nervous laugh, Bob Gray switched it on and the roll played "Moonlight and Roses" exactly as it had back in the 1930s when "the grayhound" had met his doom because of it.

I checked the data out with the librarian at the British Information Service in New York:

Lord Keyes died on December 26, 1945. His full name was Roger John Brownlow Keyes. He had been an Admiral of the Fleet, who had retired in 1935, became a Member of Parliament until 1943, although in 1940 he returned to active duty, again with the Royal Navy.

At first his job was special liaison with the King of Belgium, and it is interesting to note that Sybil Leek mentioned the words "Royalty...King..." prior to disclosing Roger Keyes' other functions. After serving as Director of Combined Naval Operations in 1940 and 1941, he became Naval Attache in various European capitals. That post is often used as a cover for the Naval Intelligence operative. Quite plainly, Lord Keyes was a Naval Intelligence officer, though not in America.

It is here that the spy's role became clear: He came from Keyes, either in his employ or on his orders, to seek out a contact in Washington. He mentioned the year 1935. Curiously, that was the year Keyes retired for the first time—to set up the intelligence service perhaps? At the time of sudden death, important dates sometimes become embedded in the mind of the victim and are remembered more than a less impressive later date.

I still wondered about the term "grayhound." But what I had suspected about its true meaning was confirmed by the *Dictionary of Slang and Unconventional English* (Eric Partridge, 1938):

"Grayhound: a hammock with little bedding, unfit for storage; a nautical term."

Was that it? Not quite.

"Ocean greyhound; a fast Atlantic liner."

That was it, then. The spy was a fast courier between Europe and America, truly a gray hound—quiet and fast, bent on his mission.

The missing papers, of course, were never found nor did Bob Gray make any attempt to locate the body, if there was one, in the closed-off tunnel. He was too fond of his beautiful house in the woods to start tearing down the wall just because a lowly British courier had met his death somewhere in it.

I suppose the "grayhound" isn't running any more, either, as I heard nothing further from either Gray or Ruth Montgomery on this. Perhaps he met up with his employer, Lord Keyes, in the land where missing documents don't mean a thing.

A CONNECTICUT
STAY-BEHIND

*O*ne of the more amazing stories that has come my way concerns a family of farmers in central Connecticut. Some people have a ghost in the house, a stay-behind who likes the place so much he or she doesn't want to leave. But this family had entire groups of ghosts staying on simply because they liked the sprawling farmhouse, and simply because it happened to be their home too. The fact that they had passed across the threshold of death did not deter them in the least. To the contrary, it seemed a natural thing to stay behind and watch what the young ones were doing with the house, possibly help them here and there, and at the very least, have some fun with them by causing so-called "inexplicable" phenomena to happen.

After all, life can be pretty dull in central Connecticut, especially in the winter. It isn't any more fun being a ghost in central Connecticut, so one cannot really hold it against these stay-behinds if they amuse themselves as best they could in the afterlife. When I was there, the house was showing its age; it wasn't in good condition, and needed lots of repairs, The family wasn't as large as it was before some of the younger generation moved out to start lives of their own, but it was still a busy house and a friendly one, ghosts or no ghosts. It stood on a quiet country road, off the main route, and on a clear day you could see the Massachusetts border in the distance—that is, if you were looking for it. It was hardly noticeable, for, in this part of the country, all New England looked the same.

Because of the incredible nature of the many incidents, the family wanted no publicity, no curious tourists, and especially no reporters. To defer to their wishes, I have changed the family name to help them retain that anonymity and the peace and quiet of their country house. The house in question was already old when a map of the town, drawn in 1761, showed it. The owners, the Harveys, had lived in it all their lives, with an interruption. Mrs. Harvey's great-great-grandparents bought it from the original builder, and when her great-great-grandfather died in 1858, it happened at the old homestead. Likewise, her great-great-grandmother passed on in 1871, aged eighty, and again it happened at home. One of their children died at the age of ninety-one in 1921, also at home.

This is important, you see, because it accounts for the events which transpired later in the lives of their descendants. A daughter named Julia married an outsider and moved to another state, but she considered herself part of the family just the same, so much so that her second home was still the old homestead in central Connecticut. Another daughter, Martha, was Mrs. Harvey's great-grandmother. Great-grandmother Martha died at age ninety-one, also in the house. Then there was an aunt, a sister of her great-great-grandfather's, by the name of Nancy, who came to live with them, being a widow; she lived to be ninety and died in the house. They still had some of her furniture there. Mrs. Harvey's grandparents had only one child, Viola, who became her mother, but they took in boarders, mostly men working in the nearby sawmills. One of these boarders died in the house too, but his name is unknown. Possibly several others died there too.

Of course the house didn't look the way it originally did;

additions were built onto the main part, stairs were moved, a well in the cellar was filled in because members of the family going down for cider used to fall into it, and many of the rooms which later became bedrooms originally had other purposes. For instance, daughter Marjorie's bedroom was once called the harness room because horses' harnesses were once made in it, and the room of one of the sons used to be called the cheese room for obvious reasons. What became a sewing room was originally used as a pantry with shelves running across the south wall. The fact that stairs were changed throughout the house is important, because in the mind of those who lived in the past, the original stairs would naturally take precedence over later additions or changes. Thus phantoms may appear out of the wall, seemingly without reason, except that they would be walking up staircases which no longer exist. Mrs. Harvey was born in this house but at age four her parents moved away from it, and did not return until much later. But even then, Mrs. Harvey recalled an incident which she was never to forget. When she was only four years old, she remembered very clearly an old lady she had never seen before appeared at her crib. She cried, but when she told her parents about it, they assured her it was just a dream. But Mrs. Harvey knew she had not dreamt the incident; she remembered every detail of the old lady's dress.

When she was twelve years old, at a time when the family had returned to live in the house, she was in one of the upstairs bedrooms and again the old lady appeared to her. But when she talked about it to her parents, the matter was immediately dropped. As Frances Harvey grew up in the house, she couldn't help but notice some strange goings-on. A lamp moved by itself, without anyone being near it. Many times she could feel a presence walking close behind her in the upstairs part of the house, but when she turned around, she was alone. Nor was she the only one to notice the strange goings-on. Her brothers heard footsteps around their beds, and complained about someone tending over them, yet no one was to be seen. The doors to the bedrooms would open by themselves at night, so much so that the boys tied the door latches together so that the doors could not in fact open by themselves. Just the same, when morning came, the doors were wide open with the knot still in place.

It was at that time that her father got into the habit of taking an after dinner walk around the house before retiring. Many times he told the family of seeing a strange light going through the upstairs rooms, a glowing luminosity for which there was no rational explanation. Whenever Frances Harvey had to be alone upstairs she felt uncomfortable, but when she mentioned this to her parents she was told that all old houses made one feel like that and to never mind. One evening Frances was playing a game with her grandfather when both of them clearly heard footsteps corning up the back stairs. But her grandfather didn't budge. When Frances asked him who this could possibly be, he merely shrugged and said there was plenty of room for everyone.

As the years passed, the Harveys would come back to the house from time to time to visit. On one of these occasions, Frances would wake up in the night because someone was bending over her. At other times there was a heavy depression on the bed as if someone were sitting there! Too terrified to tell anyone about it, she kept her experiences to herself for the time being. Then, in the early 1940s, Frances married; with her husband and two children she eventually returned to the house to live there with her grandparents. No sooner had they moved in than the awful feeling came back in the night. Finally she told her husband, who of course scoffed at the idea of ghosts. The most active area in the house seemed to be the upstairs, roughly from her son Don's closet, through Lolita, the daughter's room, and especially the front hall and stairs. It felt as if someone were standing on the landing on the front stairs, just watching. This goes back a long time. Mrs. Harvey's mother frequently complained, when working in the attic, that all of a sudden she would feel someone next to her, someone she could not see.

One day Mrs. Harvey and her youngest daughter went grocery shopping. After putting the groceries away, Mrs. Harvey reclined on the living room couch while the girl sat in the dining room, reading. Suddenly they heard a noise like thunder even though the sky outside was clear. It came again, only this time it sounded closer as if it were upstairs! When it happened the third time, it was accompanied by a sound as if someone were making up the bed in Mrs. Harvey's son's room upstairs.

Now, they had left the bed in disorder, because they had been in a hurry to go shopping. No one else could have gone upstairs, and yet when they entered the son's room, the bed was made up as smoothly as possible. Yet still, part of the family scoffed at the idea of having ghosts in the house and considered the mother's ideas as dreams or hallucinations. They were soon to change their minds, however, when it happened to them as well.

The oldest daughter felt very brave and called up the stairs, "Little ghosties, where are you?" Her mother told her she had better not challenge them, but the others found it amusing. That night she came downstairs a short time after she had gone to bed, complaining that she felt funny in her room but thought it was just her imagination. The following night, she awoke to the feeling that someone was bending over her. One side of her pillow was pulled away from her head as though a hand had pushed it down. She called out and heard footsteps receding from her room, followed by heavy rumbling in the attic above. Quickly she ran into her sister's room where both of them lay awake the rest of the night listening to the rumbling and footsteps walking around overhead. The next day she noticed a dusty, black footprint on the light colored scatter rug next to her bed. It was in the exact location where she had felt someone standing and bending over her. Nobody's footprint in the house matched the black footprint, for it was long and very narrow. At this point the girls purchased special night lights and left them on all night in the hope of sleeping peacefully.

One day Mrs. Harvey felt very brave and started up the stairs in response to footsteps coming from her mother's bedroom. She stopped—she heard the pocket watch. Quickly she ran down the stairs and outside to get her son to be a witness to it. Sure enough, he too could hear the ticking noise. This was followed by doors opening and closing by themselves. Finally, they dared to go upstairs, and when they entered the front bedroom they noticed a very strong, sweet smell of perfume. When two of the daughters came home from work that evening the family compared notes and it developed that they, too, had smelled the strange perfume and heard the ticking noise upstairs. They concluded that one of their ghosts, at least, was a woman.

About the time, the youngest daughter reported seeing an old woman in her room, standing at a bureau with something shiny in her hand. The ghost handed it to her but she was too frightened to receive it. Since her description of the woman had been very detailed, Mrs. Harvey took out the family album and asked her daughter to look through it in the hope that she might identify the ghostly visitor. When they came to one particular picture, the girl let out a small cry: that was the woman she had seen! It turned out to be Julia, a great-great-aunt of Mrs. Harvey's, the same woman whom Mrs. Harvey herself had seen when she was twelve years old. Evidently the lady was still staying around.

Mrs. Harvey's attention was deflected from the phenomena in the house by her mother's illness. Like a dutiful daughter, she attended to her to the very last, but in March of 1966 her mother passed away. Whether there is any connection with her mother's death or not, the phenomena started to increase greatly, both in volume and intensity in July of that same year—to be exact, on July 20, 1966. Mrs. Harvey was hurrying one morning to take her daughter Lolita to the center of town so she could get a ride to work. Her mind was preoccupied with domestic chores, when a car came down the road, brakes squealing. Out of habit, she hurried to the living room window to make sure that none of their cats had been hit by the car. This had been a habit of her mother's and hers whenever there was the sound of sudden brakes outside.

As she did so, for just a fleeting glance, she saw her late mother looking out of the window that was her favorite one. It didn't register at first, then Mrs. Harvey realized her mother couldn't possibly have been there. However, since time was of the essence, Mrs. Harvey and her daughter Lolita left for town without saying anything to any of the others in the house. When they returned, her daughter Marjorie was standing outside waiting for them. She complained of hearing someone moving around in the living room just after they had left, and it sounded just like Grandma when she straightened out the couch and chair covers.

It frightened her, so she decided to wait in the dining room for her mother's return. But while there, she heard footsteps coming from the living room and go into the den, then she heard the sound of clothes being folded. This was something Mrs. Harvey's mother was also in the habit of doing there. It was enough for Marjorie to run outside the house and wait there. Together with her sister and her mother she returned to the living room, only to find the chair cover straightened. The sight of the straightened chair cover made the blood freeze in Mrs. Harvey's veins; she recalled vividly how she had asked her late mother not to bother straightening the chair covers during her illness, because it hurt her back. In reply, her mother had said, "Too bad I can't come back and do it after I die."

Daughter Jane was married to a Navy man, who used to spend his leaves at the old house. Even during his courtship days, he and Mrs. Harvey's mother got along real fine, and they used to do crossword puzzles together. He was sleeping at the house some time after the old lady's death when he awoke to see her standing by his bed, with her puzzle book and pencil in hand. It was clear to Mrs. Harvey by now that her late mother had joined the circle of dead relatives to keep a watch on her and the family. Even while she was ill, Mrs. Harvey's mother wanted to help in the house. One day after her mother's death, Mrs. Harvey was baking a custard pie and lay down on the couch for a few minutes while it was baking.

She must have fallen asleep, for she awoke to the voice of her mother saying, "Your pie won't burn, will it?" Mrs. Harvey hurriedly got up and checked, the pie was just right and would have burned if it had been in any longer. That very evening something else happened. Mrs. Harvey wanted to watch a certain program on television which came on at seven-thirty p.m. But she was tired and fell asleep on the couch in the late afternoon. Suddenly she heard her mother's voice say to her, "It's time for your program, dear." Mrs. Harvey looked at the clock, it was exactly seven-thirty p.m. Of course, her mother did exactly the same type of thing when she was living, so it wasn't too surprising that she should continue with her concerned habits after she passed on into the next dimension.

But if Mrs. Harvey's mother had joined the ghostly crew in the house, she was by no means furnishing the bulk of the phenomena, not by a long shot. Lolita's room upstairs seemed to be the center of many activities, with her brother Don's room next to hers also very much involved. Someone was walking from her bureau to her closet and her brother heard the footsteps, too. Lolita looked up and saw a man in a uniform with gold buttons standing in the back of her closet. At other times she smelled perfume and heard the sound of someone dressing near her bureau. All the time she heard people going up the front stairs, mumbling, go into her closet, where the sound stopped abruptly. Yet, they could not see anyone on such occasions.

Daughter Jane wasn't left out of any of this either. Many nights she would feel someone standing next to her bed, between the bed and the wall. She saw three different people and felt hands trying to lift her out of bed. To be sure, she could not see their faces; their shapes were like dark shadows. Marjorie, sleeping in the room next to Jane's, also experienced an attempt by some unseen forces to get her out of bed. She grabbed the headboard to stop herself from falling.

One night she awoke to catch a glimpse of someone in a long black coat hurrying through the hall. Mumbling was heard in that direction, so she put her ear against the door to see if she could hear any words, but she couldn't make out any. Marjorie, too, saw the old woman standing at the foot of her bed—the same old woman whom Mrs. Harvey had seen when she was twelve years old. Of course, that isn't too surprising; the room Marjorie slept in was Julia's a long time ago. Lolita also had her share of experiences: sounds coming up from the cellar bothering her, footsteps, voices, even the sound of chains. It seemed to her that they came right out of the wall by her head, where there used to be stairs but are no more. Finally, it got so bad that Lolita asked her mother to sleep with her. When Mrs. Harvey complied the two women clearly saw a glow come in from the living room and go to where the shelves used to be. Then there was the sound of dishes, and even the smell of food.

Obviously, the ghostly presences were still keeping house in their own fashion, reliving some happy or at least busy moments from their own past. By now Mr. Harvey was firmly convinced that he shared the house with a number of dead relatives, if not friends. Several times he woke to the sound of bottles being placed on the bureau. One night he awoke because the bottom of their bed was shaking hard; as soon as he was fully awake, it stopped. This was followed by a night in which Mrs. Harvey could see a glow pass through the room at the bottom of the bed. When "they" got to the hall door, which was shut, she could hear it open, but it actually did not move. Yet the sound was that of an opening door. Next she heard several individuals walk up the stairs, mumbling as they went.

The following night a light stopped by their fireplace and, as she looked closely, it resembled a figure bending down. It got so that they compared notes almost every morning to see what had happened next in their very busy home. One moonlight night Mrs. Harvey woke to see the covers of her bed folded in half, the entire length of the bed. Her husband was fully covered, but she was totally uncovered. At the same time she saw some dark shadows by the side of the bed. She felt someone's hand holding her own, pulling her gently. Terrified, she couldn't move, wondering what would happen next. Then the blankets were replaced as before, she felt something cold touch her forehead, and the ghosts left. But the stay-behinds were benign, and meant no harm. Some nights Mrs. Harvey would hear some one putting things on Jane's bureau, so she tried to go up and see what it was. Carefully tiptoeing up the stairs to peek into her door to see if she could actually trap a ghost, she found herself halfway along the hall when she heard footsteps along the foot of son Don's bed, coming in her direction. Quickly, she hurried back down the stairs and stopped halfway. The footsteps sounded like a woman's, and suddenly there was the rustle of a taffeta gown. With a whooshing sound she passed Mrs. Harvey and went into Jane's room. Mrs. Harvey waited, rooted to the spot on the stairs.

A moment later the woman's footsteps came back, only this time someone walked with her, someone heavier. They went back through Don's room, and ended up in Lolita's closet—the place where Lolita had seen the man in the uniform with the shining gold buttons. Mrs. Harvey did not follow immediately but that night she decided to go up to Lolita's room and have another look at the closet. As she approached the door to the room, it opened, which wasn't unusual, since it was in the habit of opening at the slightest vibration. But before Mrs. Harvey could close it, it shut itself tight and the latch moved into place of its own volition. Mrs. Harvey didn't wait around for anything further that night.

For awhile, there was peace. In October the phenomena resumed. One night Mrs. Harvey woke up when she saw a shadow blocking the light coming from the dining room. She looked towards the door and noticed a lady dressed all in black come into her bedroom and stand close to her side of the bed. This time she clearly heard her speak.

"Are you ready? It is almost time to go."

With that, the apparition turned and started up the stairs. The stairs looked unusually light, as if moonlight were illuminating them. When the woman in black got to the top step, all was quiet and the stairs were dark again, as before. Mrs. Harvey could see her clothes plainly enough, but not her face. She noticed that the apparition had carried a pouch-style pocketbook, which she had put over her arm, so that her hands would be free to lift up her skirt as she went up the stairs. The next morning, Mrs. Harvey told her husband of the visit. He assured her she must have dreamed it all. But before she could answer, her daughter Marjorie came in and said that she had heard someone talking in the night, something about going, and it being almost time. She saw a figure at the foot of her bed, which she described as similar to what Mrs. Harvey had seen.

The night before Thanksgiving, 1967, Marjorie heard footsteps come down the stairs. She was in bed, and tried to get up to see who it was, but somehow couldn't move at all, except to open her eyes to see five people standing at the foot of her bed! Two of them were women, the others seemed just outlines or shadows. One of the two women wore a hat shaped like an old-fashioned one, and she looked very stern. As Marjorie was watching the group, she managed to roll over a little in her bed and felt someone next to her. She felt relieved at the thought that it was her mother, but then whoever it was got up and left with the others in the group. All the time they kept talking among themselves, but Marjorie could not make out what was being said. Still talking, the ghostly visitors went back up the stairs.

Nothing much happened until Christmastime. Again the footsteps running up and down the stairs resumed, yet no one was seen. On Christmas night Jane and her mother heard walking in the room above the living room where Mrs. Harvey's mother used to sleep. At that time Mr. Harvey was quite ill and was sleeping in what used to be the sewing room, so as not to awake when his wife got up early.

On two different occasions Mrs. Harvey had "visitors." The first time someone lifted her a few inches off the bed. Evidently someone else was next to her in bed, for when she extended her hand that person got up and left. Next she heard footsteps going up the stairs and someone laugh, then all was quiet again. About a week later she woke one night to feel someone pulling hard on her elbow and ankle. She hung onto the top of her bed with her other hand, but the unseen entities pushed, forcing her to brace herself against the wall.

Suddenly it all stopped. Yet there were no sounds of anyone leaving. Mrs. Harvey jumped out of bed and tried to turn the light on. It wouldn't go on. She went back to bed when she heard a voice telling her not to worry, that her husband would be all right. She felt relieved at the thought, until the voice added, "But you won't be." Then the unseen voice calmly informed her that she would die in an accident caused by a piece of bark of some sort of tree. That was all the voice chose to tell her, but it was enough to start her worrying. Under the circumstances, and in order not to upset her family, she kept quiet about it, eventually thinking that she had dreamed the whole incident. After all, if it were just a dream there was no point in telling anyone, and if it were true, there was nothing she could do anyway, so there was no point in worrying her family. She had almost forgotten the incident, when she did have an accident about a week later. She hurt her head rather badly in the woodshed, requiring medical attention. While she was still wondering whether that was the incident referred to by the ghostly voice, she had a second accident: a heavy branch fell on her and knocked her unconscious.

But the voice had said that she would die in an accident, so Mrs. Harvey wasn't at all sure that the two incidents, painful though they had been, were what the voice had referred to. Evidently some ghosts get a vicarious thrill out of making people worry, because Mrs. Harvey was still alive and well, many years after the unseen voice had told her she would die in an accident.

But if it were not enough to cope with ghost people, Mrs. Harvey also had the company of a ghost dog. Their favorite pet, Mabel, passed into eternal dogdom in March, 1967. Having been treated as a member of the family, Mabel had been permitted to sleep in the master bedroom, but as she became older she started wetting the rug, so eventually she had to be kept outside,

After the dog's death, Marjorie offered to get her mother another dog, but Mrs. Harvey didn't want a replacement for Mabel—no other dog could take her place. Shortly after the offer, and its refusal, Lolita heard a familiar scratch at the bathroom door. It sounded exactly as Mabel had always sounded when Lolita came home late at night. At first, Mrs. Harvey thought her daughter had just imagined it, but then the familiar wet spot reappeared on the bedroom rug again. They tried to look for a possible leak in the ceiling but could find no rational cause for the rug to be wet. The wet spot remained for about a month. During that time several of the girls heard a noise which reminded them of Mabel walking about. Finally the rug dried out and Mabel's ghost stopped walking.

And then, the house became quiet. Had the ghosts gone on to their just rewards, been reincarnated, or simply tired of living with flesh-and-blood relatives? Stay-behinds generally stay indefinitely; unless, of course, they feel they are really not wanted. Or perhaps they just get bored with it all.

THE LADY HAS BEEN DEAD FOR SOME TIME

*M*aurice O. was an elderly man of Polish extraction, healthy, vigorous, and strong, despite his years. He was firmly rooted in the Roman Catholic faith but was also aware of the psychic world around him. Mr. O. operated a workshop located in a loft occupying the second story of a house in lower Broadway, in one of the oldest parts of New York City. This case was brought to my attention by the man's nephew, a teacher on Long Island, who had developed an interest in historical research, especially research pertaining to the American Revolutionary period.

When I met Mr. O., he was at first very suspicious of me and my psychic friend, Ingrid Beckman. He didn't understand what parapsychology was or what we were going to do to his place. Patiently, I explained that I wanted Ingrid to get her bearing and to see whether she could pick up something from the atmosphere. While Ingrid was puttering around in the rear of the place, I convinced Mr. O. that I had to know what had happened to him, so that I could judge the case fairly. He explained that he had been in the neighborhood for fifty-five years. He remembered that, when he was a small boy, another building had stood on the same spot. "I came here from Poland in 1913, when I was ten years old," Mr. O. explained in a halting, heavily accented voice. "In this spot there was an old red brick building with few windows. On the corner there was a United cigar store. Down the block was a saloon. They had girls there; customers would come into the saloon, talk to the girls, and then go upstairs with them. In those days it cost them fifty cents or a dollar. There also used to be a barber shop in the building. In 1920 they tore down the old building and built the present factory loft, but they used the same foundations."

When Mr. O. moved his business into a building he had known all his life, it was a little like a homecoming for him. He was in the business of servicing high-speed sewing machines, which were sent to him from all over the country. Most of the time he did the work alone; for a while, his brother Frank had assisted him. In those days he never gave psychic phenomena any thought, and the many strange noises he kept hearing in the loft didn't really bother him. He thought there must be some natural explanation for them, although there were times when he was sure he heard heavy footsteps going up and down the stairs when he was alone in the building. One Saturday afternoon around four o'clock, as he was ready to wash up and go home, he walked back into the shop to wipe his hands. All of a sudden he saw a heavy iron saw fly up into the air on its own volition. It fell down to the floor, broken in two. Mr. O. picked up the pieces and said to nobody in particular, "Ghost, come here. I am not afraid of you; I want to talk to you." However, there was no answer.

"See that latch on the door," Maurice O. said to us, and showed us how he locked up the place so that nobody could come in. "Many times I've seen that latch move up and down, as if someone wanted to get in, and when I went outside there was no one there."

Often he would hear footsteps overhead in the loft above his. When he would go upstairs to check what the noise was all about, he would find the third floor loft solidly locked up and no one about. Once, when he went to the toilet between 1:30 and 2:00 p.m., at a time when he knew he was alone in the building, he found himself locked out of his place, yet he knew he had left the door open. Someone, nevertheless, had locked the latch from the inside. Finally, with the help of a friend, he broke the door open and of course found the place empty. The incident shook Mr. O. up considerably, as he couldn't explain it, no matter how he tried. During this time, too, he kept seeing shadows, roughly in the shape of human beings. They would move up and down in the back of the workshop and were of a grayish color. "It was the shape of a banana," Mr. O. commented. Curiously, during the first eight years of his occupancy—he had been across the street for forty years before—Mr. O. had had no such problems. It was only in the last two years that he began to notice things out of the ordinary.

However, Mr. O. had heard rumors of strange goings-on in the building. A previous owner of the loft building had a music store and was in the habit of spending Saturday nights in his shop with some invited friends, listening to music. One night, so the story goes, around midnight, everything started to pop out of the shelves, merchandise went flying through the air, and the entire building began to shake as if there had been an earthquake. While all this was going on, the people in the music store heard a tremendous noise overhead. They became frightened and called the police. Several radio cars responded immediately but could not find out what was wrong. Everything seemed normal upstairs. Shortly after, the owner sold the building and moved to California.

Mr. O.'s workshop was L-shaped, with a small office immediately behind the heavy steel door that gave access to the corridor, and then to a steep staircase that led out into the street. The machine shop itself was to the left and in back of the office. Thus, it was possible to work in the back of the shop and not see anyone coming in through the entrance door. But it was not possible to escape hearing any noises on the floor, since the entire building was not very large.

The day after Thanksgiving, 1971, Maurice was alone in the shop, working quietly on some orders he wanted to get out of the way. Since it was the day after Thanksgiving and just before the weekend, the building was very quiet. There was no one upstairs, and Maurice was sure he was the only one in the building at the time. Suddenly, he saw a lady walk into his office. Since he hadn't heard the heavy door slam, which it always does when someone walks in, he wondered how she had gotten into the building and into his office. She wore what to Maurice seemed a very old-fashioned, but very chic, dress, white gloves, and a bonnet, and she smelled of a sweet fragrance that immediately captured him. What was so nice a lady doing in his sewing machine shop?

Maurice did not pursue his line of thought, how she had gotten in in the first place, but asked her what she wanted. But, he felt a little frightened. He had noticed that her face was more like a skeleton covered with skin than the face of a flesh-and-blood person. The lady seemed unusually white. There was no reply; she simply stood there, looking around the place. Maurice repeated his question.

"Well," she said finally, in a faraway tone of voice, "I just came here to look at the place. I used to live in this building." Then she went to the window and pointed to the street. "I used to play over there; these houses are all new brick houses. My father and mother had a corn farm where the Federal Building is now, downtown."

"Was there anything peculiar about her tone of voice?" I asked.

"No, it sounded pretty clear to me, real American," Mr. O. replied. "She said, 'You know, all these new buildings weren't here during Revolutionary times.' Then she added, rather apologetically, 'I just came around to look.'"

Maurice was standing in back of the counter that separated his office from the short stretch of corridor leading from the entrance door. The lady was standing on the other side of the counter, so Maurice could get a good look at her; but he was too frightened to look her in the face. When he backed up, she started to talk rapidly. "I just wanted to visit the neighborhood. I used to live here." Then, pointing her hand toward the window, she said, "The headquarters of the British Army used to be across the street."

The statement made no impression on Mr. O. Besides, he was much too upset by all this to wonder how a woman standing before him in the year 1971 could know the location of the headquarters of the British Army, which had left New York almost two hundred years before.

"What did she look like?" I asked.

"She was dressed very nicely, and she looked just like any other person except for her face. I didn't see her hands, but she had on brand new gloves, her dress looked new, and the hat was real nice."

"Did you see her walking?"

"Yes, she was walking."

"What happened next?"

"Well," Maurice explained, swallowing hard at the memory of his experience, "I finally got up enough courage to ask her, 'Where are you going now?'"

The question had seemed to make the lady sad, even upset. "I'm leaving to visit relatives on Long Island," she said finally. "In the cemetery. My relatives, my friends, my father and mother."

Maurice became more and more uneasy at all this. He pretended that he had some business in the rear of the shop and started to back up from the counter.

"I'm going to visit you again," the lady said and smiled.

For about a minute, Mr. O. busied himself in the back of his workshop, then returned to the office. The woman was gone.

"Was the door still closed?"

"The door was closed. No one could have left without slamming the door, and I would have heard it. I quickly opened the door to convince myself that I had really spoken to a person. I looked around; there was nobody outside. Nobody."

Maurice checked both his door and the door downstairs. Neither door had been opened, so he went back up to continue working. He was still very much upset but decided to stay until about five o'clock. When he was ready to go home and had put the keys into the door, he suddenly began to smell the same perfume again. She's back again, he thought, and he looked everywhere. But there was no one about. Quickly he locked the door and ran downstairs.

A year to the day after the apparition, Maurice decided to work late—more out of curiosity than out of any conviction that she would return. But the lady never did.

Mr. O.'s nephew, who was a teacher and a researcher, commented, "With reference to the British headquarters being across the street, I have checked this fact out and have found that during the Revolution the British headquarters were across the street from this same building my uncle now occupies. This is a fact I know my uncle couldn't possibly have known."

"Ingrid," I said, after I had asked her to join me and Mr. O. in the front of the workshop, "what do you feel about this place?"

"There is a lot of excitement here," she replied. "I think there is a man who is kind of dangerous, very treacherous, and I think someone might have been injured here. This happened about twenty-five years ago."

"Do you think there is an earlier presence in this house?"

"I feel that this was a prosperous place, an active, busy spot. A lot of people were coming here. It was part home, part business. Before that I think this building was something else.

I think a family lived here. They may have been foreigners, and I think the man was killed. I feel that this man came to this country and invested his savings here. He wanted to build up a family business. I also think there is a woman connected with it. She wears a longish dress, going below the knees."

"What is her connection with this place?"

"She may have spent her childhood here—what happened here might have happened to her father. Perhaps she came here as a young child and spent many years in this building. She has some connection with this man, I feel."

"Does she have any reason to hang onto this place?"

'Maybe she doesn't understand why all this has happened, and she can't accept it yet. Perhaps she has lost a loved one."

Every year, around Thanksgiving, Maurice O. waited for the lady to come back and talk to him again. After he knew that she was "just a ghost," he wasn't afraid of her any longer. As far as the lady was concerned, she needn't worry either; when the British Army headquarters stood across the street, the area was a lot safer than it became in the 1970s—especially at night. But, she really didn't need to worry about muggings either, things being as they are.

THE FERRYHOUSE PHANTOM

*H*averstraw was a sleepy little town about an hour's ride north of New York City, perched high on the west side of the Hudson River. As its name implies, it was originally settled by the Dutch. On the other side of the river, not far away, was Colonel Beverley Robinson's house, where Benedict Arnold made his headquarters. The house burned down some years ago, and there were only a few charred remnants to be seen on the grounds. At Haverstraw also was the house of Joshua Smith, the man who helped Major John Andre escape, having been entrusted with the British spy's care by his friend, Benedict Arnold. At Haverstraw, too, was one of the major ferries to cross the Hudson River, for during the Revolutionary period there were no bridges to go from one side to the other.

I had never given Haverstraw any particular thought, although I had passed through it many times on my way upstate. In August 1966 I received a letter from a gentleman named Jonathan Davis, who had read some of my books and wanted to let me in on an interesting case he thought worthy of investigation. The house in question stood directly on the river, overlooking the Hudson and, as he put it, practically in the shadow of High Tor Mountain. Including the basement, there were four floors in all. But rather than give me the information secondhand, he suggested to the owner, a friend, that she communicate with me directly. The owner of the house turned out to be Laurette Brown, an editor of a national women's magazine in New York City.

"I believe my house is haunted by one or possibly two ghosts: a beautiful thirty-year-old woman and her two-year-old daughter," she explained. Ms. Brown had shared the house with another career woman, Kaye S., since October 1965. Kaye, a lovely blonde woman who came from a prominent family, was extremely intelligent and very creative. She adored the house overlooking the river, which the two women had bought on her instigation. Strangely, though, Kaye frequently said she would never leave it again alive. A short time later, allegedly because of an unhappy love affair, she drove her car to Newburgh, rigged up the exhaust pipe, and committed suicide, along with the child she had had by her second husband.

"After she died, and I lived here alone, I was terribly conscious of a spirit trying to communicate with me," Ms. Brown explained. "There was a presence, there were unnatural hangings of doors and mysterious noises, but I denied them. At the time, I wanted no part of the so-called supernatural." Since then, Ms. Brown has had second thoughts about the matter, especially as the phenomena continued. She began to wonder whether the restless spirit wanted something from her, whether there was something she could do for the spirit. One day, her friend Jonathan Davis was visiting and mentioned that he very much wanted the red rug on which he was standing at the time and which had belonged to Kaye. Before Ms. Brown could answer him, Davis had the chilling sensation of a presence and the impression that a spirit was saying to him, "No, you may not take my rug."

"Since that time, I have also heard footsteps, and the crying of a child. Lately, I wake up, out of a deep sleep, around midnight or 2:00 a.m., under the impression that someone is trying to reach me. This had never happened to me before."

Ms. Brown then invited me to come out and investigate the matter. I spoke to Jonathan Davis and asked him to come along on the day when my medium and I would pay the house a visit. Davis contributed additional information. According to him, on the night of August 6, 1966, when Ms. Brown had awakened from deep sleep with particularly disturbed thoughts she had gone out on the balcony overlooking the Hudson River. At the same time, she mixed herself a stiff drink to calm her nerves. As she stood on the balcony with her drink in hand, she suddenly felt another presence with her, and she knew at that instant, had she looked to the right, she would have seen a person. She quickly gulped down her drink and went back to sleep. She remembered, as Mr. Davis pointed out, that her former housemate had strongly disapproved of her drinking.

"It may interest you to know," Ms. Brown said, "that the hills around High Tor Mountain, which are so near to our house, are reputed to be inhabited by a race of dwarfs that come down from the mountains at night and work such mischief as moving road signs, et cetera. That there is some feeling of specialness, even enchantment, about this entire area, Kaye always felt, and I believe that, if spirits can roam the earth, hers is here at the house she so loved."

The story sounded interesting enough, even though I did not take Ms. Brown's testimony at face value. As is always the case when a witness has preconceived notions about the origin of a psychic disturbance, I assume nothing until I have investigated the case myself. Ms. Brown had said nothing about the background of the house. From my knowledge of the area, I knew that there were many old houses standing on the river front.

Ethel Johnson Meyers was my medium, and my wife Catherine drove the car. Catherine, who had by then become extremely interested in the subject, helped me with the tape recording equipment and the photography. Mr. Davis could not make it after all, owing to some unexpected business in the city.

Riverside Avenue runs along the river but is a little hard to locate if you don't know your way around Haverstraw. The house turned out to be quite charming, perched directly on the water's edge. Access to it was now from the street side, although I felt pretty sure that the main entrance had been either from around the comer or from the water itself. From the looks of the house, it was immediately clear to me that we were dealing with a pre-Revolutionary building.

Ms. Brown let us into a long veranda running alongside the house, overlooking the water. Adjacent to it was the living room, artistically furnished and filled with antiquities, rugs, and pillows. Ethel Meyers sat down in a comfortable chair in the corner of the living room, taking in the appointments with the eye of a woman who has furnished her own home not so long before. She knew nothing about the case or the nature of our business here.

"I see three men and a woman," she began. "The woman has a big nose and is on the older side; one of the men has a high forehead; and then there is a man with a smallish kind of nose, a round face, and long hair. This goes back some time, though."

"Do you feel an actual presence in this house?"

"I feel as if someone is looking at me from the back," Ethel replied. "It might be a woman. I have a sense of disturbance. I feel as if I wanted to run away—I'm now speaking as if I were her, you understand—I'm looking for the moment to run, to get away ."

Ethel took a deep breath and looked toward the veranda, and beyond it to the other side of the Hudson River. "Somebody stays here who keeps looking out a window to see if anyone is coming. I can't seem to find the window. There is a feeling of panic. It feels as if I were afraid of somebody's coming. A woman and two men are involved. I feel I want to protect someone."

"Let the individual take over them, Ethel," I suggested, hoping that trance would give us further clues.

But Ethel wasn't quite ready for it. "I've got to find that window," she said. "She is full of determination to find that window."

"Why is the window so important to her?"

"She wants to know if someone is coming. She's got to look out the window."

I instructed Ethel to tell the spirit that we would look for the window, and to be calm. But to the contrary, Ethel seemed more and more agitated. "Got to go to the window...the window...the window. The window isn't here anymore, but I've got to find it. Who took away the...No, it is not here. It is not this way. It is that way." By now Ethel was gradually sinking into trance, although by no means a complete one. At certain moments she was still speaking as herself, giving us her clairvoyant impressions, while at other moments some alien entity was already speaking through her directly.

"Very sick here, very sick," she said, her words followed by deep moaning. For several minutes I spoke to the entity directly, explaining that whatever he was now experiencing was only the passing symptoms remembered and had no validity in the present. The moaning, however, continued for some time. I assured the entity that he could speak to me directly, and that there was nothing to be afraid of, for we had come as friends.

Gradually, the moaning became quieter, and individual words could be understood. "What for? What for? The other house..." This was immediately followed by a series of moans. I asked who the person was and why he was here, as is my custom. "Why are you bringing him here?" the entranced medium said. "That man, that man, why are you bringing him here? Why? Why?" This was followed by heavy tears.

As soon as I could calm the medium again, the conversation continued. "What troubles you? What is your problem? I would like to help you," I said.

"Talk, talk, talk...too many...too many."

"Be calm, please."

"No! Take him away! I can't tell. They have left. Don't touch me! Take it away! Why hurt me so?"

"It's all right now; much has happened since," I began.

Heavy tears was the response. "They went away. Don't bother me! They have gone. Don't touch! Take him away! Take them off my neck!"

"It's all right," I said again, in as soothing a tone of voice as I could muster. "You are free. You need not worry or fear anything."

Ethel's voice degenerated into a mumble now. "Can't talk...so tired...go away."

"You may talk freely about yourself."

"I'll tell you when they've gone. I didn't help...I didn't help...I didn't know."

"Who are the people you are talking about?"

"I don't know. They took it over."

"Tell me what happened."

"They went away over the water. Please take this off so I can talk better."

Evidently, the entity thought that it was still gagged or otherwise prevented from speaking clearly. In order to accommodate him, I told him I was taking off whatever was bothering him, and he could speak freely and clearly now. Immediately, there was a moaning sound, more of relief than of pain. But the entity would not believe that I had taken "it" off and called me a liar instead. I tried to explain that he was feeling a memory from the past, but he did not understand that. Eventually he relented.

"What is your name?" I asked.

"You know, you know." Evidently he had mistaken me for

someone else. I assured him that I did not know his name.

"You are a bloody rich man, that is what you are," he said, not too nicely. Again, he remembered whatever was preventing him from speaking, and, clutching his throat, cried, "I can't speak...the throat..." Then suddenly, he realized there was no pain and calmed down considerably. "I didn't have that trouble after all," he commented.

"Exactly. That is why we've come to help you."

"Enough trouble...I saw them come up, but they went away."

All along I had assumed that we were talking to a male. Since the entity was using Ethel's voice, there were of course some female tinges to it, but somehow it sounded more like a masculine voice than that of a woman. But it occurred to me that I had no proof one way or another.

"What is your name? Are you a gentleman or..."

"Defenseless woman. Defenseless. I didn't take anyone. But you won't believe me."

I assured her that I would.

"You won't believe me...It was dark. It was dark here...I told him, take care of me."

"Is this your house?"

"Yes."

"What is your name?"

"My name is Jenny."

"Why are you here?"

"Where is my window? Where is it?"

I ignored the urgency of that remark and continued with my questioning "What is your family name?"

"Smith...Smith."

"Where and when were you born?"

There was no reply.

"What day is this today?" I continued.

"July."

"What year are we in?"

"80."

"What went on in this house? Tell me about it."

"They brought him here. They came here." Evidently the woman wasn't too happy about what she was about to tell me.

"Whose house is this?"

"Joshua. Joshua Smith."

"How is he related to you?"

"Husband. They brought him...I told them, tell them! No...no one was coming. That is all I told them. I don't know why they hurt me."

"You mean, they thought you knew something?"

"Yah...my friends. All that noise. Why don't they stop? Oh, God, I feel pain. They got away. I told you they got away."

"Who are the people you fear?"

"Guns—I must look in the window. They are coming. All is clear...time to go...they got away...they got away...See, look, they got away. It is dark. They are near the water. I get the money for it."

"What is the money for?"

"For helping."

At the time, I hadn't fully realized the identity of the speaker. I therefore continued the interrogation in the hope of ferreting out still more evidential material from her. "Who is in charge of this country?"

"George...George...nobody...everybody is fighting."

"Where were you born?"

"Here."

"Where was your husband born?"

Instead of answering the question, she seemed to say, faintly but unmistakably, "Andre."

"Who is Andre?"

"He got away. God Bless His Majesty. He got away."

"You must go in piece from this house," I began, feeling

that the time had come to free the spirit from its compulsion. "Go in peace and never return here, because much time has gone on since, and all is peaceful now. You mustn't come back. You mustn't come back."

"They will come back."

"Nobody will come. It all happened a long time ago. Go away from here."

"Johnny...Johnny..."

"You are free, you are free. You can go from this house."

"Suckers...bloody suckers...They are coming, they are coming now. I can see them. I can see them! God Bless His Majesty. They got away, they got away!"

It was clear that Jenny was reliving the most dramatic moment of her life. Ethel, fully entranced now, sat up in the chair, eyes glazed, peering into the distance, as if she were following the movements of people we could not see!

"There is the horse," the spirit continued. "Quick, get the horse! I am a loyal citizen. Good to the Crown. They got away. Where is my window?" Suddenly, the entity realized that everything wasn't as it should be. An expression of utter confusion crept over Ethel's face. "Where am I, where am I?"

"You are in a house that now belongs to someone else," I explained.

"Where is that window? I don't know where I am."

I continued to direct her away from the house, suggesting that she leave in peace and go with our blessing. But the entity was not quite ready for that yet, She wouldn't go out the window, either—soldiers are there."

"Only in your memory," I assured her, but she continued to be very agitated.

"Gone...a rope...My name is Jenny...Save me, save me!"

At this point, I asked Ethel's spirit control, Albert, to help me free the entity, who was tremendously embroiled in her emotional memories. The appeal worked. A moment later,

Albert's crisp, matter-of-fact voice broke through. "We have taken the entity who was lost in space and time," he commented.

If ever there was proof that a good trance medium does not draw upon the unconscious minds of the sitters—that is to say, those in the room with her—then this was it. Despite the fact that several names had come through Ethel's entranced lips, I must confess they did not ring a bell with me. This is the more amazing as I have studied history and should have recognized the name Joshua Smith. But the fact is, in the excitement of the investigation, I did not, and I continued to press for better identification and background. In face, I did not even connect John with Andre and continued to ask who John was. Had we come to the house with some knowledge that a Revolutionary escape had taken place here, one might conceivably attribute the medium's tremendous performance to unconscious or even conscious knowledge of what had occurred in the place. As it was, however, we had come because of a suspected ghost created only a few years ago—a ghost that had not the slightest connection with pre-Revolutionary America. No one, including the owner of the house had said anything about any historical connotations of the house. Yet, instead of coming up with the suspected restless woman who had committed suicide, Mrs. Meyers went back into the eighteenth century and gave us authentic information—information I am sure she did not possess at the time, since she is neither a scholar specializing in pre-Revolutionary Americana nor familiar with the locality or local history.

When Albert took over the body of the instrument, I was still in the dark about the connections between this woman and Smith and Andre. "Albert," I therefore asked with some curiosity, "who is this entity?"

"There are three people here," Albert began. "One is gone on horseback, and one went across. They came here to escape because they were surrounded. One of them was Major Andre."

"The historical Major Andre?" I asked incredulously.

"Yes," Albert replied. "They took asylum here until the coast was clear, but as you may well know, Andre did not get very far, and Arnold escaped across the water."

"What about the woman? Is her real name Smith?"

"Yes, but she is not related to Joshua Smith. She is a woman in charge of properties, living here."

"Why does she give the name Jenny Smith?"

"She was thinking more of her employer than of herself. She worked for Joshua Smith, and her name was Jennifer."

"I see," I said, trying to sort things out. "Have you been able to help her?"

"Yes, she is out of a vacuum now, thanks to you. We will of course have to watch her until she makes up her mind that it is no longer 1780."

"Are there any others here in the house?" I asked.

"There are others. The Tories were always protected around this neck of the woods, and when there was an escape, it was usually through here."

"Are all the disturbances in this house dating back to the colonial period?"

"No, there are later disturbances here right on top of old disturbances."

"What is the most recent disturbance in this house?"

"A woman and a child."

Immediately this rang a bell. It would have been strange if the medium had not also felt the most recent emotional event in this house, that involving a woman and a child. According to Jonathan Davis, Ms. Brown had heard the sound of a child in a room that was once used as a nursery. Even her young daughter, then age five, had heard the sounds and been frightened by them. But what about the woman?

"The woman became very disturbed because of the entity you have just released," Albert responded. "In fact, she had been taken over. This was not too long ago."

"What happened to her?"

"She became possessed by the first woman, Jennifer, and as a result felt very miserable."

"Am I correct in assuming that Jennifer, the colonial woman, was hanged?"

"That is right."

"And am I further correct is assuming that the more recent woman took on the symptoms of the unfortunate Jennifer?"

"That is right, too."

"I gather Jennifer died in this house. How?"

"Strangulation."

"What about the more recent case? How did she die?"

"Her inner self was tortured. She lost her breath. She was badly treated by men who did not understand her aberration, the result of her possession by the first spirit in the house. Thus, she committed suicide: It was poison or strangulation or both, I am not sure."

"Do you still sense her in the house now?"

"Yes. She is always following people around. She is here all right, but we did not let her use the instrument, because she could stay on, you know. However, we have her here, under control. She is absolutely demented now. At the time she committed suicide, she was possessed by this woman, but we cannot let her speak because she would possess the instrument. Wait a moment. All right, thank you, they have taken her." Evidently, Albert had been given the latest word by his helpers on the Other Side. It appeared that Kaye was in safe hands, after all.

"Is there any connection between this woman and the present occupants of the house?" I asked.

"Yes, but there will be no harm. She was not in the right

mind when she died, and she is not yet at rest. I'm sure she would want to make it clear that she was possessed and did not act as herself. Her suicide was not of her own choosing. I am repeating words I am being told: it was not of her own volition. She suffered terribly from the possession, because the colonial woman had been beaten and strangled by soldiers."

"Before you withdraw, Albert, can we be reasonably sure that the house will be quiet from now on?"

"Yes. We will do our best."

With that, Albert withdrew, and Ethel returned to her own self, seemingly a bit puzzled at first as to where she was, rubbing her eyes, yawning a couple of times, then settling back into the comfortable chair and waiting for me to ask further questions, if any. But for the moment I had questions only for the owner of the house. "How old is this house, and what was on the spot before it was built?"

"It is at least a hundred years old, and I remember someone telling me that something special happened down here on this spot, something historical, like an escape. There were soldiers here during the Revolutionary War, but I really don't know exactly what happened."

It is important to point out that even Ms. Brown, who had lived in the area for some time, was not aware of the full background of her house. The house, in fact, was far more than a hundred years old. It stood already in September 1780, when Major John Andre had visited it. At that time, there was a ferry below the house that connected with the opposite shore, and the house itself belonged to Joshua Smith, a good friend of General Benedict Arnold. It was to Joshua Smith that Arnold had entrusted the escape of Major Andre. Everything Ethel had said was absolutely true. Three people had tried to escape: Andre, a servant, and of course, General Arnold, who succeeded. Smith was a Loyalist and considered his help a matter of duty. To the American Army he was a traitor. Even though

Andre was later captured, the Revolutionary forces bore down heavily on Smith and his property. Beating people to death in order to elicit information was a favorite form of treatment used in the eighteenth century by both the British and the American armies. Undoubtedly, Jennifer had been the victim of Revolutionary soldiers, and Kaye, perhaps psychic herself, the victim of Jennifer. Ethel Meyers had once again shown what a superb medium she was. But there were still some points to be cleared up.

"How long have you had the house now, Ms. Brown?" I asked.

"A year and a half. Kaye's suicide took place after we had been here for two months .We had bought the house together. She had been extremely upset because her husband was going to cut off his support. Also, he had announced a visit, and she didn't want to see him. So she took off on a Sunday with her child, and in Newburgh she committed suicide along with the child. They didn't find her until Thursday."

"After her death, what unusual things did you experience in the house?"

"I always felt that someone was trying to communicate with me, and I was fleeing from it in terror. I still feel her presence here, but now I want it to be here. She always said that she wanted to stay here, that she loved this river bank. We both agreed that she would always stay here. When I heard all sorts of strange noises after her death, such as doors closing by themselves and footsteps where no one could be seen walking, I went into an alcoholic oblivion and on a sleeping pill binge, because I was so afraid. At the time, I just didn't want to communicate."

"Prior to these events, did you have any psychic experiences?"

"I had many intuitive things happen to me, such as knowing things before they happened. I would know when someone was dead before I got the message; for instance, prior to your coming, I had heard noises almost every night and felt the presence of people. My little girl says there is a little Susan upstairs, and sometimes I too hear her cry. I hear her call and the way she walks up and down the stairs."

"Did you ever think that some of this might come from an earlier period?"

"No, I never thought of that."

"Was Kaye the kind of person who might commit suicide?"

"Certainly not. It would be completely out of character for her. She used to say, there was always a way, no matter what the problem, no matter what the trouble. She was very optimistic, very reliable, very resourceful. And she considered challenges and problems things one had to surmount. After her death, I looked through the mail, through all her belongings. My first impression was that she had been murdered, because it was so completely out of character for her. I even talked to the police about it. Their investigation was in my opinion not thorough enough. They never looked into the matter of where she had spent the four days and four nights between Sunday and Thursday, before she was found. But I was so broken up about it myself, I wasn't capable of conducting an investigation on my own. For a while I even suspected her husband of having killed her."

"But now we know, don't we," I said.

That particular ferry at Haverstraw hasn't run in a long time. The house on Riverside Avenue still stands, quieter than it used to be, and it is keeping its secrets locked up tight now. The British and the Americans have been fast friends for a long time now, and the passions of 1780 belong to history.

THE HAUNTED TRAILER

*S*ometimes, one would think, the work of a Psychic Investigator must be downright drab. Little old ladies having nightmares, imaginative teenagers letting off steam over frustrations in directions as yet unexplored, neurotics fantasizing about their special roles and talents. All this is grist for the investigator's mill, poor chap, and he has to listen and nod politely, for that's how he gets information. (As when Peter Lorre whispered across the screen, "Where is the information?" this question is the beacon onto which the psychic sleuth must be drawn.)

And in fact it is perfectly possible for such people to have genuine ESP experiences. Anybody can play this game. All he's got to be is alive and kicking. ESP comes to just about everyone, and there's nothing one can do about it one way or the other.

It is therefore necessary to have a completely open mind as to the kind of individual who might have a psychic experience of validity. I can attest to this need to my regret. Several years ago, people approached me who had witnessed the amazing Ted Serios demonstrate his thought photography and who wanted me to work with the fellow. But my quasi-middle-class sense of propriety shied away from the Midwestern bellhop when I realized that he drank and was not altogether of drawing-room

136

class. How wrong I was! A little later, Professor Jule Eisenbud of the University of Colorado showed better sense and less prejudice as to a person's private habits, and his work with Serios was not only a scientific breakthrough of the first order, but was turned into a successful book for Eisenbud as well.

Of course I don't expect my subjects to be proprietors of New England mansions about to collapse, or Southern plantation owners drinking mint juleps on their lawns, but I have yet to hear from a truck driver who has seen a ghost, or a State Department man with premonitions. Hindsight maybe, but not precognition.

So it was with more than casual interest that I received a communication (via the U.S. mail) from a comely young lady named Rita Atlanta. That she was indeed comely I found out later from her Christmas cards. Christmas cards don't hardly come any comelier. Hers show all of Rita in a champagne glass (a very large champagne glass without champagne in it—only Rita) underneath a Christmas tree

Her initial letter, however, had no such goodies in it, but merely requested that I help her get rid of her ghost. Such requests are of course not unusual, but this one was—and I am not referring to the lady's occupation, which was that of an exotic dancer in sundry nightclubs around the more or less civilized world.

What made her case unusual was the fact that "her" ghost appeared in a thirty-year-old trailer near Boston.

"When I told my husband that we had a ghost," she wrote, "he laughed and said, 'Why should a respectable ghost move into a trailer? We have hardly room in it ourselves with three kids.'"

It seemed the whole business had started in the summer, when the specter made its first, sudden appearance. Although her husband could not see what she saw, Miss Atlanta's pet skunk evidently didn't like it and moved into another room.

Three months later, her husband passed away, and Miss Atlanta was kept busy hopping the Atlantic (hence her stage name) in quest of nightclub work.

Ever since her first encounter with the figure of a man in her Peabody, Massachusetts trailer, the dancer had kept the lights burning all night long. As someone once put it, "I don't believe in ghosts, but I'm scared of them."

Despite the lights, Miss Atlanta always felt a presence at the same time her initial experience had taken place—between three and three-thirty in the morning. It would awaken her with such regularity that at last she decided to seek help.

At the time she contacted me she was appearing nightly at the Imperial in Frankfurt, taking a bath onstage in an oversize champagne glass with under-quality champagne. The discriminating clientele that frequented the Imperial of course loved the "French touch," and Rita Atlanta was a wow.

I discovered that her late husband was Colonel Frank Bane, an Air Force ace, who had originally encouraged the Vienna-born woman to change from ballet dancer to belly dancer and eventually to what is termed "exotic" dancing, but which is better described as stripping.

(Not that there is anything wrong with it *per se*, although the Air Force never felt cool under the collar about the whole thing. But the Colonel was a good officer and the boys thought the Colonel's Missus was a good sport—so nobody did anything about it.)

I decided to talk to the "Champagne Bubble Girl" on my next overseas trip. She was working at that time in Stuttgart, but she came over to meet us at our Frankfurt hotel, and my wife was immediately taken with her pleasant charm, her lack of "show business" phoniness. We repaired for lunch to the terrace of a nearby restaurant to discuss the ups and downs of a hectic life in a champagne glass, not forgetting three kids in a house trailer.

I asked Rita to go through an oriental dance for my camera (minus champagne glass, but not minus anything else) and then we sat down to discuss the ghostly business in earnest. In September of the previous year she and her family had moved into a brand-new trailer in Peabody, Massachusetts. After her encounter with the ghost, Rita made some inquiries about the nice, grassy spot she had chosen to set down the trailer as her home. Nothing had ever stood on the spot before. No ghost stories. Nothing. Just one little thing...

One of the neighbors in the trailer camp, which was at the outskirts of greater Boston, came to see her one evening. By this time Rita's heart was already filled with fear, fear of the unknown that had suddenly come into her life here. She freely confided in her neighbor, a woman by the name of Birdie Gleason.

To her amazement, the neighbor nodded with understanding. She, too, had felt "something," an unseen presence, in her house trailer next to Rita's.

"Sometimes I feel someone is touching me," she added.

"What exactly did *you* see?" I interjected, while outside the street noises of Frankfurt belied the terrifying subject we were discussing.

"I saw a big man, almost seven feet tall, about three hundred to three hundred fifty pounds, and he wore a long coat and a big hat."

But the ghost didn't just stand there glaring at her. Sometimes he made himself comfortable on her kitchen counter. With his ghostly legs dangling down from it. He was as solid as a man of flesh and blood, except that she could not see his face clearly since it was in the darkness of early morning.

Later, when I visited the house trailer with my highly sensitive camera, I took some pictures in the areas indicated by Miss Atlanta—the bedroom, the door to it, and the kitchen counter. In all three areas, strange phenomena manifested on my film. Some mirrorlike transparencies developed in normally opaque areas, which could not and cannot be explained by ordinary facts.

When it happened the first time, she raced for the light, turned the switch, her heart beating in her mouth. The yellowish light of the electric lamp bathed the bedroom in a nightmarish twilight. But the spook had vanished. There was no possible way a real intruder could have come and gone so fast. No way out, no way in. Because this was during the time Boston was being terrorized by the infamous Boston Strangler, Rita had taken special care to double-lock the doors and secure all windows. Nobody could have entered the trailer without making a great deal of noise. I examined the locks and the windows—not even Houdini could have done it.

The ghost, having once established himself in Rita's bedroom, returned for additional visits—always in the early morning hours. Sometimes three times a week, sometimes even more often.

"He was staring in my direction all the time," Rita said with a slight Viennese accent, and one could see that the terror had never really left her eyes. Even three thousand miles away, the spectral stranger had a hold on her.

Was he perhaps looking for something? No, he didn't seem to be. In the kitchen, he either stood by the table or sat down on the counter. Ghosts don't need food—so why the kitchen?

"Did he ever take his hat off?" I wondered.

"No, never," she said and smiled. Imagine a ghost doffing his hat to the lady of the trailer!

What was particularly horrifying was the noiselessness of the apparition. She never heard any footfalls. No rustling of his clothes as he silently passed by. No clearing of the throat as if he wanted to speak. Nothing. Just silent stares. When the visitations grew more frequent, Rita decided to leave the lights on all night. After that, she did not *see* him any more. But he was still there, at the usual hour, standing behind the bed, staring at her. She knew he was. She could almost feel the sting of his gaze.

One night she decided she had been paying heavy light bills long enough. She hopped out of bed, turned the light switch to the off position, and as the room was plunged back into semidarkness, she lay down in bed again. Within a few moments, her eyes had gotten accustomed to the dark. Her senses were on the alert, for she was not at all sure what she might see. Finally, she forced herself to turn her head in the direction of the door. Was her mind playing tricks on her? There, in the doorway, stood the ghost. As big and brooding as ever.

With a scream, she dove under the covers. When she came up, eternities later, the shadow was gone from the door.

The next evening, the lights were burning again in the trailer, and every night thereafter, until it was time for her to fly to Germany for her season's nightclub work. Then she closed up the trailer, sent her children to stay with friends, and left, with the faint hope that on her return in the winter the trailer might be free of its ghost. But she wasn't at all sure.

It was getting dark outside now, and I knew Miss Atlanta had to fly back to Stuttgart for her evening's work soon. It was obvious to me that this exotic dancer was a medium, as only the psychic can "see" apparitions.

I queried her about the past, and reluctantly she talked of her earlier years in Austria.

When she was a school girl of eight, she suddenly felt herself impelled to draw a picture of a funeral. Her father was puzzled by the choice of the so somber a subject by a little girl. But as she pointed out who the figures in her drawing were, ranging from her father to the more distant relatives, her father listened with lips tightly drawn. When the enumeration was over he inquired in a voice of incredulity mixed with fear, "But who is being buried?"

"Mother," the little girl replied, without a moment's hesitation, and no more was said about it.

Three weeks to the day later, her mother was dead.

The war years were hard on the family. Her father, a postal employee, had a gift for playing the numbers, allegedly upon advice from his deceased spouse. But the invasion by Germany ended all that, and eventually Rita found herself in the United States and married to an Air Force Colonel.

She had forgotten her psychic experiences of the past, when the ghost in the trailer brought them all back only too vividly. She was frankly scared, knowing her abilities to receive messages from beyond the veil. But who was this man?

I decided to visit Peabody with a medium and see what we could learn, but it wasn't until the winter of that year that I met Rita and she showed me around her trailer. It was a cold and moist afternoon.

Her oldest son greeted us at the door. He had seen nothing and neither believed nor disbelieved his mother. But he was willing to do some legwork for me, to find out who the shadowy visitor might be.

It was thus that we learned that a man had been run over by a car very close by, a few years ago. Had the dead man, confused about his status, sought refuge in the trailer—the nearest "house" in his path?

Was he trying to make contact with what he could sense was a medium, able to receive his anxious pleas?

It was at this time that I took the unusual photographs in Rita's presence of the areas indicated by her as being haunted. Several of these pictures show unusual mirrorlike areas, areas in which "something" must have been present in the atmosphere. But the ghost did not appear for me, or, for that matter, for Rita.

Perhaps our discovery of his "problem" and our long and passionate discussion of this had reached his spectral consciousness and he knew that he was out of his element in a trailer belonging to people not connected with his world.

Was this his way of finally, belatedly, doffing his hat to the lady of the house trailer with an apology for his intrusions?

I didn't hear again from Rita Atlanta, but the newspapers carried oversize ads now and then telling this or that city of the sensational performance of the woman in the champagne glass.

It is safe to assume that she took her baths in the glass completely alone, something she could not be sure of in the privacy of her Massachusetts trailer. For the eyes of a couple of hundred visiting firemen in a Frankfurt nightclub were far less bothersome than one solitary pair of eyes staring at you from another world.

A NEW HAMPSHIRE ARTIST AND HER GHOSTS

*E*lizabeth Nealon Weistrop was a renowned sculptress who lived far away from the mainstream of city life in rural New Hampshire. I talked to her when I had occasion to admire a particularly striking bronze medallion she had created for the Society of Medallists. It was a squirrel, such as abound in her New England woods.

Mrs. Weistrop's experiences had given her a sense of living with the uncanny, far from being afraid of it or worried.

"What were the most striking examples of your brush with the uncanny—that is of yourself or your family?" I queried her.

"There are many," Mrs. Weistrop replied, "but I'll try to give you the most evidential incidents. For example, when our Debby was six years old, the doctor decided she should be taken out of the first grade and remain at home to recover from nervousness that resulted from a serious infection from which she had recently recovered. She missed going to school with her sister Betsy, two years older, but played every day with five-year-old Donna Esdale, a neighbor's little girl.

"Our family—my husband, our two girls, and I—was living in a cottage in West Dennis on Cape Cod at the time but we located a better place in Yarmouthport—a warmer house with a studio that I could use for sculpture. Donna's father owned a truck, so we paid him to move us to the new house.

"Three weeks later (we had seen no one from West Dennis), Betsy, Debby, and I were eating breakfast and Debby said, 'What happened to Donna?' I said, 'What do you mean?' Debby said, 'Why was Donna's face all covered with blood?' Then Betsy and I explained to Debby that she had just had a bad dream and that Donna was all right, but Debby insisted with questions. 'Did a truck hit her?' 'Did someone hit her in the face?' 'Why was her face all covered with blood?' And no matter how Betsy and I explained about dreams, Debby refused to understand and asked the same questions.

"Finally, the school bus came. Betsy went to school and Debby looked after her wistfully, wanting to go to school too.

"During the day Debby played with her new black puppy, and I was busy working at sculpture, and the breakfast session left my mind.

"About nine o'clock that evening, Donna's father, Ralph, came to the studio and asked how everyone was. I said we were all fine and automatically asked after his family. He said, 'All right, except that last night my wife and I were up all night. Donna had nose bleeds all night and her face was just covered with blood!'

"Debby was asleep but Betsy was standing near me, and we turned and stared at each other in wonder.

"While living on Cape Cod in 1956, we rented a house from a Mrs. Ridley in West Hyannisport. The house she rented to us had belonged to her mother, a woman in her eighties who had recently died. Mrs. Ridley lived next door with her husband and a daughter, Rodella. I found them pleasant people, proud of their American Indian ancestry and sadly missing the grandmother fondly referred to as 'Gunny.' They spoke of her so often and of her constant activity making repairs on the home she loved that I almost felt I knew her. When they told me of their own supernatural experiences, they did not find a skeptic in me, as my own mother whom I had loved dearly had been gifted with ESP. My mother had been the old child born with a caul {veil} in an Irish family of eleven children, and as I grew up I became very familiar with my mother's amazing and correct predictions. My own experiences with the unknown had been limited to a strong feeling of a force or power leading and directing me in my work as a sculptor.

"One sunny fall afternoon, I was alone concentrating on a sculpture of St. Francis. My husband, Harry, was away for the day and our two girls were in school, when I heard a loud thump from the bedroom that our girls shared. This room had been the large sunny bedroom of 'Gunny' and within easy view of where I was working. I stopped work to investigate, expecting to see that a large piece of furniture had collapsed or been overturned. As I searched the room and looked out of the window, I could discover nothing that could have made such a sound. Still puzzled, I walked into the next room, the kitchen, and noted that our highly nervous dog was sleeping soundly—a dog who was always on her feet barking at the slightest sound. The clock in the kitchen said 2:30 and that would give me one half hour more to concentrate on St. Francis, so I went back to work, still wondering.

"That evening after the girls were asleep I walked outside in back of the house, and Mrs. Ridley, who was sitting on her back porch, invited me into her house to have coffee with her, her daughter, and her daughter's fiancé.

"While we chatted around the table, Mrs. Ridley told of sitting by her kitchen window that afternoon and having seen her mother, 'Gunny,' just as clear as day, walk up the path from the woods to our house and go over and knock on her own bedroom window at our house.

"I asked, 'What time was that?' and Mrs. Ridley answered, 'At 2:30.'"

JOHN, UP IN VERMONT

*T*his isn't exactly a ghost story, if ghosts are troubled individuals unaware of their passing and status, with some sort of compulsion unresolved. But then again, it is, if you consider the afterlife full of fine distinctions as to who is a ghost and who is simply a troubled spirit.

Not far from Stowe, Vermont, in what I have long thought of as the most beautiful part of New England, there was a country house that once belonged to the late lyricist John LaTouche. He and a friend, who shall remain nameless, co-owned the place, and for all I know, the friend still lives there. But John hadn't really left entirely either. He was buried up there in Vermont in a flowerbed, amid his favorite trees and hills. That is, his body was. As for the rest, well now, that is another matter entirely.

I first met John LaTouche through the late medium and psychic investigator Eileen Garrett over lunch at the Hotel St. Regis in New York. She thought, and rightly so, that we would become friends since we had in common not only our professional pursuits—I, too, am a lyricist, among other professional aspects—but also our intense involvement with the paranormal. Soon after this initial meeting, John invited me to a private dinner party at his home on East 55th Street, right across from an ancient FDNY firehouse, where he occupied the magnificent penthouse—at the time he was doing well financially (which was not always the case) because his "Ballad for Americans" and the musical *The Legend of Baby Doe* were paying him handsomely.

At the party were also my late friend and medium Ethel Johnson Meyers and the Broadway actress Future Fulton, who was very psychic, and the four of us held a séance after dinner.

Picture my surprise when it was John who went under first, showing he had trance abilities also. Regrettably, I do not have an exact transcript of what came through him at that time, but it seemed that a distant ancestor of his, a Breton lady, wanted to manifest and reassure him in his work and quest for success. No sooner had he returned to his normal state, than Ethel described in great detail what the spirit looked like, and considering that Ethel would not have known the details of an eighteenth century Breton woman's costume, this seemed rather interesting to me at the time.

Sometimes, when people with psychic gifts link up, the mediumship goes back and forth as the case may require. Several months after this initial get-together, I was in rehearsal with a musical revue, one of my first theatrical involvements, in which Future Fulton had a singing role. I had made an appointment with John to see him the Friday of that week. "Are you fry Freeday?" I asked, "I mean, are you free Friday?" We set a meeting for three o'clock. Unfortunately, it slipped my mind in the heat of rehearsals until about 2 on Friday. It became impossible for me to break away from the goings-on and get to a phone, and I had visions of John never wanting to speak to me again for having stood him up. When Future noticed my distress, she inquired as to its cause, and when I told her, she said, "Oh well, that's nothing. I will get through to John."

With that she sat down on a bench, leaned back, closed her eyes for a moment, and then said cheerfully, "It is done. Don't worry about it."

Being forever the scientific investigator, I was not really relieved. As soon as I could, at around seven o'clock. I rushed to the nearest telephone and called John. Before he could say a word, I began to apologize profusely for the missed appointment, and my inability to notify him.

"What are you babbling about?" John interjected, when I caught my breath for a moment. "Of course you called me."

"I did not."

"No? Then why is there a message on my answering machine from you telling me you could not make it?"

"There is?"

"Yes...must have been around two or so because I got back in time for our meeting a little after that, and it was on the tape."

I did not know what to say. Later, I told John, who just shook his head and smiled.

Time went on, and we met now and again, usually at his house. On one occasion, we were invited for a run-through of a new work he and his friend with whom he shared the house in Vermont had written. John seemed in the best of health and creative activity.

It was in August of 1956, and I had just come home from the opening night of my play *Hotel Excelsior*, a less than brilliant piece of mine at the Provincetown Theatre in Greenwich Village, and I checked my answering service, as was my custom.

"Only one message," the operator said laconically. "John LaTouche has died."

I was in a state of shock. But as I found out, John had gone to his Vermont retreat that weekend and nothing had been wrong. Now John was overweight, and he liked to eat well. Apparently too well, for after a heavy meal he had had a heart attack and died. Or rather, his body gave out.

For it was not the end of our friendship by a long shot. I did not attend the funeral up in Vermont, which was for close family only. His mother Effy did, and Effy and I were friendly for a while after, until she too passed into the Great Beyond.

Maybe three or four months passed.

Ethel Meyers and I were doing a routine investigation of a haunted house somewhere in Connecticut. Picture my surprise when she suddenly went into trance, and the next voice I heard was not some obscure ghostly person stuck in that particular house for whatever personal reasons, but my old friend John LaTouche!

"Greetings, Hans," he said in almost his usual voice, and then went on to explain how touched he was by his funeral amid the flowers up in Vermont. But he was not there. Not John.

After that time, John communicated with me now and again, telling me that he had adjusted to his sudden departure from the physical world—he was only 39 at the time of his death—and that he was still creating works of art for the stage, Over There.

Then, too, he became sort of an adviser to me, especially in matters theatrical, and he began to use not only Ethel Meyers as his channel, but also others.

I don't know when the celestial Board of Directors will want to send John back to earth in his next incarnation, but he seems to be a free spirit doing his thing, communicating hither and yon, apparently able to drop in, so to speak, at séances and investigations, at will. The only place I am sure he is not at, is up in Vermont under the flowers.

GHOSTS AROUND BOSTON

*S*ometime back, I often went to Boston to appear on radio or television, and as a result people kept telling me of their own psychic adventures—and problems. I tried to follow up many of these cases, but there were limits even to my enthusiasm.

Since having a ghostly experience is not necessarily what people like to advertise—especially to the neighbors—some of these stories, which are all true, contain only the initials of the people involved. I, of course, know them but promised not to divulge their full names, or heaven forbid, exact addresses.

Mrs. Geraldine W. was a graduate of Boston City Hospital and worked as a registered nurse; her husband was a teacher, and they had four children. Neither Mr. nor Mrs. W. ever had the slightest interest in the occult; in fact, Mrs. W. remembers hearing some chilling stories about ghosts as a child and considering them just so many fairy tales.

One July, the W.'s decided to acquire a house about twenty miles from Boston, as the conditions in the city seemed inappropriate for bringing up their four children. They chose a Victorian home sitting on a large rock overlooking a golf course in a small town.

Actually, there were two houses built next door to each other by two brothers. The one to the left had originally been used as a winter residence, while the other, their choice, was used as a summer home. It was a remarkable sight, high above the other houses in the area. The house so impressed the W.'s that they immediately expressed their interest in buying it. They were told that it had once formed part of the H. estate, and had remained in the same family until nine years prior to their visit. Originally built by a certain Ephraim Hamblin, it had been sold to the H. family and remained a family property until it passed into the hands of the P. family. It remained in the P.'s possession until the W.'s acquired it that spring.

Prior to obtaining possession of the house, Mrs. W. had a strange dream in which she saw herself standing in the driveway, looking up at the house. In the dream she had a terrible feeling of foreboding, as if something dreadful had happened in the house. On awakening the next morning, however, she thought no more about it and later put it out of her mind.

Shortly after they moved in on July 15, Mrs. W. awoke in the middle of the night for some reason. She looked up to the ceiling and saw what looked to her like a sparkler. It swirled about in a circular movement, and then disappeared. On checking, Mrs. W. found that all the shades were drawn in the room, so it perplexed her how such a light could have appeared on the ceiling. But the matter quickly slipped from her mind.

Several days later, she happened to be sitting in the living room one evening with the television on very low since her husband was asleep on the couch. Everything was very quiet. On the arm of a wide-armed couch there were three packages of cigarettes side by side. As she looked at them, the middle package suddenly flipped over by itself and fell to the floor. Since Mrs. W. had no interest in psychic phenomena, she dismissed this as probably due to some natural cause. A short time thereafter, she happened to be sleeping in her daughter's room, facing directly alongside the front hall staircase. The large hall light was burning since the lamp near the children's rooms had burned out. As she lay in the room, she became aware of heavy, slow, plodding footsteps coming across the hallway.

Terrified, she kept her eyes closed tight because she thought there was a prowler in the house. Since everyone was accounted for, only a stranger could have made the noises. She started to pray over and over in order to calm herself, but the footsteps continued on the stairs, progressing down the staircase and around into the living room where they faded away. Mrs. W. was thankful that her prayers had been answered and that the prowler had left.

Just as she started to doze off again the footsteps returned. Although she was still scared, she decided to brave the intruder, whoever he might be. As she got up and approached the area where she heard the steps, they resounded directly in front of her—yet she could see absolutely no one. The next morning she checked all the doors and windows and found them securely locked, just as she had left them the night before. She mentioned the matter to her husband, who ascribed it to nerves. A few nights later, Mrs. W. was again awakened in the middle of the night, this time in her own bedroom. As she woke and sat up in bed, she heard a woman's voice from somewhere in the room. It tried to form words, but Mrs. W. could not make them out. The voice was hollow and sounded like something from an echo chamber. It seemed to her that the voice had come from an area near the ceiling over her husband's bureau. The incident did not prevent her from going back to sleep, perplexing though it was.

By now Mrs. W. was convinced that they had a ghost in the house. She was standing in her kitchen, contemplating where she could find a priest to have the house exorcised, when all of a sudden a trash bag, which had been resting quietly on the floor, burst open, spilling its contents all over the floor. The disturbances had become so frequent that Mrs. W. took every opportunity possible to leave the house early in the morning with her children, and not go home until she had to. She did not bring in a priest to exorcise the house, but managed to obtain a bottle of blessed water from Lourdes. She went through each room, sprinkling it and praying for the soul of whoever was haunting the house.

One evening, Mr. W. came home from work around six o'clock and went upstairs to change his clothes while Mrs. W. was busy setting the table for dinner. Suddenly Mr. W. called his wife and asked her to open and close the door to the back hall stairs. Puzzled by his request, she did so five times, each time more strenuously. Finally she asked her husband the purpose of this exercise. He admitted that he wanted to test the effect of the door being opened and closed in this manner because he had just observed the back gate to the stairs opening and closing by itself!

This was as good a time as any to have a discussion of what was going on in the house, so Mrs. W. went upstairs to join Mr. W. in the bedroom where he was standing. As she did so, her eye caught a dim, circular light that seemed to skip across the ceiling in two strokes; at the same time, the shade at the other end of the room suddenly snapped up, flipping over vigorously a number of times. Both Mr. and Mrs. W. started to run from the room; then, catching themselves, they returned to the bedroom.

On looking over these strange incidents, Mrs. W. admitted that there had been some occurrences that could not be explained by natural means. Shortly after they had moved to the house, Mr. W. had started to paint the interior, at the same time thinking about making some structural changes in the house because there were certain things in it he did not like.

As he did so, two cans of paint were knocked out of his hands, flipping over and covering a good portion of the living room and hall floors.

Then there was that Saturday afternoon when Mr. W. had helped his wife vacuum the hall stairs. Again he started to talk about the bad shape the house was in, in his opinion, and as he condemned the house, the vacuum cleaner suddenly left the upper landing and traveled over the staircase all by itself, finally hitting him on the head with a solid thud!

But their discussion did not solve the matter; they had to brace themselves against further incidents, even though they did not know why they were happening or who caused them.

One evening Mrs. W. was feeding her baby in the living room near the fireplace, when she heard footsteps overhead and the dragging of something very heavy across the floor. This was followed by a crashing sound on the staircase, as if something very heavy had fallen against the railing. Her husband was asleep, but Mrs. W. woke him up and together they investigated, only to find the children asleep and no stranger in the house.

It was now virtually impossible to spend a quiet evening in the living room without hearing some uncanny noise. There was scratching along the tops of the doors inside the house, a rubbing sound along the door tops, and once in a while the front doorknob would turn by itself, as if an unseen hand were twisting it. No one could have done this physically because the enclosed porch leading to the door was locked and the locks were intact when Mrs. W. examined them.

The ghost, whoever he or she was, roamed the entire house. One night Mrs. W. was reading in her bedroom at around midnight when she heard a knocking sound halfway up the wall of her room. It seemed to move along the wall and then stop dead beside her night table. Needless to say, it did not contribute to a peaceful night. By now the older children were also aware of the disturbances. They, too, heard knocking on doors with no one outside, and twice Mrs. W.'s little girl, then seven years old, was awakened in the middle of the night because she heard someone walking about the house. Both her parents were fast asleep.

That year, coming home on Christmas night to an empty house, or what they presumed to be an empty house, the W.'s noticed that a Christmas light was on in the bedroom window. Under the circumstances, the family stayed outside while Mr. W. went upstairs to check the house. He found everything locked and no one inside. The rest of the family then moved into the lower hall, waiting for Mr. W. to come down from upstairs. As he reached the bottom of the stairs, coming from what he assured his family was an empty upper story, they all heard footsteps overhead from the area he had just examined.

On the eve of St. Valentine's Day, Mrs. W. was readying the house for a party the next evening. She had waxed the floors and spruced up the entire house, and it had gotten late. Just before going to bed, she decided to sit down for a while in her rocking chair. Suddenly she perceived a moaning and groaning sound coming across the living room from left to right. It lasted perhaps ten to fifteen seconds, and then ended as abruptly as it had begun.

During the party the next evening, the conversation drifted to ghosts, and somehow Mrs. W. confided in her sister-in-law about what they had been through since moving to the house. It was only then that Mrs. W. found out from her sister-in-law that her husband's mother had had an experience in the house while staying over one night during the summer. She, too, had heard loud footsteps coming up the hall stairs; she had heard voices, and a crackling sound as if there had been a fire someplace. On investigating these strange noises, she had found nothing that could have caused them. However, she had decided not to tell Mrs. W. about it, in order not to frighten her.

Because of her background and position, and since her husband was a respected teacher, Mrs. W. was reluctant to discuss their experiences with anyone who might construe them as imaginary, or think the family silly. Eventually, however, a sympathetic neighbor gave her one of my books, and Mrs. W. contacted me for advice. She realized, of course, that her letter would not be read immediately, and that in any event, I might not be able to do anything about it for some time. Frightening though the experiences had been, she was reconciled to living with them, hoping only that her children would not be hurt or frightened.

On March 3, she had put her three young boys to bed for a nap and decided to check if they were properly covered. As she went up the stairway, she thought she saw movement out of the corner of her eye. Her first thought was that her little boy, then four years old, had gotten up instead of taking his nap. But, on checking, she found him fast asleep.

Exactly one week later, Mrs. W. was in bed trying to go to sleep when she heard a progressively louder tapping on the wooden mantle at the foot of the bed. She turned over to see where the noise was coming from or what was causing it when it immediately stopped. She turned back to the side, trying to go back to sleep, when suddenly she felt something or someone shake her foot as though trying to get her attention. She looked down at her foot and saw absolutely nothing.

Finally, on March 26, she received my letter explaining some of the phenomena to her and advising her what to do. As she was reading my letter, she heard the sound of someone moving about upstairs, directly over her head. Since she knew that the children were sleeping soundly, Mrs. W. realized that her unseen visitor was not in the least bit put off by the advice dispensed her by the ghost hunter. Even a dog the W.'s had acquired around Christmas had its difficulty with the unseen forces loose in the house.

At first, he had slept upstairs on the rug beside Mrs. W.'s bed. But a short time after, he began to growl and bark at night, especially in the direction of the stairs. Eventually he took to sleeping on the enclosed porch and refused to enter the house, no matter how one would try to entice him. Mrs. W. decided to make some inquiries in the neighborhood, in order to find out who the ghost might be or what he might want.

She discovered that a paper-hanger who had come to do some work in the house just before they had purchased it had encountered considerable difficulties. He had been hired to do some paper hanging in the house, changing the decor from what it had been. He had papered a room in the house as he had been told to, but on returning the next day found that some of his papers were on upside down, as if moved around by unseen hands. He, too, heard strange noises and would have nothing further to do with the house. Mrs. W. then called upon the people who had preceded them in the house, the P. family, but the daughter of the late owner said that during their stay in the house they had not experienced anything unusual. Perhaps she did not care to discuss such matters. At any rate, Mrs. W. discovered that the former owner, Mr. P., had actually died in the house three years prior to their acquisition of it. Apparently, he had been working on the house, which he loved very much, and had sustained a fracture. He recovered from it, but sustained another fracture in the same area of his leg. During the recovery, he died of a heart attack in the living room.

It was conceivable that Mr. P. did not like the rearrangements made by the new owners and resented the need for repapering or repainting, having done so much of that himself while in the flesh. But if it was he who was walking up and down the stairs at night, turning doorknobs, and appearing as luminous balls of light—who, then, was the woman whose voice has also been heard?

So it appeared that the house overlooking the golf course for the past hundred and twenty-two years had more than one spectral inhabitant in it. Perhaps Mr. P. was only a Johnny-come-lately, joining the earlier shades staying on in what used to be their home. As far as the W.'s were concerned, the house was big enough for all of them, so long as they know their place!

Peter Q. came from a devout Catholic family, part Scottish, and part Irish. One June, Peter Q. was married, and his brother Tom, with whom he had always maintained a close and cordial relationship, came to the wedding. That was the last time the two brothers were happy together.

Two weeks later Tom and a friend spent a weekend on Cape Cod. During that weekend, Tom lost his prize possession, his collection of record albums worth hundreds of dollars were stolen. Being somewhat superstitious, he feared that his luck had turned against him and, sure enough, a hit-and-run driver struck his car shortly afterwards.

Then in August of the same year, Tom and his father caught a very big fish on a fishing trip and was to win a prize, consisting of a free trip during the season. As he was cleaning the fish to present it to the jury, the line broke and Tom lost the prize fish. But his streak of bad luck was to take on ominous proportions soon after. Two weeks later, Tom Q. died instantly, and his friend David died the next day.

Even before the bad news was brought home to Peter Q. and the family, an extraordinary thing happened at their house. The clock in the bedroom stopped suddenly. When Peter checked it and wound it again, he found nothing wrong with it. Shortly after, word of Tom's death came, and on checking the time, Peter found that the clock had stopped at the very instant of his brother's death.

During the following days, drawers in what used to be their bedroom would open by themselves when there was no one about. This continued for about four weeks, then it stopped again. On the anniversary of Tom's death, Peter, who was then a junior at the university, was doing some studying and using a fountain pen to highlight certain parts in the books. Just then, his mother called him and asked him to help his father with his car. Peter placed the pen inside the book to mark the page and went to help his father. On returning an hour later, he discovered that a picture of his late brother and their family had been placed where Peter had left the pen, and the pen was lying outside the book next to it. No one had been in the house at the time since Peter's wife was out working.

Under the influence of Tom's untimely death and the phenomena taking place at his house, Peter Q. became very interested in life after death and read almost everything he could, talking with many of his friends about the subject, and becoming more and more convinced that man does in some mysterious way survive death. His wife disagreed with him and did not wish to discuss the matter.

One night, while her husband was away from the house, Peter's wife received a telepathic impression concerning continuance of life, and as she did so, a glowing object about the size of a softball appeared next to her in her bed. It was not a dream, for she could see the headlights from passing cars shining on the wall of the room, yet the shining object was still there next to her pillow, stationary and glowing. It eventually disappeared.

Many times since, Peter Q. felt the presence of his brother, a warm, wonderful feeling; yet it gave him goose bumps all over. As for the real big send-off Tom had wanted from this life, he truly received it. The morning after his accident, a number of friends called the house without realizing that anything had happened to Tom. They had felt a strong urge to call, as if someone had communicated with them telepathically to do so.

Tom Q. was a collector of phonograph records and owned many, even though a large part of his collection had been stolen. The night before his fatal accident, he had played some of these records.

When Peter later checked the record player, he discovered that the last song his brother had played was entitled, "Just One More Day." Of the many Otis Redding recordings his brother owned, why had he chosen that one?

Mr. Harold B. was a professional horse trainer who traveled a good deal of the time. When he did stay at home, he lived in an old house in a small town in Massachusetts. Prior to moving to New England, he and his wife lived in Ohio, but he was attracted by the Old World atmosphere of New England and decided to settle down in the East. They found a house that was more than two hundred years old, but unfortunately it was in dire need of repair. There was neither electricity nor central heating, and all the rooms were dirty, neglected, and badly in need of renovating. Nevertheless, they liked the general feeling of the house and decided to take it.

The house was in a sad state, mostly because it had been lived in for fifty-five years by a somewhat eccentric couple who had shut themselves off from the world. They would hardly admit anyone to their home, and it was known in town that three of their dogs had died of starvation. Mr. and Mrs. B. moved into the house on Walnut Road in October. Shortly after their arrival, Mrs. B. fractured a leg, which kept her housebound for a considerable amount of time. This was unfortunate since the house needed so much work. Nevertheless, they managed. With professional help, they did the house over from top to bottom, putting in a considerable amount of work and money to make it livable, until it became a truly beautiful house.

Although Mrs. B. was not particularly interested in the occult, she had had a number of psychic experiences in the past, especially of a precognitive nature, and had accepted her psychic powers as a matter of course. Shortly after the couple had moved into the house on Walnut Road, they noticed that there was something peculiar about their home.

One night, Mrs. B. was sleeping alone in a downstairs front room off the center entrance hall. Suddenly she was awakened by the sensation of a presence in the room, and as she looked up she saw the figure of a small woman before her bed, looking right at her. She could make out all the details of the woman's face and stature, and noticed that she was wearing a veil, as widows sometimes did in the past. When the apparition became aware of Mrs. B.'s attention, she lifted the veil and spoke to her, assuring her that she was not there to harm her but that she came as a friend. Mrs. B. was too overcome by it all to reply, and before she could gather her wits, the apparition drifted away.

Immediately, Mrs. B. made inquiries in town, and since she was able to give a detailed description of the apparition, it was not long until she knew who the ghost was. The description fit the former owner of the house, Mrs. C., to a tee. Mrs. C. died at age eighty-six, shortly before the B.'s moved into what was her former home. Armed with this information, Mrs. B. braced herself for the presence of an unwanted inhabitant in the house. A short time afterwards, she saw the shadowy outline of what appeared to be a heavy-set person moving along the hall from her bedroom. At first she thought it was her husband so she called out to him, but she soon discovered that her husband was actually upstairs. She then examined her room and discovered that the shades were drawn, so there was no possibility that light from traffic on the road outside could have cast a shadow into the adjoining hall. The shadowy figure she had seen did not, however, look like the outline of the ghost she had earlier encountered in the front bedroom.

While she was wondering about this, she heard the sound of a dog running across the floor. Yet there was no dog to be seen. Evidently her own dog also heard or sensed the ghostly dog's doings because he reacted with visible terror.

Mrs. B. was still wondering about the second apparition when her small grandson came and stayed overnight. He had never been to the house before and had not been told of the stories connected with it. As he was preparing to go to sleep, but still fully conscious, he saw a heavy-set man wearing a red shirt standing before him in his bedroom. This upset him greatly, especially when the man suddenly disappeared without benefit of a door. He described the apparition to his grandparents, who reassured him by telling him a white lie: namely, that he had been dreaming. To this the boy indignantly replied that he had not been dreaming, but, in fact, he had been fully awake. The description given by the boy not only fitted the shadowy outline of the figure Mrs. B. had seen along the corridor, but was a faithful description of the late Mr. C., the former owner of the house.

Although the ghost of Mrs. C. had originally assured the B's that she meant no harm and that she had come as a friend, Mrs. B. had her doubts. A number of small items of no particular value disappeared from time to time and were never found again. This was at times when intruders were completely out of the question.

Then Mrs. B. heard the pages of a wallpaper sampler lying on the dining room table being turned one day. Thinking her husband was doing it, she called out to him, only to find that the room was empty. When she located him in another part of the house, he reported having heard the pages being turned also, and this reassured Mrs. B. since she now had her husband's support in the matter of ghosts. It was clear to her that the late owners did not appreciate the many changes they had made in the house. But Mrs. B. also decided that she was not about to be put out of her home by a ghost. The changes had been made for the better, she decided, and the C.'s, even in their present ghostly state, should be grateful for what they had done for the house and not resent them. Perhaps these thoughts somehow reached the two ghosts telepathically; at any rate, the atmosphere in the house became quiet after that.

Barbara was a young woman with a good background who saw me on a Boston television program and volunteered her own experiences as a result. The following week, she wrote to me.

My family home, in Duxbury, Massachusetts, which is near Plymouth and the home of such notables as Myles Standish and John Alden, is one of the oldest houses in town although we do not know just how old it is.

Last February my brother Edward and his wife Doris and their family moved into the house. Before this my brother Carl and my father were there alone after my mother's death nearly a year ago.

The first occasion of odd happenings was on March 17, St. Patrick's Day. We are a very small part Irish—the name is about all that is left, O'Neil. A friend of mine and I went up to the farm to visit. Shortly after we arrived we heard a noise, which to me sounded like a baby whimpering as it awoke and to my sister-in-law as a woman moaning. I spoke to Doris, something about her baby being awake. She said no and let it pass until later when she told us that she had heard the same noise earlier in the morning and had gone upstairs to check on the baby. As she stood beside the crib, the baby sleeping soundly, she heard the noise again. She then called to the barn to see if all the dogs were accounted for—which they were.

Since this first noticed phenomenon the following things have occurred.

My sister-in-law is keeping a log—I may have omissions.

1.   The upstairs door opened and closed (the latch type door) and a shadow filed the whole staircase. It was a calm, cloudy day, and the possibility of a draft is somewhat unlikely. Witnessed by Doris.

2.   My brother Carl heard a voice saying, "Bring it back." This went on for several minutes but it was clear for the full time.

3.   Footsteps upstairs heard by Doris.

4.   Doris went into the front room to see the overstuffed rocker rocking as though someone was in it. After she entered the chair began to stop as though someone got up.

5. July 4, Doris went upstairs and saw the outline of a man which just seemed to disappear.

Before Edward and Doris moved in, Carl and my father were living there alone (all are in the house now). There was no one in the house most of the time since my mother died nearly a year ago. During this time the girl who rents the other house on the farm twice saw the outline of a man over there—once sitting in a chair and another time she woke my brothers about this. She is very jittery about it and as a result does not know about the other things.

I suppose I could go on a bit about the family history. My grandmother traces her ancestry back to Myles Standish and John Alden; my grandfather from Nova Scotia of Scots-Irish ancestry. I don't know who it was, but someone who lived in the house hanged himself in the barn.

Carl is a sensible, hard-working dairyman who graduated from the University of Massachusetts. Edward is a scoffer since he has observed nothing, recently discharged from the Navy as a lieutenant and is a graduate of Tufts University.

Doris is a very intelligent, levelheaded girl who, before these events, would have called herself a scoffer or disbeliever.

I graduated from Bridgewater Teachers College and at first tried to say that there was a logical explanation to these things but there have just been too many things.

My friend is an intelligent, clear thinking person.

I give you this background on the witnesses, not as a bragger or being vain, but to give you an idea of the type of witnesses. We are not the hysterical, imagining type.

The house has thirteen rooms (not all original) and the ghost seems to roam around at will.

It has been said that the people of Boston—proper Bostonians—are a breed all their own: polite, erudite, and very determined to have things their own way. I have found that these proper Bostonian ghosts are no different in the afterlife. Some of them may not be exactly erudite, but neither are they insolent or, Heaven forbid, dumb.

HUNGRY LUCY

"*J*une Havoc's got a ghost in her townhouse," Gail Benedict said cheerily on the telephone. Gail was in public relations, and a devoted ghost-finder ever since I had been able to rid her sister's apartment of a poltergeist years before.

The house in question was 104 years old, stashed away in what New Yorkers then called "Hell's Kitchen," the area in the 40s between Ninth and Tenth Avenues, not far from the theater district. Built on the corner of Forty-fourth Street and Ninth Avenue, it had been in the possession of the Rodenberg family until a Mr. Payne bought it. He remodeled it carefully, with a great deal of respect for the old plans. He did nothing to change its quaint Victorian appearance, inside or out.

About three years later, glamorous stage and television star June Havoc bought the house, and rented the upper floors to various tenants. She herself moved into the downstairs apartment, simply because no one else wanted it. It didn't strike her as strange at the time that no tenant had ever renewed the lease on that floor-through downstairs apartment, but now she knows why—it was all because of Hungry Lucy.

The morning after Gail's call, June Havoc telephoned me, and a séance was arranged for Friday of that week. I immediately reached British medium Sybil Leek, but I gave no details. I merely invited her to help me get rid of a noisy ghost. Noise was what June Havoc complained about.

"It seems to be a series of insistent sounds," she said. "First, they were rather soft. I didn't really notice them three years ago. Then I had the architect who built that balcony in the back come in and asked him to investigate these sounds. He said there was nothing whatever the matter with the house. Then I had the plumber up, because I thought it was the steam pipes. He said it was not that either. Then I had the carpenter in, for it is a very old house, but he couldn't find any structural defects whatever."

"When do you hear these tapping noises?"

"At all times. Lately, they seem to be more insistent. More demanding. We refer to it as 'tap dancing,' for that is exactly what it sounds like."

The wooden floors were in such excellent state that Miss Havoc didn't cover them with carpets. The yellow pine used for the floorboards cannot be replaced today.

June Havoc's maid had heard loud tapping in Miss Havoc's absence, and many of her actor friends had remarked on it.

"It is always in this area," June Havoc pointed out, "and seems to come from underneath the kitchen floor. It has become impossible to sleep a full night's sleep in this room."

The kitchen leads directly into the rear section of the floor-through apartment, to a room used as a bedroom. Consequently, any noise disturbed her sleep.

Underneath Miss Havoc's apartment, there was another floor-through, but the tenants had never reported anything unusual there, nor had the ones on the upper floors. Only Miss Havoc's place was noisy.

We now walked from the front of the apartment into the back half. Suddenly there was a loud tapping sound from underneath the floor as if someone had shot off a machine gun. Catherine and I had arrived earlier than the rest, and there were just the three of us.

"There, you see," June Havoc said. The ghost had greeted us in style.

I stepped forward at once.

"What do you want?" I demanded.

Immediately, the noise stopped.

While we waited for the other participants in the investigation to arrive, June Havoc pointed to the rear wall.

"It has been furred out," she explained. "That is to say, there was another wall against the wall, which made the room smaller. Why, no one knows."

Soon *New York Post* columnist Earl Wilson and Mrs. Wilson, Gail Benedict, and Robert Winter-Berger, also a publicist, arrived, along with a woman from *Life* magazine, notebook in hand. A little later Sybil Leek swept into the room. There was a bit of casual conversation, in which nothing whatever was said about the ghost, and then we seated ourselves in the rear portion of the apartment. Sybil took the chair next to the spot where the noises always originated. June Havoc sat on her right, and I on her left. The lights were very bright since we were filming the entire scene for Miss Havoc's television show.

Soon enough, Sybil began to "go under."

"Hungry," Sybil mumbled faintly.

"Why are you hungry?" I asked.

"No food," the voice said.

The usually calm voice of Sybil Leek was panting in desperation now.

"I want some food, some food!" she cried.

I promised to help her and asked for her name.

"Don't cry. I will help you," I promised.

"Food...I want some food..." the voice continued to sob.

"Who are you?"

"Lucy Ryan."

"Do you live in this house?"

"No house here."

"How long have you been here?"

"A long time."

"What year is this?"

"Seventeen ninety-two."

"What do you do in this house?"

"No house...people...fields..."

"Why then are you here? What is there here for you?"

The ghost snorted.

"Hm...men."

"Who brought you here?"

"Came...people sent us away...soldiers...follow them...sent me away...."

"What army? Which regiment?"

"Napier."

"How old are you?"

"Twenty."

"Where were you born?"

"Hawthorne...not very far away from here."

I was not sure whether she said "Hawthorne" or "Hawgton," or some similar name.

"What is you father's name?"

Silence.

"Your mother's name?"

Silence.

"Were you baptized?"

"Baptized?"

She didn't remember that either.

I explained that she had passed on. It did not matter.

"Stay here...until I get some food...meat...meat and corn..."

"Have you tried to communicate with anyone in this house?"

"Nobody listens."

"How are you trying to make them listen?"

"I make noise because I want food."

"Why do you stay in one area? Why don't you move around freely?"

"Can't. Can't go away. Too many people. Soldiers."

"Where are your parents?"

"Dead."

"What is your mother's name?"

"Mae."

"Her maiden name?"

"Don't know."

"Your father's first name?"

"Terry."

"Were any of your family in the army?"

Ironical laughter punctuated her next words.

"Only...me."

"Tell me the names of some of the officers in the army you knew."

"Alfred...Wait."

"Any rank?"

"No rank."

"What regiment did you follow?"

"Just this...Alfred."

"And he left you?"

"Yes. I went with some other man, then I was hungry and I came here."

"Why here?"

"I was sent here."

"By whom?"

"They made me come. Picked me up. Man brought me here. Put me down on the ground."

"Did you die in this spot?"

"Die, die? I'm not dead. *I'm hungry.*"

I then asked her to join her parents, those who loved her, and to leave this spot. She refused. She wanted to walk by the river, she said. I suggested that she was not receiving food and could leave freely. After a while, the ghost seemed to slip away peacefully and Sybil Leek returned to her own body, temporarily vacated so that Lucy could speak through it. As usual, Sybil remembered absolutely nothing of what went on when she was in deep trance. She was crying, but thought her mascara was the cause of it.

Suddenly, the ghost was back. The floorboards were reverberating with the staccato sound of an angry tap, loud, strong, and demanding.

"What do you want?" I asked again, although I knew now what she wanted.

Sybil also extended a helping hand. But the sound stopped as abruptly as it had begun.

A while later, we sat down again. Sybil reported feeling presences.

"One is a girl, the other is a man. A man with a stick. Or gun. The girl is stronger. She wants something."

Suddenly, Sybil pointed to the kitchen area.

"What happened in the corner?"

Nobody had told Sybil of the area in which the disturbances had always taken place.

"I feel her behind me now. A youngish girl, not very well dressed, Georgian period. I don't get the man too well."

At this point, we brought into the room a small Victorian wooden table, a gift from Gail Benedict.

Within seconds after Sybil, June Havoc, and I had lightly placed our hands upon it, it started to move, seemingly of its own volition!

Rapidly, it began to tap out a word, using a kind of Morse code. While Earl Wilson was taking notes, we allowed the table to jump hither and yon, tapping out a message.

None of us touched the table top except lightly. There was no question of manipulating the table. The light was very bright, and our hands almost touched, so that any pressure by one of us would have been instantly noticed by the other two. This type of communication is slow, since the table runs through the entire alphabet until it reaches the desired letter, then the next letter, until an entire word has been spelled out.

"L-e-a-v-e," the communicator said, not exactly in a friendly mood.

Evidently she wanted the place to herself and thought we were the intruders.

I tried to get some more information about her. But instead of tapping out another word in an orderly fashion, the table became very excited—if that is the word for emotional tables—and practically leapt from beneath our hands. We were required to follow it to keep up the contact, as it careened wildly through the room. When I was speaking, it moved toward me and practically crept onto my lap. When I wasn't speaking, it ran to someone else in the room. Eventually, it became so wild, at times entirely off the floor, that it slipped from our light touch and, as the power was broken, instantly rolled into a corner—just another table with no life of its own.

We repaired to the garden, a few steps down an iron staircase, in the rear of the house.

"Sybil, what do you feel down here?" I asked.

"I had a tremendous urge to come out here. I didn't know there was a garden. Underneath my feet almost is the cause of the disturbance."

We were standing at a spot adjacent to the basement wall and close to the center of the tapping disturbance we had heard.

"Someone may be buried here," Sybil remarked, pointing to a mound of earth underneath our feet. "It's a girl."

"Do you see the wire covering the area behind you?" June Havoc said. "I tried to plant seeds there, and the wire was to protect them—but somehow nothing, nothing will grow there."

"Plant something on this mound," Sybil suggested. "It may well pacify *her.*"

We returned to the upstairs apartment, and soon after broke up the "ghost hunting party," as columnist Sheila Graham called it later.

The next morning, I called June Havoc to see how things were. I knew from experience that the ghost would either be totally gone, or totally mad, but not the same as before.

Lucy, I was told, was rather mad. Twice as noisy, she still demanded her pound of flesh. I promised June Havoc that we'd return until the ghost was completely gone.

A few days passed. Things became a little quieter, as if Lucy were hesitating. Then something odd happened the next night. Instead of tapping from her accustomed corner area, Lucy moved away from it and tapped away from above June's bed. She had never been heard from that spot before.

I decided it was time to have a chat with Lucy again. Meanwhile, corroboration of the information we had obtained had come to us quickly. The morning after our first séance, Bob Winter-Berger called. He had been to the New York Public Library and checked on Napier, the officer named by the medium as the man in charge of the soldier's regiment.

The *Dictionary of National Biography* contained the answer. Colonel George Napier, a British officer, had served on the staff of Governor Sir Henry Clinton. How exciting, I thought. The Clinton mansion once occupied the very ground we were having the séance on. As far as I knew, the place was still not entirely free of the uncanny, for reports continued to reach me of strange steps and doors opening by themselves.

Although the mansion itself no longer stands, the carriage house in the rear was now part of Clinton Court, a reconstructed apartment house on West Forty-sixth Street. How could Sybil Leek, only recently arrived from England, have known of these things?

Napier was indeed the man who had charge of a regiment on this very spot, and the years 1781–1782 are given as the time when Napier's family contracted the dreaded yellow fever and died. Sir Henry Clinton forbade his aide to be in touch with them, and the Colonel was shipped off to England, half-dead himself, while his wife and family passed away on the spot that later became Potter's Field.

Many Irish immigrants came to the New World in those years. Perhaps the Ryan girl was one of them, or her parents were. Unfortunately, history does not keep much of a record of camp followers.

On January 15, 1965, precisely at midnight, I placed Sybil Leek into deep trance in my apartment on Riverside Drive. In the past we had succeeded in contacting *former* ghosts once they had been pried loose in an initial séance in the haunted house itself. I had high hopes that Lucy would communicate and I wasn't disappointed.

"Tick, tock, tickety-tock, June's clock stops, June's clock stops," the entranced medium murmured, barely audibly.

"Tickety-tock, June's clock stops, tickety-tock…"

"Who are you?" I asked.

"Lucy."

"Lucy, what does this mean?"

"June's clock stops, June's clock stops, frightened June, frightened June," she repeated like a child reciting a poem.

"Why do you want to frighten June?"

"Go away."

"Why do you want her to go away?"

"People there…too much house…too much June…too many clocks…she sings, dances, she makes a lot of noise…I'm hungry, I'm always hungry. You don't do a thing about it…"

"Will you go away if I get you some food? Can we come to an agreement?"

"Why?"

"Because I want to help you, help June."

"Ah, same old story."

"You're not happy. Would you like to see Alfred again?"

"Yes...he's gone."

"Not very far. I'll get you together with Alfred if you will leave the house."

"Where would I go?"

"Alfred has a house of his own for you."

"Where?"

"Not very far."

"Frightened to go...don't know where to go...nobody likes me. She makes noises, I make noises. I don't like that clock."

"Where were you born, Lucy?"

"Larches by the Sea...Larchmont...by the Sea...people disturb me."

Again I asked her to go to join her Alfred, to find happiness again. I suggested she call for him by name, which she did, hesitatingly at first, more desperately later.

"No...I can't go from here. He said he would come. He said *wait*. Wait...here. Wait. Alfred, why don't you come? Too many clocks. Time, time, time...noisy creature. Time, time...three o'clock."

"What happened at three o'clock?" I demanded.

"He said he'd come," the ghost replied. "I waited for him."

"Why at three o'clock in the middle of the night?"

"Why do you think? Couldn't get out. Locked in. Not allowed out at night. I'll wait. He'll come."

"Did you meet any of his friends?"

"Not many...what would I say?"

"What was Alfred's name?"

"Bailey...Alfred said 'Wait, wait...I'll go away,' he said. 'They'll never find me.'"

"Go to him with my love," I said, calmly repeating over

and over the formula used in rescue circle operations to send the earthbound ghost across the threshold.

As I spoke, Lucy slipped away from us, not violently as she had come, but more or less resignedly.

I telephoned June Havoc to see what had happened that night between midnight and 12:30. She had heard Lucy's tapping precisely then, but nothing more as the night passed—a quiet night for a change.

Was Lucy on her way to her Alfred?

We would know soon enough.

In the weeks that followed, I made periodic inquiries of June Havoc. Was the ghost still in evidence? Miss Havoc did not stay at her townhouse all the time, preferring the quiet charm of her Connecticut estate. But on the nights when she did sleep in the house on Forty-fourth Street, she was able to observe that Lucy Ryan had changed considerably in personality—the ghost had been freed, yes, but had not yet been driven from the house. In fact, the terrible noise was now all over the house, although less frequent and less vehement—*as if she were thinking things over.*

I decided we had to finish the job as well as we could and another séance was arranged for late March, 1965. Present were—in addition to our hostess and chief sufferer—my wife Catherine and myself; Emory Lewis, editor of *Cue* magazine; Barry Farber, WOR radio commentator; and two friends of June Havoc. We grouped ourselves around a table in the *front room* this time. This soon proved to be a mistake. No Lucy Ryan. No ghost. We repaired to the other room where the original manifestations had taken place, with more luck this time.

Sybil, in trance, told us that the girl had gone, but that Alfred had no intention of leaving. He was waiting for *her* now. I asked for the name of his commanding officer and was told it was Napier. This we knew already. But who was the next in rank?

"Lieutenant William Watkins."

"What about the commanding general?"

He did not know.

He had been born in Hawthorne, just like Lucy, he told Sybil. I had been able to trace this Hawthorne to a place not far away in Westchester County.

There were people all over, Sybil said in trance, and they were falling down. They were ill.

"Send Alfred to join his Lucy," I commanded, and Sybil in a low voice told the stubborn ghost to go.

After an interlude of table tipping, in which several characters from the nether world made their auditory appearance, she returned to trance. Sybil in trance was near the river again, among the sick.

But no Lucy Ryan. Lucy's gone, she said.

"The smell makes me sick," Sybil said, and you could see stark horror in her sensitive face.

"Dirty people, rags, people in uniform too, with dirty trousers. There is a big house across the river."

"Whose house is it?"

"Mr. Dawson's. Doctor Dawson. Dr. James Dawson…Lee Point. Must go there. Feel sick. Rocks and trees, just the house across the river."

"What year is this?"

"Ninety-two."

She then described Dr. Dawson's house as having three windows on the left, two on the right, and five above, and said that it was called Lee Point—Hawthorne. It sounded a little like Hawgton to me, but I can't be sure.

Over the river, she said. She described a "round thing on a post" in front of the house, like a shell. For messages, she thought.

"What is the name of the country we're in?" I asked.

"Vinelands. Vinelands."

I decided to change the subject back to Hungry Lucy. How did she get sick?

"She didn't get any food, and then she got cold, by the river.

... Nobody helped them there. Let them die. Buried them in a pit."

"What is the name of the river?"

"Mo...Mo-something."

"Do you see anyone else still around?"

"Lots of people with black faces, black shapes."

The plague, I thought, and how little the doctors could do in those days to stem it.

I asked about the man in charge and she said "Napier" and I wondered who would be left in command after Napier left, and the answer this time was, "Clinton...old fool. Georgie."

There were a Henry Clinton and a George Clinton, fairly contemporary with each other.

"What happened after that?"

"Napier died."

"Any other officers around?"

"Little Boy Richardson...Lieutenant."

"What regiment?"

"Burgoyne."

Sybil, entranced, started to hiss and whistle. "Signals," she murmured. "As the men go away, they whistle."

I decided the time had come to bring Sybil out of trance. She felt none the worse for it, and asked for something to drink. *Hungry*, like Lucy, she wasn't.

We began to evaluate the information just obtained. Dr. James Dawson may very well have lived. The A.M.A. membership directories weren't that old. I found the mention of Lee Point and Hawthorne interesting, inasmuch as the two locations were quite close. Lee, of course, would be Fort Lee, and there was a "point" or promontory in the river at that spot.

The town of Vinelands does exist in New Jersey, but the river beginning with "Mo-" may be the Mohawk. That

Burgoyne was a general in the British army during the Revolution is well known.

So there you have it. Sybil Leek knew very little, if anything, about the New Jersey and Westchester countryside, having only recently come to America. Even I, then a New York resident for 27 years, had never heard of Hawthorne before. Yet there it was on the way to Pleasantville, New York.

The proof of the ghostly pudding, however, was not the regimental roster, but the state of affairs at June Havoc's house.

A later report had it that Lucy, Alfred, or whoever was responsible had quieted down considerably.

They were down, but not out.

I tactfully explained to June Havoc that feeling sorry for a hungry ghost makes things tough for a parapsychologist. The emotional pull of a genuine attachment, no matter how unconscious it may be, can provide the energies necessary to prolong the stay of the ghost.

Gradually, as June Havoc—wanting a peaceful house, especially at 3 A.M.—allowed practical sense to outweigh sentimentality, the shades of Hungry Lucy and her soldier-boy faded into the distant past, whence they came.

THE **BURNING GHOST**

I treat each case reported to me on an individual basis. Some I reject on the face of the report, and others only after I have been through a long and careful investigation. But other reports have the ring of truth about them and are worthy of belief, even though some of them were no longer capable of verification because witnesses have died, or sites have been destroyed.

A good example was the case reported to me by Mrs. Edward Needs, Jr., of Canton, Ohio. In a small town by the name of Homeworth, there was a stretch of land near the highway that had become nothing more than a neglected farm with a boarded-up old barn still standing. The spot was actually on a dirt road, and the nearest house was half a mile away, with wooded territory in between. This was important, you see, for the spot was isolated, and a man might die before help could arrive. On rainy days, the dirt road was impassable. Mrs. Needs had passed the spot a number of times, and did not particularly care to go there. Somehow it always gave her an uneasy feeling. Once, their car got stuck in the mud on a rainy day, and they had to drive through open fields to get out.

It was on that adventure-filled ride that Mr. Needs confided for the first time what had happened to him at that spot on prior occasions. It was the year when Edward Needs and a friend were on a joy ride after dark. At that time Needs had not yet married his present wife, and the two men had been drinking a little, but were far from drunk. It was then that they discovered the dirt road for the first time.

On the spur of the moment, they followed it. A moment later they came to the old barn. But just as they were approaching it, a man jumped out of nowhere in front of them. What was even more sobering was the condition this man was in: engulfed in flames from head to toe! Quickly, Needs put his bright headlights on the scene, to see better. The man then ran into the woods across the road and just disappeared.

Two men never became cold sober more quickly. They turned around and went back to the main highway fast. But the first chance they had, they returned with two carloads full of other fellows. They were equipped with strong lights, guns, and absolutely no whiskey. When the first of the cars was within twenty feet of the spot where Needs had seen the apparition, they all saw the same thing: there before them was the horrible spectacle of a human being blazing from top to bottom, and evidently suffering terribly as he tried to run away from his doom. Needs emptied his gun at the figure: it never moved or acknowledged that it had been hit by the bullets. A few seconds later, the figure ran into the woods— exactly as it had when Needs had first encountered it.

Now the ghost posse went into the barn, which they found abandoned although not in very bad condition. The only strange thing was spots showing evidence of fire: evidently someone or something had burned inside the barn without, however, setting fire to the barn as a whole. Or had the fiery man run outside to save his barn from the fire?

THE **GHOST** AND THE **PUPPY**

*A*lice H., a widow, lived in a five-room bungalow flat in the Middle West. She worked part-time as a saleswoman, but lived alone. Throughout her long life she never had any real interest in psychic phenomena. She even went to a spiritualist meeting with a friend and was not impressed one way or another. She was sixty-two when she had her first personal encounter with the unknown.

One night she went to bed and awoke because something was pressing against her back. Since she knew herself to be alone in the apartment, it frightened her. Nevertheless, she turned around to look—and to her horror she saw the upper part of her late husband's body. As she stared at him, he glided over the bed, turned to look at her once more with a mischievous look in his eye, and disappeared on the other side of the bed. Mrs. H. could not figure out why he had appeared to her, because she had not been thinking of him at that time. But evidently he was to instigate her further psychic experiences.

Not much later, she had another manifestation that shook her up a great deal. She had been sound asleep when she was awakened by the whimpering of her puppy. The dog was sleeping on top of the bed covers. Mrs. H. was fully awake now and looked over her shoulder where stood a young girl of about ten years, in the most beautiful blue tailored pajamas. She was looking at the dog. As Mrs. H. looked closer, she noticed that the child had neither face nor hands nor feet showing. Shaken, she jumped out of bed and went toward the spirit. The little girl moved back toward the wall, and Mrs. H. followed her. As the little girl in the blue pajamas neared the wall, it somehow changed into a beautiful flower garden with a wide path! She walked down the path in a mechanical sort of way, with the wide cuffs of her pajamas showing, but still with no feet. Nevertheless, it was a happy walk, then it all disappeared.

The experience bothered Mrs. H. so much that she moved into another room. But her little dog stayed on in the room where the experience had taken place, sleeping on the floor under the bed. That first experience took place on a Sunday in October, at four A.M. The following Sunday, again at four o'clock, Mrs. H. heard the dog whimper, as if he were conscious of a presence. By the time she reached the other room, however, she could not see anything. These experiences continued for some time, always on Sunday at four in the morning. It then became clear to Mrs. H. that the little girl hadn't come for her—but only to visit her little dog.

THE GIRLS' SCHOOL GHOST

*I*n one of the quietest and most elegant sections of old Cincinnati, where ghosts and hauntings were rarely whispered about, stood a lovely Victorian mansion built around 1850, in what was then a wealthy suburb of the city.

The house was brought to my attention some years ago by John Strader of Clifton, a descendant of one of the early Dutch families who settled Cincinnati, and himself a student of the paranormal. The tenants at that time were the Stenton family, or rather, of one of the apartments in the mansion, for it had long been subdivided into a number of apartments lived in by various people.

Soon after they had taken up residence in the old house, the Stentons were startled by noises, as if someone were walking in the hall, and when they checked, there was never anyone about who could had caused the walking. Then, two weeks after they had moved in, and always at exactly the same time—2:10 A.M.—they would hear the noise of a heavy object hitting the marble floor; of course there was nothing that could have caused it.

Shortly thereafter, while Mrs. Stenton and her father were doing some research work in the flat, someone softly called out her name, Marilyn. Both heard it. What really upset them was the sound of arguing voices coming from the area of the

185

ceiling in their bedroom: Mrs. Stenton had the impression that there were a group of young girls up there.

But the most dramatic event was to transpire a couple of weeks later. Someone had entered the bedroom, and although she knew she had been alone, her family being in other parts of the house, she was frightened—especially when she saw what appeared to be a misty figure. As soon as she had made eye contact with it, the figure shot out of the room, through the French doors leading to a studio, managing to knock the Venetian blinds on the doors, causing them to sway back and forth.

Shortly before I visited Cincinnati to deal with this case, Mrs. Stenton had another eerie experience. It was winter and it had been snowing the night before. When Mrs. Stenton stepped out onto their front porch, she immediately noticed a fresh set of footprints on the porch, heading *away* from the house.

The house was originally built in 1850 as a large private home; later it became a girls' school, and much later an apartment house of sorts. The Stenton's apartment, encompassing seven rooms, was the largest in the house.

When I looked into the case I discovered some additional details. In 1880 a young man of the Henry family had committed suicide in the house by shooting himself, and after the family moved; the house could not be sold for a long time. It became known as being haunted and was boarded up. Finally a girls' school, the Ealy School, bought it in 1900.

Other tenants had also encountered unusual phenomena ranging from "presences" to noises of objects hitting floors, and footsteps following one around when no one was, in fact, doing so. Even the dog owned by one of the tenants would under no condition enter the area of the disturbances and would put up a fearsome howl.

But the item most likely to have an answer to the goings-on came to me by talking to some of the oldsters in the area: one of the young girls in the school was said to have hanged herself upstairs, right above the Stenton's apartment. Was it her ghost or that of young Henry who could not leave well enough alone?

A VISIT WITH THE SPIRITED JEFFERSON

"*T*his typical pre-Revolutionary tavern was a favorite stopping place for travelers," the official guide to Charlottesville says. "With its colonial furniture and china, its beamed and paneled rooms, it appears much the way it did in the days when Jefferson and Monroe were visitors. Monroe writes of entertaining Lafayette as his guest at dinner here, and General Andrew Jackson, fresh from his victory at New Orleans, stopped over on his way to Washington."

The guide, however, does not mention that the tavern was moved a considerable distance from its original place to a much more accessible location where the tourist trade could better benefit. Regardless of this comparatively recent change of position, the tavern was exactly as it had been, with everything inside—including its ghosts—intact. At the original site, it was surrounded by trees, which framed it and sometimes towered over it. At the new site, facing the road, it looks out into the Virginia countryside almost like a manor house. One walks up to the wooden structure over a number of steps and enters the old tavern to the left or, if one prefers, the pub to the right, which had become a coffee shop. Taverns in the eighteenth and early nineteenth centuries were not simply bars or inns; they were meeting places where people could talk freely, sometimes about political subjects. They were used as headquarters for Revolutionary movements or for invading military forces. Most taverns of any size had ballrooms in which the social functions of the area could be held. Only a few private individuals were wealthy enough to have their own ballrooms built into their manor houses.

What was fortunate about Michie Tavern was the fact that everything was pretty much as it was in the eighteenth century, and whatever restorations have been undertaken are completely authentic. The furniture and cooking utensils, the tools of the innkeeper, the porcelain, the china, the metal objects are all of the period, whether they had been in the house or not. As was customary with historical restorations or preservations, whatever was missing in the house was supplied by painstaking historical research, and objects of the same period and the same area are substituted for those presumably lost during the intervening period.

On my first visit to Charlottesville in 1964, Virginia Cloud had wanted me to visit the tavern, but somehow the schedule did not permit it then. This time the four of us arrived in mid-morning, in order to see the tavern before the tourists came— the luncheon crowd might make an interview with the current manager of the coffee shop difficult. The tavern has three floors and a large number of rooms, so we would need the two hours we had allowed ourselves for the visit. After looking at the downstairs part of the tavern, with its "common" kitchen and the over-long wooden table where two dozen people could be fed, we mounted the stairs to the second floor.

Ingrid kept looking into various rooms, sniffing out the psychic presences, as it were, while I followed close behind. Horace Burr and Virginia Cloud kept a respectable distance, as if trying not to "frighten" the ghosts away. That was all right with me, because I did not want Ingrid to tap the unconscious of either one of these very knowledgeable people.

Finally we arrived in the third-floor ballroom of the old

tavern. I asked Ingrid what she had felt in the various rooms below. "In the pink room on the second floor I felt an argument or some sort of strife but nothing special in any of the other rooms."

"What about this big ballroom?"

"I can see a lot of people around here. There is a festive atmosphere, and I think important people came here; it is rather exclusive, this room. I think it was used just on special occasions."

By now I had waved Horace and Virginia to come closer, since it had become obvious to me that they wanted very much to hear what Ingrid was saying. Possibly new material might come to light, unknown to both of these historians, in which case they might verify it later on or comment upon it on the spot.

"I'm impressed with an argument over a woman here," Ingrid continued. "It has to do with one of the dignitaries, and it is about one of their wives."

"How does the argument end?"

"I think they just had a quick argument here, about her infidelity."

"Who are the people involved?"

"I think Hamilton. I don't know the woman's name."

"Who is the other man?"

"I think Jefferson was here."

"Try to get as much of the argument as you can."

Ingrid closed her eyes, sat down in a chair generally off limits to visitors, and tried to tune in on the past. "I get the argument as a real embarrassment," she began. "The woman is frail, she has a long dress on with lace at the top part around the neck, her hair is light brown."

"Does she take part in the argument?"

"Yes she has to side with her husband."

"Describe her husband."

"I can't see his face, but he is dressed in a brocade jacket pulled back with buttons down the front and breeches. It is a very fancy outfit."

"How does it all end?"

"Well, nothing more is said. It is just a terrible embarrassment."

"Is this some sort of special occasion? Are there other people here?"

"Yes, oh, yes. It is like an anniversary or something of that sort. Perhaps a political anniversary of some kind. There is music and dancing and candlelight."

While Ingrid was speaking, in an almost inaudible voice, Horace and Virginia were straining to hear what she was saying but not being very successful at it. At this point Horace waved to me, and I tiptoed over to him. "Ask her to get the period a little closer," he whispered in my ear.

I went back to Ingrid and put the question to her. "I think it was toward the end of the war," she said, "toward the very end of it. For some time now I've had the figure 1781 impressed on my mind."

Since nothing further seemed to be forthcoming from Ingrid at this point, I asked her to relax and come back to the present, so that we could discuss her impressions freely.

"The name Hamilton is impossible in this connection," Horace Burr began. But I was quick to interject that the name Hamilton was fairly common in the late eighteenth and early nineteenth centuries and that Ingrid need not have referred to *the* Alexander Hamilton. "Jefferson was here many times, and he could have been involved in this," Burr continued. "I think I know who the other man might have been. But could we try questioning the medium on specific issues?"

Neither Ingrid nor I objected, and Horace proceeded to ask Ingrid to identify the couple she had felt in the ballroom. Ingrid threw her head back for a moment, closed her eyes, and then replied, "The man is very prominent in politics, one of the big three or four at the time, and one of the reasons this is all so embarrassing, from what I get, is that the other man is of much lower caliber. He is not one of the big leaders; he may be an officer or something like that."

While Ingrid was slowly speaking, I again felt the strange sense of transportation, of looking back in time, which had been coming to me more and more often, always unsought and usually one of fleeting duration. "For what it is worth," I said, "while Ingrid is speaking, I also get a very vague impression that all this has something to do with two sisters. It concerns a rivalry between two sisters."

"The man's outfit," Ingrid continued her narrative, "was sort of gold and white brocade and very fancy. He was the husband. I don't see the other man."

Horace seemed unusually agitated at this. "Tell me, did this couple live in this vicinity or did they come from far away on a special anniversary?"

"They lived in the vicinity and came just for the evening."

"Well, Horace?" I said, getting more and more curious, since he was apparently driving in a specific direction. "What was this all about?"

For once, Horace enjoyed being the center of attraction. "Well, it was a hot and heavy situation, all right. The couple were Mr. and Mrs. John Walker—he was the son of Dr. Walker of Castle Hill. And the man, who wasn't here, was Jefferson himself. Ingrid is right in saying that they lived in the vicinity—Castle Hill is not far away from here."

"But what about the special festivity that brought them all together here?"

Horace wasn't sure what it could have been, but Virginia, in great excitement, broke in here. "It was in this room that the waltz was danced for the first time in America. A young man had come from France dressed in very fancy clothes. The lady he danced with was a closely chaperoned girl from

Charlottesville. She was very young, and she danced the waltz with this young man, and everybody in Charlottesville was shocked. The news went around town that the young lady had danced with a man holding her, and that was just terrible at the time. Perhaps that was the occasion. Michie Tavern was a stopover for stagecoaches, and Jefferson and the local people would meet here to get their news. Downstairs was the meeting room, but up there in the ballroom the more special events took place, such as the introduction of the waltz."

I turned to Horace Burr. "How is it that this tavern no longer stands on the original site? I understand it has been moved here for easier tourist access."

"Yes," Horace replied. "The building originally stood near the airport. In fact, the present airport is on part of the old estate that belonged to Colonel John Henry, the father of Patrick Henry. Young Patrick spent part of his boyhood there. Later, Colonel Henry sold the land to the Michies. This house was then their main house. It was on the old highway. In turn, they built themselves an elaborate mansion which is still standing and turned this house into a tavern. All the events we have been discussing took place while this building was on the old site. In 1926 it was moved here. Originally, I think the ballroom we are standing in now was just the loft of the old Henry house. They raised part of the roof to make it into a ballroom because they had no meeting room in the tavern."

In the attractively furnished coffee shop to the right of the main tavern, Mrs. Juanita Godfrey, the manager, served us steaming hot black coffee and sat down to chat with us. "Had anyone ever complained about unusual noises or other inexplicable manifestations in the tavern?" I asked.

"Some of the employees who work here at night do hear certain sounds they can't account for," Mrs. Godrey replied. "They will hear something and go and look, and there will be nothing there."

"In what part of the building?"

"All over, even in this area. This is a section of the slave quarters, and it is very old."

Mrs. Godfrey did not seem too keen on psychic experiences, I felt. To the best of her knowledge, no one had had any unusual experiences in the tavern. "What about the lady who slept here one night recently?" I inquired.

"You mean Mrs. Milton—yes, she slept here one night." But Mrs. Godfrey knew nothing of Mrs. Milton's experiences.

However, Virginia had met the lady, who was connected with the historical preservation effort of the community. "One night when Mrs. Milton was out of town," Virginia explained, "I slept in her room. At the time she confessed to me that she had heard footsteps frequently, especially on the stairway down."

"That is the area she slept in, yes," Mrs. Godfrey confirmed. "She slept in the ladies' parlor on the first floor."

"What about yourself, Virginia? Did *you* hear anything?"

"I heard noises, but the wood sometimes behaves very funny. She, however, said they were definitely footsteps. That was in 1961."

What had Ingrid unearthed in the ballroom of Michie Tavern? Was it merely the lingering imprint of America's first waltz, scandalous to the early Americans but innocent in the light of today? Or was it something more—an involvement between Mrs. Walker and the illustrious Thomas Jefferson? My image of the great American had always been that of a man above human frailties. But my eyes were to be opened still further on a most intriguing visit to Monticello, Jefferson's home.

"You're welcome to visit Monticello to continue the parapsychological research which you are conducting relative to the personalities of 1776," wrote James A. Bear, Jr., of the Thomas Jefferson Memorial Foundation, and he arranged for us to go to the popular tourist attraction after regular hours, to permit

Ingrid the peace and tranquility necessary to tune in on the very fragile vibrations that might hang on from the past.

Jefferson, along with Benjamin Franklin, has become a popular historical figure these days: a play, a musical, and a musical film have brought him to life, showing him as the shy, dedicated, intellectual architect of the Declaration of Independence. Jefferson, the gentleman Virginia farmer, the man who wants to free the slaves but is thwarted in his efforts by other Southerners; Jefferson, the ardent but bashful lover of his wife; Jefferson, the ideal of virtue and American patriotism—these are the images put across by the entertainment media, by countless books, and by the tourist authorities which try to entice vistors to come to Charlottesville and visit Jefferson's home, Monticello.

Even the German tourist service plugged itself into the Jefferson boom. "This is like a second mother country for me," Thomas Jefferson is quoted as saying while traveling down the Rhine. "Everything that isn't English in our country comes from here." Jefferson, compared the German Rhineland to certain portions of Maryland and Pennsylvania and pointed out that the second largest ethnic group in America at the time were Germans. In an article in the German language weekly *Aufbau,* Jefferson is described as the first prominent American tourist in the Rhineland. His visit took place in April 1788. At the time Jefferson was ambassador to Paris, and the Rhine journey allowed him to study agriculture, customs, and conditions on both sides of the Rhine. Unquestionably, Jefferson, along with Washington, Franklin, and Lincoln, represents one of the pillars of the American edifice.

Virginia Cloud, ever the avid historian of her area, points out that not only did Jefferson and John Adams have a close relationship as friends and political contemporaries but there were certain uncanny "coincidences" between their lives. For instance, both Jefferson and Adams died within hours of each other, Jefferson in Virginia and Adams in Massachusetts, on July 4, 1826—exactly fifty years to the day they had both signed the Declaration of Independence. Adams's last words were, "But Jefferson still lives." At the time that was no longer true, for Jefferson had died earlier in the day.

Jefferson's imprint is all over Charlottesville. Not only did the talented "Renaissance man" design his own home, Monticello, but he also designed the Rotunda, the focal point of the University of Virginia. Jefferson, Madison, and Monroe were members of the first governing board of the University, which is justly famous for its academics and the school of medicine—and which, incidentally, was then the leading university in the study of parapsychology, since Dr. Ian Stevenson taught there.

On our way to Monticello we decided to visit the old Swan Tavern, which had some important links with Jefferson. The tavern was then used as a private club, but the directors graciously allowed us to come in, even the ladies, who were generally not admitted. Nothing in the appointments reminds one of the old taverns, since the place has been extensively remodeled to suit the requirements of the private club. At first we inspected the downstairs and smiled at several elderly gentlemen who hadn't the slightest idea why we were there. Then we went to the upper story and finally came to rest in a room to the rear of the building. As soon as Ingrid had seated herself in a comfortable chair in a corner, I closed the door and asked her what she felt about this place, of which she had no knowledge.

"I feel that people came here to talk things over in a lighter vein, perhaps over a few drinks."

"Was there anyone in particular who was outstanding among these people?"

"I keep thinking of Jefferson, and I'm seeing big mugs; most of the men have big mugs in front of them."

Considering that Ingrid did not know the past of the

building as a tavern, this was pretty evidential. I asked her about Jefferson.

"I think he was the figurehead. This matter concerned him greatly, but I don't think it had anything to do with his own wealth or anything like that."

"At the time when this happened, was there a warlike action in progress?"

"Yes, I think it was on the outskirts of town. I have the feeling that somebody was trying to reach this place and that they were waiting for somebody, and yet they weren't really expecting that person."

Both Horace Burr and Virginia Cloud were visibly excited that Ingrid had put her finger on it, so to speak. Virginia had been championing the cause of the man about whom Ingrid had just spoken. "Virginians are always annoyed to hear about Paul Revere, who was actually an old man with a tired horse that left Revere to walk home," Virginia said, somewhat acidly, "while Jack Jouett did far more—he saved the lives of Thomas Jefferson and his legislators. Yet, outside of Virginia, few have ever heard of him."

"Perhaps Jouett didn't have as good a press agent as Paul Revere had in Longfellow, as you always say, Virginia," Burr commented. I asked Virginia to sum up the incident that Ingrid had touched on psychically.

"Jack Jouett was a native of Albermarle County and was of French Huguenot origin. His father, Captain John Jouette, owned this tavern."

"We think there is a chance that he also owned the Cuckoo Tavern in Louisa, forty miles from here," Burr interjected.

"Jouett had a son named Jack who stood six feet, four inches and weighed over two hundred pounds. He was an expert rider and one of those citizens who signed the oath of intelligence to the Commonwealth of Virginia in 1779.

"It was June 3, 1781, and the government had fled to

Charlottesville from the advancing British troops. Most of Virginia was in British hands, and General Cornwallis very much wanted to capture the leaders of the Revolution, especially Thomas Jefferson, who had authored the Declaration of Independence, and Patrick Henry, whose motto, 'Give me liberty or give me death,' had so much contributed to the success of the Revolution. In charge of 250 cavalrymen was Sir Banastre Tarleton. His mission was to get to Charlottesville as quickly as possible to capture the leaders of the uprising. Tarleton was determined to cover the seventy miles' distance between Cornwallis's headquarters and Charlottesville in a single twenty-four-hour period, in order to surprise the leaders of the American independence movement.

"In the town of Louisa, forty miles distant from Charlottesville, he and his men stopped into the Cuckoo Tavern for a brief respite. Fate would have it that Jack Jouett was at the tavern at that moment, looking after his father's business. It was a very hot day for June, and the men were thirsty. Despite Tarleton's orders, their tongues loosened, and Jack Jouett was able to overhear their destination. Jack decided to outride them and warn Charlottesville. It was about ten P.M. when he got on his best horse, determined to take short cuts and side roads, while the British would have to stick to the main road. Fortunately, it was a moonlit night; otherwise he might not have made it in the rugged hill country.

"Meanwhile the British were moving ahead too, and around eleven o'clock they came to a halt on a plantation near Louisa. By two A.M. they had resumed their forward march. They paused again a few hours later to seize and burn a train of twelve wagons loaded with arms and clothing for the Continental troops in South Carolina. When dawn broke over Charlottesville, Jouette had left the British far behind. Arriving at Monticello, he dashed up to the front entrance to rouse Jefferson; however, Governor Jefferson, who was an early riser, had seen the rider tear up his driveway and met him at the door. Ever the gentleman, Jefferson offered the exhausted messenger a glass of wine before allowing him to proceed to Charlottesville proper, two miles farther on. There he roused the other members of the government, while Jefferson woke his family. Two hours later, when Tarleton came thundering into Charlottesville, the government of Virginia had vanished."

"That's quite a story, Virginia," I said.

"Of course," Burr added, "Tarleton and his men might have been here even earlier if it hadn't been for the fact that they first stopped at Castle Hill. Dr. and Mrs. Walker entertained them lavishly and served them a sumptuous breakfast. It was not only sumptuous but also delaying, and Dr. Walker played the perfect host to the hilt, showing Tarleton about the place despite the British commander's impatience, even to measuring Tarleton's orderly on the living-room door jamb. This trooper was the tallest man in the British army and proved to be six feet, nine and one-quarter inches in height. Due to these and other delaying tactics—and there are hints that Mrs. Walker used her not inconsiderable charms as well to delay the vistors—the Walkers made Jack Jouett's ride a complete success. Several members of the legislature who were visiting Dr. Walker at the time were captured, but Jefferson and the bulk of the legislature, which had just begun to convene early in the morning, got away.

"You see, the legislature of Virginia met in this building, and Ingrid was entirely correct with her impressions. The members of the legislature knew, of course, that the British were not far away, but they weren't exactly expecting them here."

After Thomas Jefferson had taken refuge at the house of a certain Mr. Cole, where he was not likely to be found, Jouett went to his room at his father's tavern, the very house we were in. He had well deserved his rest. Among those who were hiding from British arrest was Patrick Henry. He arrived at a certain farmhouse and identified himself by saying, "I'm Patrick Henry." But the farmer's wife replied, "Oh, you couldn't be, because my husband is out there fighting, and Patrick Henry would be out there too." Henry managed to convince the farmer's wife that his life depended on his hiding in her house, and finally she understood. But it was toward the end of the Revolutionary War and the British knew very well that they had for all intents and purposes been beaten. Consequently, shortly afterward, Cornwallis suggested to the Virginia legislators that they return to Charlottesville to resume their offices.

It was time to proceed to Monticello; the afternoon sun was setting, and we would be arriving just after the last tourists had left. Monticello, which every student knows from its representation on the American five-cent piece, is probably one of the finest examples of American architecture, designed by Jefferson himself, who lies buried here in the family graveyard. It stands on a hill looking down into the valley of Charlottesville, perhaps fifteen minutes from the town proper. Carefully landscaped grounds surround the house. Inside, the house is laid out in classical proportions. From the entrance hall with its famous clock, also designed by Jefferson, one enters a large, round room, the heart of the house. On both sides of this central area are rectangular rooms. To the left was a corner room, used as a study and library from where Jefferson, frequently early in the morning before anyone else was up, used to look out on the rolling hills of Virginia. Adjacent to it was a very small bedroom, almost a bunk. Thus, the entire west wing of the building was a self-contained apartment in which Jefferson could be active without interfering with the rest of his family. On the other side of the round central room was a large dining room leading to a terrace which, in turn, continues into an open walk with a magnificent view of the hillside. The furniture was Jefferson's own, as are the silver and china, some of it returned to Monticello in recent years by history-conscious citizens of the area who had purchased it in various ways.

The first room we visited was Jefferson's bedroom. Almost in awe herself, Ingrid touched the bedspread of what was once Thomas Jefferson's bed, then his desk and the books he had handled. "I feel his presence here," she said, "and I think he did a lot of his work in this room, a lot of planning and working things out, till the wee hours of the night." I don't think Ingrid knew that Jefferson was in the habit of doing just that, in this particular room.

I motioned Ingrid to sit down in one of Jefferson's chairs and try to capture whatever she might receive from the past. "I can see an awful lot of hard work, sleepless nights and turmoil. Other than that, nothing."

We went into the library next to the study. "I don't think he spent much time here really, just for reference." On we went to the dining room to the right of the round central room. "I think that was his favorite room, and he loved to meet people here socially." Then she added, "I get the words plum pudding and hot liquor."

"Well," Burr commented, "he loved the lighter things of life. He brought ice cream to America, and he squirted milk directly from the cow into a goblet to make it froth. He had a French palate. He liked what we used to call floating island, a very elaborate dessert."

"I see a lot of people. It is a friendly gathering with glittering glasses and candlelight," Ingrid said. "They are elegant but don't have on overcoats. I see their white silken shirts. I see them laughing and passing things around. Jefferson is at the table with white hair pulled back, leaning over and laughing."

The sun was setting, since it was getting toward half past

six now, and we started to walk out the French glass doors onto the terrace. From there an open walk led around a sharp corner to a small building, perhaps twenty or twenty-five yards distant. Built in the small classical American style as Monticello itself, the building contained two fair-sized rooms, on two stories. The walk led to the entrance to the upper story, barricaded by an iron grillwork to keep tourists out. It allowed us to enter the room only partially, but sufficiently for Ingrid to get her bearings. Outside, the temperature sank rapidly as the evening approached. A wind had risen, and so it was pleasant to be inside the protective walls of the little house.

"Horace, where are we now?" I asked.

"We are in the honeymoon cottage where Thomas Jefferson brought his bride and lived at the time when his men were building Monticello. Jefferson and his family lived here at the very beginning, so you might say that whatever impressions there are here would be of the pre-Revolutionary part of Jefferson's life."

I turned to Ingrid and asked for her impressions. "I feel everything is very personal here and light, and I don't feel the tremendous strain in the planning of things I felt in the Monticello building. As I close my eyes, I get a funny feeling about a bouquet of flowers, some very strong and peculiar exotic flowers. They are either pink or light red and have a funny name, and I have the feeling that a woman involved in this impression is particularly fond of a specific kind of flower. He goes out of his way to get them for her, and I also get the feeling of a liking for a certain kind of chinaware or porcelain. Someone is a collector and wants to buy certain things, being a connoisseur, and wants to have little knick-knacks all over the place. I don't know if any of this makes any sense, but this is how I see it."

"It makes sense indeed," Horace Burr replied. "Jefferson did more to import rare trees and rare flowering shrubs than anyone else around here. In fact, he sent shipments back from

France while he stayed there and indicated that they were so rare that if you planted them in one place they might not succeed. So he planted only a third at Monticello, a third at Verdant Lawn, which is an old estate belonging to a friend of his, and a third somewhere else in Virginia. It was his idea to plant them in three places to see if they would thrive in his Virginia."

"The name Rousseau comes to mind. Did he know anyone by that name?" Ingrid asked.

"Of course, he was much influenced by Rousseau."

"I also get the feeling of a flickering flame, a habit of staying up to all hours of the morning. Oh, and is there any historical record of an argument concerning this habit of his, between his wife and himself and some kind of peacemaking gesture on someone else's part?"

"I am sure there was an argument," Horace said, "but I doubt that there ever was a peacemaking gesture. You see, their marriage was not a blissful one; she was very wealthy and he spent her entire estate, just as he spent Dabney Carr's entire estate and George Short's entire estate. He went through estate after estate, including his own. Dabney Carr was his cousin, and he married Jefferson's sister, Martha. He was very wealthy, but Jefferson gathered up his sister and the children and brought them here after Carr's death. He then took over all the plantations and effects of Mr. Carr.

"Jefferson was a collector of things. He wrote these catalogues of his own collection, and when he died it was the largest collection in America. You are right about the porcelain, because it was terribly sophisticated at that time to be up on porcelain. The clipper trade was bringing in these rarities, and he liked to collect them."

Since Ingrid had scored so nicely up to now, I asked her whether she felt any particular emotional event connected with this little house.

"Well, I think the wife was not living on her level, her standard, and she was unhappy. It wasn't what she was used to. It wasn't grand enough. I think she had doubts about him and his plans."

"In what sense?"

"I think she was dubious about what would happen. She was worried that he was getting too involved, and she didn't like his political affiliations too well."

I turned to Horace for comments. To my surprise, Horace asked me to turn off my tape recorder since the information was of a highly confidential nature. However, he pointed out that the material could be found in *American Heritage* magazine, and that I was free to tell the story in my own words.

Apparently, there had always been a problem between Jefferson and his wife concerning other women. His associations were many and varied. Perhaps the most lasting was with a beautiful young black woman, about the same age as his wife. She was the illegitimate natural child of W. Skelton, a local gentleman, and served as a personal maid to Mrs. Jefferson. Eventually, Jefferson had a number of children by this woman. He even took her to Paris. He would send for her. This went on for a number of years and eventually contributed to the disillusionment of this woman. She died in a little room upstairs, and they took the coffin up there some way, but when they put it together and got her into the coffin, it wouldn't come downstairs. They had to take all the windows out and lower her on a rope. And what was she doing up there in the first place? All this did not contribute to Mrs. Jefferson's happiness. There are said to be some descendants of that liaison still alive today, but you won't find any of this in American textbooks.

Gossip and legend intermingle in small towns and in the countryside. This is especially true when important historical figures are involved. So it has been said that Jefferson did not die a natural death. Allegedly, he committed suicide by cutting his own throat. Toward the end of Jefferson's life, there was a bitter feud between himself and the Lewis family. Accusations and counteraccusations are said to have gone back and forth. One such accusation is that Jefferson had Merriweather Lewis murdered and, prior to that, had accused Mr. Lewis of a number of strange things that were not true. But none of these legends and rumors can be proved in terms of judicial procedure; when it comes to patriotic heroes of the American Revolution, the line between truth and fiction is always rather indistinct.

THE MILLBRAE POLTERGEIST CASE

*O*ne wouldn't think a spanking new, modern home perched on a hill at Millbrae, a sunny little town outside San Francisco, could harbor a poltergeist case, one of those sinister disturbances often involving a teenager or otherwise emotionally unabsorbed person in the household of the living. Poltergeist only means "noisy ghost," and a ghost it was—the youngster was not playing any pranks; the youngster was being used to play them with, by a disturbed person no longer in possession of a physical body.

I heard of the Millbrae case from a young woman who used to live in that house before she decided she was old enough to have a place of her own and consequently moved out to a nearby town called Burlingame. At 20, Jean Grasso had a high school education and a big curiosity about things she could not explain. Such as ESP.

In 1964, she had an experience that particularly upset her because it did not fit in with the usual experiences of life she had been taught in school.

She was in bed at the time, just before falling asleep, or, as she puts it so poetically, "just before the void of sleep engulfs you." Ms. Grasso was not at a loss for words, and was as bright a young woman as you want to meet. Her world was very real to her and had little or no room for fantasies.

Still, there it was. Something prevented her from giving in to sleep. Before she knew what she was doing, she saw her own bare feet moving across the floor of her bedroom; she grabbed the telephone receiver and blurted into it "Jeannie, what's wrong? Did you get hurt?" The telephone had not rung. Yet her best friend, who was almost like a sister to her, was on the line. She had been in an automobile accident in which she had been run off the road and collided with a steel pole, but except for being shook up, she was all right.

What made Jean Grasso jump out of a warm bed to answer a phone that had not yet rung, to speak by name to someone who had not yet said "hello," and to inquire about an accident that no one had told her about as yet?

Ms. Grasso was a dark-haired woman of Italian and Greek background and worked as the local representative of a milk company. She was neither brooding nor particularly emotional, it seemed to me, and far from hysterical. The uncanny things that happened in her life intrigued her more in an intellectual way than in an emotional, fearful way.

When she was sixteen, she and five other girls were playing the popular parlor game of the ouija board in one of the bedrooms. Jean Grasso and Michele di Giovanni, another of the girls, were working the board when it started to move as if pushed by some force stronger than themselves.

Still very skeptical about ouija boards, Jean demanded some sign or proof of a spiritual presence. She got a quick reply: four loud knocks on the wall. There was nobody in back of the walls who could have caused them. Suddenly, the room got very cold, and they panicked and called the "séance" off then and there.

Ever since, she had heard uncanny noises in her parents' house. These had ranged from footsteps to crashing sounds as if someone or something were thrown against a wall or onto the floor. There never was a rational explanation for these sounds.

After Jean moved out to her own place in Burlingame, she returned home for occasional weekends to be with her mother. Her mother sleeps in the living-dining room area upstairs, to save her the trouble of walking up and down the stairs to the bedroom level, since she had a heart condition.

On the occasions when Jean spent a weekend at home, she would sleep in her mother's former bedroom, situated directly underneath the one fixed for her on the upper level.

One night, as Jean lay awake in bed, she heard footsteps overhead. They walked across the ceiling, "as if they had no place to go."

Thinking that her mother had breathing difficulties, she raced upstairs, but found her mother fast asleep in bed. Moreover, when questioned about the footsteps the next morning, she assured her daughter she had heard nothing.

"Were they a man's footsteps or a woman's?" I asked Jean Grasso when we discussed this after the investigation was over.

"A man's," she replied without hesitation.

Once in a while when she was in the dining area upstairs, she would see something out of the corner of an eye—a flash—something or somebody moving about—and as soon as she concentrated on it, it was not there. She chalked all that up to her imagination, of course.

"When I'm coming down the steps, in the hall, I get a chill up my spine," the young woman said, "as if I didn't want to continue on. My mother gets the same feelings there, too, I recently discovered."

That was the spot where my psychic photograph was taken, I later realized. Did these two psychic people, mother and daughter, act like living cameras?

"Do you ever have a feeling of a presence with you when you are all alone?"

"Yes, in my mother's bedroom, I feel someone is watching me and I turn but there's no one there."

I questioned her about the garden and the area around the basement. Jean confessed she did not go there often since the garden gave her an uneasy feeling. She avoided it whenever she could for no reason she could logically explain.

One night when she spent the weekend at her parents' house and was just falling asleep a little after midnight, she was awakened by the sound of distant voices. The murmur of the voices was clear enough but when she sat up to listen further, they went away. She went back to sleep, blaming her imagination for the incident. But a week later, to the day, her incipient sleep was again interrupted by the sound of a human voice. This time it was a little girl's or a woman's voice crying out, "Help...help me!"

She jumped up so fast she could hear her heart beat in her ears. Surely, her mother had called her. Then she remembered that her mother had gone to Santa Cruz. There was nobody in the house who could have called for help. She looked outside. It was way after midnight and the surrounding houses were all dark. But the voice she had just heard had not come from the outside. It was there, right in the haunted room with her!

I decided to interview Jean's mother, Mrs. Adriana Grasso, a calm pleasant woman whose skepticism in psychic matters had always been pretty strong.

"We've had this house since 1957," she explained, "but it was already five years old when we bought it. The previous owners were named Stovell and they were about to lose it when we bought it. I know nothing about them beyond that."

The very first night she went to bed in the house, something tried to prevent her from doing so. Something kept pushing her back up. On the first landing of the stairs leading down to the bedroom level, something kept her from continuing on down. She decided to fight it out. Every time after that first experience she had the same impression—that she really shouldn't be coming downstairs!

"I hear footsteps upstairs when I'm downstairs and I hear footsteps downstairs when I'm upstairs, and there never is anyone there causing them," she complained.

On several occasions, she awoke screaming, which brought her daughter running in anxiously. To calm her, she assured her she had had a nightmare. But it was not true. On several different occasions, she felt something grabbing her and trying to crush her bones. Something held her arms pinned down. Finally, she had to sleep with the lights on, and it seemed to help.

A big crash also made the family wonder what was wrong with their house. Mrs. Grasso heard it *upstairs* and her son Allen, upstairs at the same time, thought it was *downstairs*— only to discover that it was neither here nor there!

"Many times the doorbell would ring and there was no one outside," Mrs. Grasso added, "but I always assumed it was the children of the neighborhood, playing tricks on us."

Loud noises as if a heavy object had fallen brought her into the garage to investigate, but nothing had fallen, nothing was out of place. The garage was locked and so was the front door. Nobody had gotten in. And yet the noises continued; only three days before our arrival, Mrs. Grasso awoke around one in the morning to the sound of "someone opening a can in the bathroom," a metal container. In addition, there was thumping. She thought, why is my son working on his movies at this hour of the night? She assumed the can-opening noises referred to motion picture film cans, of which her son has many. But he had done nothing of the sort.

Soon even Allen and Mr. Grasso heard the loud crashes, although they were unwilling to concede that it represented anything uncanny. But the family that hears ghosts together, also finds solutions together—and the Grassos were not particularly panicky about the whole thing. Just curious.

It was at this point that I decided to investigate the case

and I so advised Jean Grasso, who greeted us at the door of her parents' house on a very warm day in October 1966. In addition to Sybil and my wife Catherine, two friends, Lori Cierf and Bill Wynn, were with us. We had Lori's car and Bill was doing the driving.

We entered the house and immediately I asked Sybil for her psychic impressions. She had not had a chance to orient herself nor did I allow her to meet the Grassos officially. Whatever she might "get" now would therefore not be colored by any rational impressions of the people she met or the house she was in.

"There is something peculiar about the lower portion of the house," Sybil began, referring to the bedroom floor. The house was built in a most peculiar manner. Because the lot was sloping toward a ravine, the top floor reached to street level on the front side of the house only. It was here that the house had its living room and entrance hall. On the floor below were the bedrooms, and finally, a garage and adjoining work room. Underneath was a basement, which, however, led to ground level in the rear, where it touched the bottom of the ravine.

At this point, however, Sybil and I did not even know if there was a lower portion to the house, but Jean Grasso assured us there was. We immediately descended the stairs into the section Sybil had felt invaded by psychic influences.

We stopped at the northeast corner of the bedroom floor where a rear entrance to the house was also situated, leading to a closed-in porch whence one could descend to the ground level outside by wooden stairs.

"What do you feel here, Sybil?" I asked, for I noticed she was getting on to something.

"Whatever I feel is below this spot," she commented. "It must have come from the old foundations, from the land."

Never let it be said that a ghost hunter shies away from dusty basements. Down we went, carrying the tape recorder and cameras. In the basement we could not stand entirely upright—at least I couldn't.

"That goes underneath the corridor, doesn't it?" Sybil said as if she knew.

"That's right," Jean Grasso confirmed.

"Somebody was chased here," Sybil commented now, "two men…an accident that should never have happened…someone died here…a case of mistaken identity."

"Can you get more?" I urged her.

"There is a lingering feeling of a man," Sybil intoned. "He is the victim. He was not the person concerned. He was running from the water's edge to a higher part of land. He was a fugitive."

Anyone coming from the San Francisco waterfront would be coming up here to higher ground.

"Whom was he running from?"

"The Law…I feel uniforms. There is an element of supposed justice in it, but…"

"How long ago was he killed?"

"1884."

"His name?"

"Wasserman…that's how I get it. I feel the influence of his last moments here, but not his body. He wants us to know he was Wasserman but not the Wasserman wanted by the man."

"What does he look like to you?"

"Ruddy face, peculiarly deep eyes…he's here but not particularly cooperative."

"Does he know he is dead?" I asked.

"I don't think he knows that. But he notices me."

I asked Sybil to convey the message that we knew he was innocent.

"Two names I have to get," Sybil insisted and started to spell, "Pottrene…P-o-t-t-r-e-n-e…Wasserman tells me these names…P-o-v-e-y…Povey…he says to find them…these people are the men who killed him."

"How was he killed?"

"They had to kill him. They thought that he was someone else."

"What was the other one wanted for?"

"He doesn't know. He was unfortunate to have been here."

"What is his first name?"

"Jan. J-a-n."

Upon my prodding, Sybil elicited also the information that this Jan Wasserman was a native of San Francisco, that his father's name was Johan or John, and he lived at 324 Emil Street.

I proceeded then to exorcise the ghost in my usual manner, speaking gently of the "other side" and what awaited him there.

Sybil conveyed my wishes to the restless one and reported that he understood his situation now.

"He's no trouble," Sybil murmured. She's very sympathetic to ghosts.

With that we left the basement and went back up the stairs into the haunted bedroom, where I took some photographs; then I moved into the living room area upstairs and took some more—all in all about a dozen black and white photographs, including some of the garage and stairs.

Imagine my pleased reaction when I discovered a week later, when the film came back from the laboratory, that two of the photographs had psychic material on them. One, taken of the stairs leading from the bedroom floor to the top floor, shows a whitish substance like a dense fog filling the front right half of my picture. The other remarkable photograph taken of Mrs. Grasso leaning against the wall in the adjoining room shows a similar substance with mirror effect, covering the front third of the area of the picture.

There was a reflection of a head and shoulders of a figure which, at first glance, I took to be Mrs. Grasso's. On close inspection, however, it was quite dissimilar and shows rather a heavy head of hair whereas Mrs. Grasso's hairdo was close to the head. Also, Mrs. Grasso wears a dark housecoat over a light dress but the image shows a woman or girl wearing a dark dress or sweater over a white blouse.

I asked Jean Grasso to report to me any changes in the house after our visit.

On November 21, 1966, I heard from her again. The footsteps were gone all right, but there was still something strange going on in the house. Could there have been two ghosts?

Loud crashing noises, the slamming of doors, noises similar to the thumping of ash cans when no sensible reason exists for the noises had been observed not only by Jean Grasso and her mother after we were there, but also by her brother and his fiancée and even the non-believing father. No part of the house seemed to be immune from the disturbance.

To test things, Jean Grasso slept at her mother's house soon after we left. At 11 P.M., the thumping started. About the same time Mrs. Grasso was awakened by three knocks under her pillow. These were followed almost immediately by the sound of thumping downstairs and movements of a heavy metallic can.

Before I could answer Jean, I had another report from her. Things were far from quiet at the house in Millbrae. Her brother's fiancée, Ellen, was washing clothes in the washing machine. She had closed and secured the door so that the noise would not disturb her intended, who was asleep in the bedroom situated next to the laundry room.

Suddenly she distinctly heard someone trying to get into the room by force, and then she felt a "presence" with her which caused her to run upstairs in panic.

About the same time, Jean and her mother had heard a strange noise from the bathroom below the floor they were then on. Jean went downstairs and found a brush on the tile floor of the bathroom. Nobody had been downstairs at the time. The brush had fallen by itself...into the middle of the floor.

When a picture in brother Allen's room lost its customary place on the wall, the thumb tack holding it up disappeared, and the picture itself somehow got to the other side of his bookcase. The frame was pretty heavy, and had the picture just fallen off it would have landed on the floor behind the bookcase; instead it was neatly leaning against the wall on top of it. This unnerved the young man somewhat, as he had not really accepted the possibility of the uncanny up to this point, even though he had witnessed some pretty unusual things himself.

Meanwhile, Jean Grasso managed to plow through the microfilm files at the San Mateo County library in Belmont. There was nothing of interest in the newspapers for 1884, but the files were far from complete.

However, in another newspaper of the area, the *Redwood City Gazette,* there was an entry that Jean Grasso thought worth passing on for my opinion. A Captain Watterman was mentioned in a brief piece, and the fact the townspeople are glad that his bill had died and they could be well rid of it.

The possibility that Sybil heard Wasserman when the name was actually Watterman was not to be dismissed—at least not until a Jan Wasserman could be identified from the records somewhere.

Since the year 1884 had been mentioned by the ghost, I looked up that year in H.H. Bancroft's *History of California,* an imposing record of that state's history published in 1890 in San Francisco.

In Volume VII, on pages 434 and 435, I learned that there had been great irregularities during the election of 1884 and political conditions bordered on anarchy. The man who had been first Lieutenant Governor and later Governor of the state was named R.W. Waterman!

This, of course, may only be conjecture and not correct. Perhaps she really did mean Wasserman with two "S's." But my search in the San Francisco Directory (*Langley's*) for 1882 and 1884 did not yield any Jan Wasserman. The 1881 *Langley* did, however, list an Ernst Wassermann, a partner in Wassermann brothers. He was located at 24th Street and Potrero Avenue.

Sybil reported that Wasserman had been killed by a certain Pottrene and a certain Povey. Pottrene as a name does not appear anywhere. Could she have meant Potrero? The name Povey, equally unusual, does, however, appear in the 1902 Langley on page 1416.

A Francis J. Povey was a foreman at Kast & Company and lived at 1 Beideman Street. It seems rather amazing that Sybil Leek would come up with such an unusual name as Povey, even if this was not the right Povey in our case. Wasserman claimed to have lived on Emil Street. There was no such street in San Francisco. There was, however, an Emma Street, listed by *Langley* in 1884 (page 118).

The city directories available to me were in shambles and plowing through them was a costly and difficult task. There were other works that might yield clues to the identity of our man. It was perhaps unfortunate that my setup did not allow for capable research assistants to help with so monumental a task, and that the occasional exact corroboration of ghostly statements was due more to good luck than to complete coverage of all cases brought to me.

Fortunately, the liberated ghosts do not really care. They know the truth already.

But I was destined to hear further from the Grasso residence.

On January 24th, 1967, all was well. Except for one thing, and that really happened back on Christmas Eve.

Jean's sister-in-law was sleeping on the couch upstairs in

the living room. It was around two in the morning, and she could not drop off to sleep, because she had taken too much coffee. While she was lying there, wide awake, she suddenly noticed the tall, muscular figure of a man, somewhat shadowy, coming over from the top of the stairs to the Christmas tree as if to inspect the gifts placed near it. At first she thought it was Jean's brother, but as she focused on the figure, she began to realize it was nobody of flesh-and-blood. She noticed his face now, and that it was bearded. When it dawned on her what she was seeing, and she began to react, the stranger just vanished from the spot where he had been standing a moment before. Had he come to say goodbye and had the Christmas tree evoked a long-ago Christmas holiday of his own?

Before the sister-in-law, Ellen, could tell Jean Grasso about her uncanny experience, Jean herself asked if she had heard the footsteps that kept her awake overhead that night. They compared the time, and it appeared that the footsteps and the apparition occurred in about the same time period.

For a few days all was quiet, as if the ghost were thinking it over. But then the pacing resumed, more furiously now, perhaps because something within him had been aroused and he was beginning to understand his position.

At this point everybody in the family heard the attention-getting noises. Mrs. Grasso decided to address the intruder and to tell him that I would correct the record of his death—that I would tell the world that he was not, after all, a bad fellow, but a case of mistaken identity.

It must have pleased the unseen visitor, for things began to quiet down again, and the house settled down to an ordinary suburban existence on the outskirts of bustling San Francisco.

But until this story made it into print, the Grassos didn't breathe with complete ease. There was always that chance that the ghost would decide that I was not telling the world fast enough. But that would have been unreasonable. After all, he had to wait an awfully long time before we took notice of him. And I jumped several ghosts to get him into print as an emergency case. So be it: Mr. Wasserman of Millbrae was not the Mr. Wasserman they were looking for, whoever they were. They just had themselves a wild ghost chase for nothing.

WHO KILLED
CAROL?

*O*ne would think that in a well arranged society such as ours the chances of murder occurring should be reasonably slim. Unfortunately, every day brings new crimes of violence, many of which are never solved. A police force hampered by inadequate funds, manpower, and frequently lacking in imagination, has become immune to the emotional aspects of so many unsolved murders. Some years ago I was able to supply the New York Police with material obtained through psychic sources pertaining to the unsolved murder of financier Serge Rubinstein. Despite the fact that the authorities acknowledged the cooperation of myself and medium Ethel Johnson Meyers, and despite their recognizing some of the names and situations as valid in the case, no culprit was ever brought into court or to justice in that bizarre case. Perhaps the public did not care, either, for Rubinstein was a brilliant sharpshooter whose career was spotty and often barely within the limits of legality. But law enforcement agencies all over the world accept the cooperation of investigators like myself, if not openly, then at least tacitly, for they often find themselves in the unpleasant position of having no place to turn for further clues.

The case which follows involves a murder which shook the world at the time it happened, because of the youth and prominence of its victim. As I wrote these lines, the culprit was still free. I have therefore changed the names somewhat, not to protect the innocent, but to avoid tipping off the guilty. Even though I changed a few names, I have reported the case exactly as it happened.

It was a chilly day in November, 1963 when the police discovered the nude body of a young woman whom I shall call Carol, in her apartment on one of the quieter streets of Hollywood. Only 22 years old, she was the daughter of a prominent businessman in the Midwest, and had come to California to seek fame and fortune, as they say.

Working as an actress when jobs were available, and as an occasional photographers' model, she lived alone in one of those two-story bungalows that make up the majority of Hollywood apartment houses. The rent was within her means, and her family back home occasionally sent her some money. She was the apple of her father and mother's eyes and their only daughter. The search for a glamorous career had been Carol's idea; the family was against it. But Carol was strong-willed and went to Hollywood over her parents' objections. They visited her frequently, and eventually the family assumed she would be all right. Carol's roles were getting larger and Carol became known as a pretty, young ingénue. Her friends in those days were many, but she introduced few of them to her parents. The world she had known at home and her new world in Hollywood were miles apart. As her career left her enough free time, she circulated widely among the young set of actors, photographers, cameramen and others who are either just within or on the fringe of the television and motion picture business in California.

She and her mother had always been very close, so Carol did confide in her when affairs of the heart came up. At one of the parties she met a young actor named Artie, with whom she was being seen more and more around town. He was then only an unknown bent on making it big; later he became a mildly successful young actor with credits known around the casting agencies.

But there were complications. Artie had an entanglement with another woman at the time he met Carol. Although he told her he would break off his relationship with the woman, he never did so entirely during the time he and Carol went together. This worried Carol and she often wrote to her mother about it. She had decided that Artie was the boy she wanted to marry, and on one occasion she introduced him to her parents.

As time went on, Carol's relationship with Artie was an "off again, on again" courtship punctuated by jealousy and occasional arguments. But neither broke off entirely with the other. Ultimately, Artie assured Carol he loved her and their relationship sailed into smoother waters. But nothing was said about marriage.

There the matter stood when the young woman's body was found dead, killed by a heavy fall or blow. Her murder electrified the movie colony, and Carol's many friends feared they would be called in by the police to testify. They were right. Dozens upon dozens of people were questioned, released, questioned, and released again. Everybody had the proper answers and alibis.

The only thing the police could establish with certainty was that Carol had had several visitors that fateful evening. Among her callers was Artie, a natural suspect, but he had left early in the evening. The doctors had fixed the time of death at around 2 A.M. Artie's alibi for that period was firm. The police had to look elsewhere for their culprit. Was it an unexpected visitor? An intruder? Or did one of her several earlier callers return later?

The investigation continued for several months, but gradually tapered off, despite the anguished demands of the parents not to let up and despite promises of a reward for any information leading to the arrest of the murderer. To be sure, the police never gave up. But they had run out of leads. Having followed up every one, and having checked out everyone Carol had known in Hollywood, they had arrived at a blank wall.

At this point the parents looked to psychic sources for help. In 1964, they brought a celebrated Dutch psychic to the scene of the crime with the full blessing of the police. The results, however, were disappointing. Carol's mother then made the rounds of assorted mediums, always hopeful that one of them might turn up a useful clue. While some of them 'saw' the tragedy clairvoyantly, nothing strong enough to be of value emerged.

She and I corresponded, and I made certain suggestions that Carol's mother try to adjust her own thinking to the inevitable reality of the situation.

Finally, I invited the parents to come to New York. We would try to have a go at the mystery with the late Betty Ritter, a medium whose accuracy I had learned to appreciate over the years. Only after Carol's parents had actually arrived in New York, did I call Betty to set the time for our experiment, which took place on January 13, 1964 at my house.

I doubted that Betty would have recognized the names of either parents or of the girl, for she did not read newspapers regularly. But to dispel all doubts, I arranged for them to arrive fifteen minutes before Betty, and then introduced them by another name.

Betty had no way of "guessing" that these people were from out of town, or that a murder was involved, or even that they had a daughter. To her, they looked like any nice, respectable middle-aged couple, friends of mine, interested in a "psychic reading."

We took our places around the dining room table and as was always the rule with my investigations, no discussion or questions of any kind were allowed.

Within a minute after we had sat down, Betty became very agitated. She remarked that she saw the spirit of a crying woman, who was not supposed "to go so soon," as she put it, and that something had happened out West that wasn't supposed to have happened. With that, she took a ring proffered her by the mother, a ring that had once belonged to the murdered girl.

"This spirit has her arms around you, sir," Betty said now, pointing to the father, "and she is crying and very upset. I see a musical clef, or something to do with entertainment." The room fell silent now with expectation.

"You are seeking a clue," Betty continued, "about the death of a woman who hasn't been gone long." The father's face remained immobile; he wasn't going to help. His wife however was quite emotional now; she realized that Betty had made some kind of contact. Clutching a pin that had once belonged to Carol, Betty, her eyes half closed, said, "It happened so fast...Stanley...I don't know what they wanted from me...He grabbed me by the neck...two men...bothering me...down the street. It was a man who whistled a lot...I was afraid to tell anybody...extort...someone was trying to take something from me...I was alone in the house, key into door. And there they were."

There were also names and initials—but I can't disclose them. All this made little, if any, sense to me at the time, but evidently the parents recognized it as valid.

The description of the attack had been graphic enough and needed no explanation, but the initials needed some placing: those named by Betty were two men on the list of potential suspects; they lived together in a house on *Stanley* Hill!

"You've come a long way, she says, and I've travelled with you on this trip," Betty continued. How could she know that the parents were not local people?

She then described the young woman as a beautiful

brunette, with a good figure, and wearing a velvet dress. At this point, the mother suppressed a little outcry.

"There are parties down the street," Betty said, "and the two men came from there. Some man made a comment. Two fish together."

Later I discovered that Carol had recently worn a velvet dress to a costume party, a dress she was particularly fond of. Carol's birth sign was Pisces.

The police had made a list of potential culprits, and since Carol was a popular girl, the list was not short. Without my questioning her, Betty Ritter now mentioned some of the men Carol might have known, not necessarily her murderers.

"Heart and S...cross him out...ring with W or M...cross it off, too...S. and W. grabbed her...but don't forget A., he was one of them, too! Down the street, third house, woman knows, photographer W., lady at house L. She was a hanger-on. J. drops in once in a while. Photographer is bearded."

Later she explained these initials. By "cross him off," Betty had meant the person was bad medicine, not necessarily guilty or innocent. I discovered there was a man initialed S., another named W.M., and Carol's landlady "living down the street" was indeed initialed L.; her husband was a bearded photographer! J. was the initial of the superintendent. How could Betty Ritter have "guessed" all these details and connected them with the murdered girl?

"Something had happened she was afraid to talk about, but she didn't think it would lead to this," Betty explained. "There was no breaking in, he had a key, and she trusted this person. She knew him, went to the kitchen while he was there. Arthur...was to have gotten married."

Carol and Artie had indeed planned to marry, but sometime before her untimely death, the engagement was broken by Artie, although Carol did not accept this as final and continued to see him.

"Keep your chin up, *Mommie*," the spirit communicator made Betty say now, "I don't want you to grieve. I'm happy here, though I'm missing music and nice things…" Nobody present had indicated at any time that the lady with me was the mother. Her daughter had always referred to her as Mommie, not Mother. "She's showing me some kind of toy animal," Betty added.

Later on the mother acknowledged this. "The toy animal still exists—it used to be her favorite knickknack."

I thanked Betty when I noticed she was getting tired, and sent her home.

A copy of the transcript was forwarded to the police, but no action could be taken. Something much more specific was needed. Still, the local police were impressed with the results and the methods I had used, and I was asked to continue, if I could, and advise them of any further findings.

In February of 1964 the parents went to California to go over the files in search of new clues. It was not easy for them to do this, for their agony was still fresh.

"Everyone and no one seems guilty," Carol's mother wrote to me afterwards. The puzzle remained. Unfortunately, there had been a time lapse of three days between the murder and the discovery of the body. The parents then offered a monetary reward to anyone coming forward with vital information about the murder. The reward was never collected.

With some difficulty, the parents contacted another famous Dutch seer, and brought him to the house. "It was not a stranger," the psychic said. Then he examined a photograph of Carol and Artie together. Feeling the boy's face with his fingertips, he suggested, "This boy is capable of murder." But he would not commit himself beyond that.

My contact with Carol's parents resumed the week before Christmas, when they paid a hurried visit to New York. On that occasion I asked for Carol's ring, so that my good friend and medium Sybil Leek could have a go at it. I introduced them to Sybil, but Mrs. Leek preferred to work on the ring at a quieter moment. Needless to say, I did not tell Sybil anything about a murder. I only told her the couple had a daughter who was dead, and that the ring had once belonged to her.

A week after Christmas Sybil had sufficiently calmed down from the hectic holiday activities that I could finally hand her the ring for a reading.

"I have the impression of a young man wearing a pinkish shirt," she began immediately, and described this person as having longish hair, with a peculiarity of the position of the eyes in relation to the rest of his face, that is, the distance between the eyes was wider than it should be. She saw him with a camera slung over the shoulder and felt he had something to do with photography. Then she got the impression of a name and started to spell it. I asked Sybil to concentrate on this man.

"This man flies a lot, brings drugged cigarettes in the bottom of his camera," Sybil said. "The girl has her picture taken by him. He is very angry, because she wants to go and he doesn't want her to go."

Then she described in horrifying, chilling detail how he placed his arm around the girl's neck and killed her, leaving her body on the floor near a fireplace. It was not premeditated murder, she explained, but the outcome of an argument between them.

I asked if the man had been alone.

"Yes," she said, her eyes closed and thoughts concentrated on the ring in her fist, "there were people there, but they went; he stayed." I asked for a description of the room in which the tragedy had occurred.

"There's a small house and you turn left when you go in. I only see one room but there are doors. A few steps up, then a little step and into the room. A music rack on the side of the fireplace."

What about the young man, what did he do after the murder? "He walked around a little road and got into a car, then went south. His own place is not far from the girl's."

Sybil also mentioned the fact that the young woman was not too cooperative, and did not wish to have the man punished for personal, sentimental reasons. This of course made things twice as difficult for me.

Then on January 9, 1968, Carol's mother came to New York again. I had offered earlier to take her to a good psychometrist if she would bring along a couple of objects that had belonged to her daughter.

I telephoned Ethel Johnson Meyers and asked if she could see me and "a friend." On January 11, we went to her apartment on the West Side. I introduced the mother by a fictitious name, then handed Ethel Carol's ring. Immediately, Mrs. Meyers "picked up" the person of the owner. "Large eyes, a good-looking individual, interested in *experiences* and seeking them, but something extraordinarily tragic about this...." And suddenly the medium grimaced with pain, complaining about being "crushed in," and exhibiting all the details of a death struggle. "I've wanted an experience, but this isn't what I wanted," Ethel said now, quoting the girl. "Five minutes before or later, it could have been avoided."

I asked for clarification of this cryptic remark. Ethel began to shiver as if in terror. Heavy breathing and inarticulate cries followed. Only gradually did the words make sense. "No, no, no...no!" She was evidently resisting an unseen but recognized attacker. "Don't—No!"

"Mommie...help..." Carol was now in control of the medium.

"Tell us who was with you...tell us who did it," I urged.

Evidently the answer involved emotional conflicts, for the medium almost choked, trying to reply. "Momma... Momma..." I asked the mother to speak up. As a result the young woman (through Ethel) broke into a series of near-hysterical laughs. Again it took some time to calm her down. No actress could have produced the utter devastation the medium now exhibited. "Where am I?" she finally said. The mother then handed Ethel a bracelet which had once been worn by her daughter. The reaction was instantaneous. "L....L...." she said, repeating it several times, then adding, "Allan...Al...don't want to...no..." "Allan" had been to the house that night but she had not let him in: he had pushed his way in. She had met him before, with Jim. The superintendent of the apartment house, Jim, liked to give parties. Was she referring to him? "What time is it, what time is it?" she kept asking, still in partial shock. She had bit the attacker in the lip. She didn't know what he did for a living. She had met him before and he lived in the same complex of buildings. But this was the first time he had ever entered her apartment. "Still there," she said, insisting he had not moved from the house after her death. She was expecting "someone" that night—but it all happened too fast. The attacker had been swarthy-complexioned, with black hair; there was something wrong with his lip; he was about forty years old.

"I hurt so...I can't think..." she exclaimed, "five minutes more...I would have had the phone off the hook..." Apparently, she had been talking to someone on the phone, and if the intruder had come five minutes before, perhaps this would have stopped him. I had rarely seen Ethel so overcome with confusion and emotional turmoil. It was very difficult to make head or tail from the testimony.

"Cover me up," she now mumbled. Ethel could not know that the woman's body was found nude. "Don't let go of me, Momma," she pleaded. "I'm sorry, forgive me."

After a few moments, the spirit left and Ethel "returned" to her old self, a little more shaken than usual. I gave a complete report to the Homicide Squad, stressing the points made by my psychic friends and their unseen "helpers."

Shortly after I had sent a detailed transcript of my various psychic investigations to the police department, I received an annotated appraisal of the same. Paragraph for paragraph, name for name, was carefully weighed by the investigating officers and evaluated as to the possible accuracy. There was no attempt to play down my contribution to a possible solution of the case nor indeed the entire field of extrasensory perception research. Nevertheless, the overall impression was one of disappointment on the part of the police that nothing more tangible had resulted from my work thus far. It should be made clear here that those named by my various psychics were not necessarily the murderer or murderers or guilty of anything illegal. It was in the nature of psychometry and other forms of mediumship to pick up names and situations from the immediate surroundings of a person, regardless of the importance of such names. Thus it may very well be that some of the individuals named by psychics may have been on the side of the angels, even good friends trying to help the murdered girl. Any inference that those names in these pages are necessarily guilty of anything would be wrong. In fact, there were so many potential suspects in this case that in the end the police were unable to pinpoint anyone sufficiently to even make a temporary arrest. Two of the more prominent individuals questioned had to be left alone eventually, since they had been completely cooperative with the authorities, even submitting to lie detector tests, which remained negative.

The case never left the dock of the police department nor indeed my own files. On November 30, 1969 I let medium Shawn Robbins hold an envelope pertaining to the case. Immediately Shawn tuned in on the situation. She described a young woman, aged twenty-three—the exact age Carol was at the time of her death. "The person you are looking for has short black hair. He is tall, slim and his hair is cut country style." On October 9, 1971 I consulted Gar Osten, a rising young astrologer whom I had met through Shawn Robbins and who worked closely with her in many instances. He and Shawn, together, decided to cast the horoscope of the late Carol and see whether in so doing they might come up with some clues as to the murderer. Osten remarked that "the planet Mercury indicates the last relationship, which was also the murderer. This was an on again, off again affair. The actor-musician is indicated." Gar and Shawn's interpretation of his chart brought up a number of interesting points. Neither knew much about Carol, except that she had been an actress and had been murdered.

"She had a subtle, versatile and changeful nature, inconstant and imitative. She was much affected by surroundings and those with whom she came in contact. A basic lack of security, lack of confidence and a feeling of unworthiness troubled her. She did not face issues squarely and had to be helped herself, although she was receptive to the needs of others. There was a great need for self expression which could have taken the direction of a creative talent. She was weak when it came to knowing when to stop which included drinking, socializing, spending, and believing the promises of others. She was attracted to the underdog and had friends among those who were weak or afflicted with emotional and physical difficulties. There was danger of being deceived by others or she suffered disillusion and the danger of scandal. She found pleasure in secret affairs of the heart. She had an eccentric tendency in regard to the use of money: She might have been generous to the wrong persons and turn away from the deserving.

"I believe this girl had four love attachments in her lifetime. The first did not turn out well and was secret in nature. Perhaps a change in schools or a move of the home of some kind ended it. The second attachment began in the last half of 1961 into early 1962. He was in a responsible position and could have been an employer or father figure. He definitely did not come from the environment where she was born. The desire was for marriage but this relationship did not work out and shortly after she entered another one. The third relationship began early in 1962. This man is shown to have been connected with the arts, music or acting. He was systematic, not reliable, and able to sense an advantage. The deception was self-inflicted on her part and from the first it was not destined to work out. There was an aspect about this man that she found difficult to deal with which frustrated her. *The fourth attachment I believe to be the murderer.* This lover is shown to be young, with intellectual leanings, possibly a student and restless and watery in nature. Theirs was an attraction through weakness rather than strength. They both had problems and they found comfort together. He seems to have had artistic leanings, musical interests, or perhaps films. Their meeting might have occurred through the career. I believe they met for the first time in August 1962. It was self-deception and the relationship seems to have been broken off about December 14, 1962, but resumed again in mid-May, 1963.

"The murder itself was set into motion by a solar eclipse on July 20, 1963." However, Shawn felt that the murderer was not a young man with whom Carol had had a long relationship. "I am sure suspicion is cast on him, I am sure the mother knows," she added, "He has been to Carol's house maybe once and she went out with him maybe three times." "Do the police suspect him?" I asked. Shawn shook her head "No. He has been interviewed, but has a perfect alibi. Also he would not have had any reason to murder her. Except of course that I don't think he is well."

A Mrs. W., resident of Hollywood, who did not know either Carol nor anyone else connected with the case but who had had psychic dreams for a number of years, communicated one particularly strong dream impression to me. She had this dream shortly after the murder had taken place. In this dream she saw a man who allegedly had been attracted to Carol at a studio where he was very important. No one knew she was seeing him and he was a challenge to her. The night he came to kill her she was very happy since he told her that they could be together always from now on. As they were making love he was kissing her and then strangled her.

Years after the murder, the police, the parents, and Carol's friends knew that there were two men who could have committed the crime. But did they? Then too, did the murderer arrive, evil intent in his heart, or did he merely come to pay a social call and wound up in the midst of a heated argument with Carol? Did he seize her body and in the heat of the discussion, cause her death? From a psychic research point of view, it seems obvious that Carol was shielding someone she loved very much. That man was Artie. Oddly enough, she may have protected him without need to. Was it possible that Carol knew her neighbor had killed her but thought at the same time that the crime would somehow be pinned on Artie, the man she very much wanted to marry? In protecting Artie, she was therefore not protecting a suspect, but merely a lover to whom she felt greater loyalty than he had shown towards her.

BANSHEES AND
OMINOUS WARNINGS

I've been all over Ireland three times and have even written a book called *The Lively Ghosts of Ireland,* but I've never met anyone in the Emerald Isle who had a banshee. Now there are things a Psychic Investigator considers legitimate and well-supported phenomena in the realm of the Uncanny, such as ghosts, haunted houses, and precognitive experiences.

Then, too, there are borderline cases involving phenomena of a more offbeat kind, such as the legendary stories about the Irish leprechauns and "little people," the fairies and brownies of the British Isles, and the dwarfs of Central Europe. To reject out of hand all such material as fantasy is of course no more scientific than to admit all spiritualist phenomena as genuine on the face of it without individual search and evaluation. What little we know of nature and our universe should have made us realize how much more there may be that is as yet unrevealed. A little humility can be most useful in modem science, but unfortunately the average physical scientist is filled with his own self-importance and has little patience with the bizarre.

The banshee is a Celtic spirit specializing in death warnings and they say it runs only in "old" Irish families. But I've heard of similar cases in other Celtic traditions and even outside of the British Isles. The banshee is usually described by those who actually have seen it as the figure of an ugly old woman, seated on the doorstep of the family about to be bereaved, and crying or screaming loudly. Banshees announce the forthcoming death of a member of the family without, however, telling the family who and when. That's part of the banshee game. Naturally the family is scared stiff when the banshee wails and everybody wonders who is next to go.

Died-in-the-wool Irish traditionalists will swear that banshees only run in the very good, ancient families and having one may be frightening, but it is also flattering: sort of a pedigree of death.

Now I have always been doubtful about the nature, though not the existence, of such strange creatures as elementals and banshees, considering them indeed part and parcel of ghostly manifestations, and thus human.

I've also learned that you can take the Irishman out of Ireland, but you can't take Ireland out of the Irishman. Even generations after, an Irish family transplanted into the New World may have the family banshee on their necks. Such was the case with the Shea family who lived a pretty prosaic life in northern Massachusetts. Joanne Shea's grandmother, and even her mother, came from Ireland, as the song goes, and with them came accounts of strange goings-on whenever death was near for a member of the family.

The grandmother's particular banshee was mild in comparison to that of others: a strange creaking noise on the stairs, which she always tried to tell herself was natural, knowing full well, however, what it meant.

One day the grandmother was visiting Mrs. Shea and her sister and, upon leaving, startled the two girls by telling them it was her last visit. She would never see them again!

The family joked about this. Then two weeks later their grandmother fell and fractured her hip, and was hospitalized with the injury.

A few days afterwards, Mrs. Shea's sister, who was a nun, was standing by a window in her chapel. Suddenly she heard a terrible scream, which she later described as sounding like the scream of a wildcat.

Terrified, she looked out the window, but could see nothing. Later, the two girls compared notes. At the exact moment when the nun had heard the scream, Grandmother had died.

A year went by. One evening, as Joanne lay in bed, she heard her brother's footsteps come up the stairs outside her room. Just then the clock chimed 11 P.M. To her surprise, Joanne clearly heard the footsteps of two people coming up the stairs, and wondered who the friend was her brother was bringing home at so late an hour. At the top of the stairs, the two pairs of footsteps separated, and one person went into the brother's room. The other footsteps came into Joanne's, and she suddenly felt petrified with fear.

Then all of a sudden, there, in front of her bed, stood her late grandmother.

Looking at the girl, the apparition turned her head a little, smiled—and then was gone like a puff of smoke.

When Joanne reported the matter to her mother the following morning, her mother brushed it aside as "probably a dream."

But then she stopped herself. What was the day's date? It was November 3—the anniversary of Grandmother's passing. Mother had forgotten to put Grandmother's name on the list of those for whom a prayer was to be said in church, as had been the custom in this Catholic family. The matter was immediately attended to, and when Joanne's brother came in that day, she questioned him about the other footsteps she had heard the night before.

He insisted that he had come in quite alone. He had not heard the ghostly steps either. Only Joanne had, and she never saw her late grandmother again after that.

Joanne's older sister, who was later to become a nun, evidently had also inherited the psychic talents so strong on the female side of the family tree.

One evening only the women were home, while the men—Joanne's father and her two brothers—were away at a ball game. Mother was downstairs, and the two girls were in bed in their room upstairs. Joanne was already beginning to doze off, when her sister suddenly jumped out of bed and ran downstairs to her mother's room.

"Did you hear the terrible scream?" the twenty-year-old woman asked her mother, who could only nod a silent yes. But Joanne had not heard it. It was a scream not unlike the cry of the wildcat, coming in from over the hill in back of the house. There was nothing outside in the yard to account for it.

For several days the women of the family were in a dither, waiting for fate to drop the other shoe. Everybody was told to be extremely careful and to avoid accidents. One could never know whom the banshee meant. On the eighth day after the unearthly scream had been heard, the waiting game was over. Joanne's uncle, her mother's brother, was hit by an automobile and died a few days later.

Just as the Germans have a peculiar name for the noisy ghost phenomena associated with disturbances of a physical nature that they call a Poltergeist, so they have a special term for the terrifying experience of a warning of impending death. These announcements of disaster or doom are called Gaenger in Central Europe, a word meaning, literally, "he who will go" (off stage), the stage being our physical world.

In a memorable but now very rare book called *Gaenger, Geister und Geslchter* (*Death Announcements, Ghosts and Visions*), Friedrich von Gaggern reported some of these occurrences that were peculiarly tied in with the Germanic mood and landscape.

I was thinking of the Gaggern work when I first heard about Jane Marquardt of Rhode Island. Not so much because of her Germanic name—after all it was her husband's—but because of the nature of the incidents that both enlivened and beclouded her life.

The most terrifying of these incidents took place when she was eighteen, at the time of World War II. Her boy friend was a bombardier overseas, while she lived with her family in Chicago. One night she awoke from deep sleep with the sudden realization that someone was pounding on her bedroom door. There was no rational explanation for the loud knocks. She got up and checked the time. It was just 3 A.M. With a vague feeling of uneasiness, she returned to bed. Somehow she connected the uncanny knocks with her boy friend. He was due to return home soon, and they would be married.

Was it fear or the natural worry about a boy overseas in the war, or was it something more?

For two days Jane lived in a state of suspended animation. Then a telegram arrived with the tragic news that her boy friend had been killed two days earlier. He and his buddies had safely completed their seventy-fourth mission and were returning home to their quarters in a bus. The bus went out of control and plunged over a cliff, killing the entire crew. Everyone on that bus was due for a furlough and return to the United States. The time of the accident was exactly 3 A.M., allowing for the difference in time zones.

The years went by and her shock wore off. She married another man, also in the military, and the family moved to New Jersey, where her husband was stationed. Jane was now twenty-five years old and the mother of a little girl. One evening they were coming back from a drive-in movie, and were within a few miles of their home, when she clearly saw a human face approaching the car on her side. As it drew near, she recognized her mother. Now she knew perfectly well that her mother was at that time in Chicago. Yet, there was her mother's face, smiling up at her and speaking to her in a clear and rather happy voice: "Jane, I'm going to die!"

With that, the vision faded quickly. Jane let out a scream. "No, dear God, no!"

Her husband, who had seen nothing, naturally assumed she was ill. Rather than alarm him, she kept her counsel. What was the point of telling him? she reasoned. Might it not make it happen in some unknown way? Also, she could tell by the way he cast sidelong glances at her that he wondered about his wife's sanity.

Jane and her mother had always been very close and had kept in frequent contact over the miles. The vision occurred on a Tuesday at midnight. On Saturday Jane received an ominous telegram advising her of her mother's sudden death. The news hit her strongly and she took it badly. But later she realized that this had been her mother's way of softening the coming blow, by forewarning her of impending death. Had her mother done this herself through subconscious channels? Had an agency out there created this vision for her benefit?

Jane was soon to learn more about her uncanny ability to tune in on distant dangers.

In 1952 she and her husband had to leave for Japan where he would hence be stationed. This was a heavy blow for her widowed father.

She was all he had left, for he, too, had taken his wife's passing badly. His tears of farewell seemed to stay in Jane's memory as she left for Japan.

She had not been in her new home more than three weeks when a strange thing happened. Her husband was downstairs, reading, while she was upstairs doing her nails. Their little girl was already asleep. Suddenly she heard clearly, so clearly it could have come from the next room, a voice calling her by name.

"Jane!" it said and at once she recognized her father's voice. She shook her head in bewilderment, wondering if she had imagined it due too her longing for her father. But again the voice called out to her. Now she dashed downstairs and questioned her husband about it. No, he had not called her. At this point she told him of her experience but he laughed it off.

A cable brought fearful news two days later. Her father had been taken ill and might not survive. But this time death did not exact the usual toll. After a long illness, Jane's father got well again. She checked the time of her experience with him and found that he had just had his first attack then. In desperation, he had actually called out to her, wishing she could be near hi>n in this difficult hour. Somehow, his voice had traveled across the Pacific in a fraction of a second and reached his favorite daughter's ears—and only hers!

Mrs. V. worked as a law secretary for a prominent attorney in the State of New Jersey. She never had had any interest in the occult, but her innate psychic sense broke through eventually whether she wanted it or not. At first, there were just trifling things. Like handing her cleaner a pair of gloves and instantly knowing he would lose them. He did. Or looking for the gravestone of a friend in a cemetery where she had never been and finding it "blindly." Then, the night her mother died, she and her sister saw the lights in the living room go on by themselves. Since these were lights that had to be turned on individually, this was indeed unusual.

Soon, Mrs. V. was to have the shock of her life. It started as an ordinary working day. Her boss was dictating to her at her desk, which was located in a long hallway leading to his private offices. During a pause in the dictation, she looked up idly and saw, to her left, through a glass separation, a woman standing in the hall. The woman looked at her, and then moved quickly behind the elevator wall and out of her line of vision.

The woman was about twelve feet away and Mrs. V. saw her clearly through the glass. Her boss was part owner of the building and often interviewed prospective tenants, so she assumed this was someone looking for office space and called his attention to the woman.

"Woman? What woman?" he demanded to know. "I don't see anyone."

"She has stepped behind the elevator wall," the secretary explained, somewhat sheepishly. The elevator was one of those older, noisy installations which one can hear approach quite clearly. Neither of them had heard the elevator coming up to the fourth floor, where they were, so they naturally felt the woman had still to be on the landing. But there was nobody there. Had she decided to walk down four flights—most unlikely in view of the elevator's presence—she could not have gotten far as yet. Also, in order to reach the stairwell, the woman would have had to brush past her employer.

Mrs. V. insisted there had been a visitor. The lawyer pressed the elevator button. The cab stopped at the fourth floor. It was empty. Evidently nobody had been riding it during the time of the incident, since the noise of the elevator's coming up could not have escaped them.

"You must have seen your own reflection in the glass partition," he reasoned. Some lawyers will reason peculiarly. Mrs. V. shook her head. She knew what she had seen was not her own image. To prove her point, she re-enacted the whole thing. From the spot she had seen the woman stand, no reflection could be gleaned from inside the office. The lawyer shrugged and went back to his work. Mrs. V. sat down quietly and tried to collect her thoughts. What had she seen? A woman of about sixty-five years of age, a little stocky in build, wearing a close-fitting hat and a brown, tweedy coat.

Moreover, something about the woman's appearance seemed to be vaguely familiar. Then all at once it hit her who the woman was!

It was none other than her late mother, Mrs. T., who had been dead for thirteen years. She had owned a coat similar to the one Mrs. V. had seen and always favored close-fitting hats. Why had her mother's ghost appeared to her at this moment? she wondered.

Was it because her father was in ill health? Was this an omen, a warning of his impending death?

Grimly preparing for the unwanted, Mrs. V. went through her work rather mechanically for the next few days.

The following week, she received a phone call from one of her sisters. Her mother's favorite sister, their aunt, had suffered a stroke. One week to the day of her mother's appearance, Mrs. V.'s aunt was dead.

THE WHALEY HOUSE GHOSTS

I first heard about the ghosts at San Diego's Whaley House through an article in Cosmic Star, Merle Gould's psychic newspaper, back in 1963. The account was not too specific about the people who had experienced something unusual at the house, but it did mention mysterious footsteps, cold drafts, unseen presences staring over one's shoulder and the scent of perfume where no such odor could logically be—the gamut of uncanny phenomena, in short. My appetite was whetted. Evidently the curators, Mr. and Mrs. James Redding, were making some alterations in the building when the haunting began.

I marked the case as a possibility when in the area, and turned to other matters. Then fate took a hand in bringing me closer to San Diego.

I had appeared on Regis Philbin's network television show and a close friendship had developed between us. When Regis moved to San Diego and started his own program there, he asked me to be his guest.

We had already talked of a house he knew in San Diego that he wanted me to investigate with him—it turned out to be the same Whaley House. Finally we agreed on June 25th as the night we would go to the haunted house and film a trance session with Sybil Leek, then talk about it the following day on Regis' show.

Sybil Leek had come over from England a few years earlier, after a successful career as a producer and writer of television documentaries, as well as an author of a number of books on animal life and antiques. At one time she ran an antique shop in her beloved New Forest area of southern England, but her name came to the attention of Americans primarily because of her religious convictions—she happened to be a witch. Not a Hallowe'en type witch, to be sure, but a follower of "the Old Religion," the pre-Christian Druidic cult which is still being practiced in many parts of the world. Her personal involvement with witchcraft was of less interest to me than her great abilities as a trance medium. I tested her and found her capable of total "dissociation of personality," which is the necessary requirement for good trance work. She can get "out of her own body" under my prodding, and lend it to whatever personality might be present in the atmosphere of our quest. Afterwards, she will remember nothing and merely continue pleasantly where we left off in conversation prior to trance—even if it is two hours later! Sybil Leek lent her ESP powers exclusively to my research and confined her "normal" activities to a career in writing and business.

We arrived in sunny San Diego ahead of Regis Philbin, and spent the day loafing at the Half Moon Inn, a romantic luxury motel on a peninsula stretching out into San Diego harbor. Regis could not have picked a better place for us—it was almost like being in Hawaii. We dined with Kay Sterner, president and chief sensitive of the local California Parapsychology Foundation, a charming and knowledgeable woman who had been to the haunted Whaley House, but of course she did not talk about it in Sybil's presence. In deference to my policy, she waited until Sybil left us. Then she told me of her forays into Whaley House, where she had felt several presences. I thanked her and decided to do my own investigating from scratch.

My first step was to contact June Reading, who was not only the director of the house but also its historian. She asked me to treat confidentially whatever I might find in the house through psychic means. This I could not promise, but I offered to treat the material with respect and without undue sensationalism, and I trust I have not disappointed Mrs. Reading too much. My readers are entitled to all the facts as I find them.

Mrs. Reading herself was the author of a booklet about the historic house, and a brief summary of its development also appeared in a brochure given to visitors, who keep coming all week long from every part of the country. I quote from the brochure:

The Whaley House, in the heart of Old Town, San Diego—restored, refurnished and opened for public viewing—represents one of the finest examples extant of early California buildings.

Original construction of the two-story mansion was begun on May 6, 1856, by Thomas Whaley, San Diego pioneer. The building was completed on May 10, 1857. Bricks used in the structure came from a clay-bed and kiln—the first brick-yard in San Diego—which Thomas Whaley established 300 yards to the southwest of his projected home.

Much of 'Old San Diego's' social life centered around this impressive home. Later the house was used as a theater for a traveling company, 'The Tanner Troupe,' and at one time served as the San Diego County Court House.

The Whaley House was erected on what is now the corner of San Diego Avenue and Harney Street, on a 150-by-217-foot lot, which was part of an 8 1/2-acre parcel purchased by Whaley on September 25, 1855. The North room originally was a granary without flooring, but was remodeled when it became the County Court House on August 12,1869.

Downstairs rooms include a tastefully furnished parlor, a music room, a library and the annex, which served as the County Court House. There are four bedrooms upstairs, two of which were leased to 'The Tanner Troupe' for theatricals.

Perhaps the most significant historical event involving the Whaley House was the surreptitious transfer of the county court records from it to 'New Town,' present site of downtown San Diego, on the night of March 31, 1871.

Despite threats to forcibly prevent even legal transfer of the court house to 'New Town,' Col. Chalmers Scott, then county clerk and recorder, and his henchmen removed the county records under cover of darkness and transported them to a 'New Town' building at 6th and G Streets.

The Whaley House would be gone today but for a group of San Diegans who prevented its demolition in 1956 by forming the Historical Shrine Foundation of San Diego County and buying the land and the building.

Later, the group convinced the County of San Diego that the house should be preserved as an historical museum, and restored to its early-day splendor. This was done under the supervision and guidance of an advisory committee including members of the Foundation, which today maintains the Whaley House as an historical museum.

Most of the furnishings, authenticated as in use in Whaley's time, are from other early-day San Diego County homes and were donated by interested citizens.

The last Whaley to live in the house was Corinne Lillian Whaley, youngest of Whaley's six children. She died at the age of 89 in 1953. Whaley himself died December 14, 1890, at the age of 67. He is buried in San Diego in Mount Hope Cemetery, as is his wife, Anna, who lived until February 24, 1913.

When it became apparent that a thorough investigation of the haunting would be made, and that all of San Diego would be able to learn of it through television and newspapers, excitement mounted to a high pitch.

Mrs. Reading kept in close touch with Regis Philbin and me, because ghosts have a way of "sensing" an impending attempt to oust them—and this was not long in coming. On May 24th the "activities" inside the house had already increased to a marked degree; they were of the same general nature as previously noticed sounds.

Was the ghost getting restless?

I had asked Mrs. Reading to prepare an exact account of all occurrences within the house, from the very first moment on, and to assemble as many of the witnesses as possible for further interrogation.

Most of these people had worked part time as guides in the house during the five years since its restoration. The phenomena thus far had occurred, or at any rate been observed, mainly between 10 a.m. and 5:30 pm, when the house closed to visitors. There is no one there at night, but an effective burglar alarm system is in operation to prevent flesh-and-blood intruders from breaking in unnoticed. Ineffective with the ghostly kind—as we were soon to learn!

I shall now quote the director's own report. It vouches for the accuracy and calibre of witnesses.

Phenomena Observed at Whaley House
By Visitors

Oct. 9, 1960—Dr. & Mrs. Kirbey, of New Westminster, B.C., Canada. 1:30-2:30 pm (He was then Director of the Medical Association of New Westminster.)

While Dr. Kirbey and his wife were in the house, he became interested in an exhibit in one of the display cases and she asked if she might go through by herself, because she was familiar with the Victorian era, and felt very much at home in these surroundings. Accordingly, I remained downstairs with the Doctor, discussing early physicians and medical practices.

When Mrs. Kirbey returned to the display room, she asked me in hesitating fashion if I had ever noticed anything unusual about the upstairs. I asked her what she had noticed. She reported that when she started upstairs, she felt a breeze over her head, and though she saw nothing, realized a pressure against her, seemed to make it hard to go up. When she looked into the rooms, had the feeling that someone was standing behind her, in fact so close to her that she turned around several times to look. Said she expected someone would tap her on the shoulder. When she joined us downstairs, we all walked toward the courtroom. As we entered, again Mrs. Kirbey turned to me and asked if I knew that someone inhabited the courtroom. She pointed to the bailiff's table, saying as she did, "Right over there." I asked her if the person was clear enough for her to describe, and she said:

"I see a small figure of a woman who has a swarthy complexion. She is wearing a long full skirt, reaching to the floor. The skirt appears to be a calico or gingham, small print. She has a kind of cap on her head, dark hair and eyes and she is wearing gold hoops in her pierced ears. She seems to stay in this room, lives here, I gather, and I get the impression we are sort of invading her privacy."

Mrs. Kirbey finished her description by asking me if any of the Whaley family were swarthy, to which I replied, "No."

This was, to my knowledge, the only description given of an apparition by a visitor, and Mrs. Kirbey the only person who brought up the fact in connection with the courtroom. Many of the visitors have commented upon the atmosphere in this room, however, and some people attempting to work in the room comment upon the difficulty they have in trying to concentrate here.

By Persons Employed at Whaley House
April, 1960
10:00 a.m. By myself, June A. Reading, 3447 Kite St. Sound of Footsteps—in the Upstairs

This sound of someone walking across the floor, I first heard in the morning, a week before the museum opened to the public. County workmen were still painting some shelving in the hall, and during this week often arrived before I did, so it was not unusual to find them already at work when I arrived.

This morning, however, I was planning to furnish the downstairs rooms, and so hurried in and down the hall to open the back door awaiting the arrival of the trucks with the furnishings. Two men followed me down the hall; they were going to help with the furniture arrangement. As I reached up to unbolt the back door, I heard the sound of what seemed to be someone walking across the bedroom floor. I paid no attention, thinking it was one of the workmen. But the men, who heard the sounds at the time I did, insisted I go upstairs and find out who was in the house. So, calling out, I started to mount the stairs. Halfway up, I could see no lights, and that the outside shutters to the windows were still closed. I made some comment to the men who had followed me, and turned around to descend the stairs. One of the men joked with me about the spirits coming in to look things over, and we promptly forgot the matter.

However, the sound of walking continued. And for the next six months I found myself going upstairs to see if someone was actually upstairs. This would happen during the day, sometimes when visitors were in other parts of the house, other times when I was busy at my desk trying to catch up on correspondence or bookwork. At times it would sound as though someone were descending the stairs, but would fade away before reaching the first floor. In September, 1962, the house was the subject of a news article in the *San Diego Evening Tribune,* and this same story was reprinted in the September 1962 issue of *Fate* magazine.

Oct. & Nov. 1962. We began to have windows in the upper part of the house open unaccountably. We installed horizontal bolts on three windows in the front bedroom, thinking this would end the matter. However, the really disturbing part of this came when it set off our burglar alarm in the night, and we were called by the Police and San Diego Burglar Alarm Co. to come down and see if the house had been broken into. Usually, we would find nothing disturbed. (One exception to this was when the house was broken into by vandals, about 1963, and items from the kitchen display were stolen.)

In the fall of 1962, early October, while engaged in giving a talk to some school children, a class of 25 pupils, I heard a sound of someone walking, which seemed to come from the roof. One of the children interrupted me, asking what that noise was, and excusing myself from them, I went outside the building, down on the street to see if workmen from the County were repairing the roof. Satisfied that there was no one on the roof of the building, I went in and resumed the tour.

Residents of Old Town are familiar with this sound, and tell me that it has been evident for years. Miss Whaley, who lived in the house for 85 years, was aware of it. She passed away in 1953.

Mrs. Grace Bourquin, 2938 Beech St.
Sat. Dec. 14, 1963, noon—Was seated in the hall downstairs having lunch, when she heard walking sound in upstairs.

Sat. Jan. 10, 1964, 1:30 P.M. Walked down the hall and looked up the staircase. On the upper landing she saw an apparition—the figure of a man, clad in frock coat and pantaloons, the face turned away from her, so she could not make it out. Suddenly it faded away.

Lawrence Riveroll, resides on Jefferson St., Old Town.
Jan. 5, 1963, 12:30 noon
Was alone in the house. No visitors present at the time. While seated at the desk in the front hail, heard sounds of music and singing, described as a woman's voice. Song "Home Again." Lasted about 30 seconds.
Jan. 7, 1963, 1:30 P.M.
Visitors in upstairs. Downstairs, he heard organ music, which seemed to come from the courtroom, where there is an organ. Walked into the room to see if someone was attempting to play it. Cover on organ was closed. He saw no one in the room.
Jan. 19, 1963, 5:15 P.M.
Museum was closed for the day. Engaged in closing shutters downstairs. Heard footsteps in upper part of house in the same area as described. Went up to check, saw nothing.
Sept. 10-12, 1964—at dusk, about 5:15 P.M.
Engaged in closing house, together with another worker. Finally went into the music room, began playing the piano. Suddenly felt a distinct pressure on his hands, as though someone had their hands on his. He turned to look toward the front hall, in the direction of the desk, hoping to get the attention of the person seated there, when he saw the apparition of a slight woman dressed in a hoop skirt. In the dim light was unable to see clearly the face. Suddenly the figure vanished.

J. Milton Keller, 4114 Middlesex Dr.
Sept. 22, 1964, 2:00 P.M.
Engaged in tour with visitors at the parlor, when suddenly he, together with people assembled at balustrade, noticed crystal drops hanging from lamp on parlor table begin to swing back and forth. This occurred only on one side of the lamp. The other drops did not move. This continued about two minutes.

Dec. 15, 1964, 5:15 P.M.

Engaged in closing house along with others. Returned from securing restrooms, walked down hall, turned to me with the key, while I stepped into the hall closet to reach for the master switch which turns off all lights. I pulled the switch, started to turn around to step out, when he said, "Stop, don't move, you'll step on the dog!" He put his hands out, in a gesture for me to stay still. Meantime, I turned just in time to see what resembled a flash of light between us, and what appeared to be the back of a dog, scurry down the hall and turn into the dining room. I decided to resume a normal attitude, so I kidded him a little about trying to scare me. Other people were present in the front hall at the time, waiting for us at the door, so he turned to them and said in a rather hurt voice that I did not believe him. I realized then that he had witnessed an apparition, so I asked him to see if he could describe it. *He said he saw a spotted dog, like a fox terrier, that ran with his ears flapping, down the hall and into the dining room.*

May 29,1965, 2:30 P.M.

Escorting visitors through house, upstairs. Called to me, asking me to come up. Upon going up, he, I, and visitors all witnessed a black rocking chair, moving back and forth as if occupied by a person. It had started moving unaccountably, went on about three minutes. Caused quite a stir among visitors.

Dec. 27, 1964, 5:00 P.M.

Late afternoon, prior to closing, *saw the apparition of a woman dressed in a green plaid gingham dress.* She had long dark hair, coiled up in a bun at neck, was seated on a settee in bedroom.

Feb. 1965, 2:00 P.M.

Engaged in giving a tour with visitors, when two elderly ladies called and asked him to come upstairs, and step over to the door of the nursery. These ladies, visitors, called his attention to a sound that was like the cry of a baby, about 16 months old. All three reported the sound.

March 24, 1965, 1:00 P.M.

He, together with Mrs. Bourquin and his parents, Mr. & Mrs. Keller, engaged in touring the visitors, when for some reason his attention was directed to the foot of the staircase. He walked back to it, and heard the sound of someone in the upper part of the house whistling. No one was in the upstairs at the time.

Mrs. Suzanne Pere, 106 Albatross, El Cajon.

April 8, 1963, 4:30 P.M.

Was engaged in typing in courtroom, working on manuscript. Suddenly she called to me, calling my attention to a noise in the upstairs. We both stopped work, walked up the stairs together, to see if anyone could possibly be there. As it was near closing time, we decided to secure the windows. Mrs. Pere kept noticing a chilly breeze at the back of her head, had the distinct feeling that someone, though invisible, was present and kept following her from one window to another.

Oct. 14, 21; Nov. 18, 1964

During the morning and afternoon on these days, called my attention to the smell of cigar smoke, and the fragrance of perfume or cologne. This occurred in the parlor, hall, upstairs bedroom. In another bedroom she called my attention to something resembling dusting powder.

Nov. 28, 1963, 2:30 P.M.

Reported seeing an apparition in the study. A group of men there, dressed in frock coats, some with plain vests, others figured material. One of this group had a large gold watch chain across vest. Seemed to be a kind of meeting; all figures were animated, some pacing the floor, others conversing; all serious and agitated, but oblivious to everything else. One figure in this group seemed to be an official, and stood off by himself. This person was of medium stocky build, light brown hair, and mustache which was quite full and long. He had very piercing light blue eyes, penetrating gaze. Mrs. Pere sensed that he was some kind of official, a person of importance. He seemed about to speak. Mrs. Pere seemed quite exhausted by her experience witnessing this scene, yet was quite curious about the man with the penetrating gaze. I remember her asking me if I knew of anyone answering this description, because it remained with her for some time.

Oct. 7., 1963, 10:30 A.M.

Reported unaccountable sounds issuing from kitchen, as though someone were at work there. Same day, she reported smelling the odor of something baking.

Nov. 27, 1964, 10:15 A.M.

Heard a distinct noise from kitchen area, as though something had dropped to the floor. I was present when this occurred. She called to me and asked what I was doing there, thinking I had been rearranging exhibit. At this time I was at work in courtroom, laying out work. Both of us reached the kitchen, to find one of the utensils on the shelf rack had disengaged itself, fallen to the floor, and had struck a copper boiler directly below. No one else was in the house at the time, and we were at a loss to explain this.

Mrs. T.R. Allen, 3447 Kite Street

Was present *Jan. 7, 1963, 1:30 P.M.* Heard organ music issue from courtroom, when Lawrence Riveroll heard the same (see his statement).

Was present *Sept. 10-12, 1964,* at dusk, with Lawrence Riveroll, when he witnessed apparition. Mrs. Allen went upstairs to close shutters, and as she ascended them, described a chill breeze that seemed to come over her head. Upstairs, she walked into the bedroom and toward the windows. Suddenly she heard a sound behind her, as though something had dropped to the floor. She turned to look, saw nothing, but again experienced the feeling of having someone, invisible, hovering near her. She had a feeling of fear. Completed her task as quickly as possible, and left the upstairs hastily. Upon my return, both persons seemed anxious to leave the house.

May, 1965 (the last Friday), 1:30 P.M.

Was seated in downstairs front hall, when she heard the sound of footsteps.

Regis Philbin himself had been to the house before. With him on that occasion was his wife, who was highly sensitive to psychic emanations, and a teacher-friend of theirs considered an amateur medium.

They observed, during their vigil, what appeared to be a white figure of a person, but when Regis challenged it, unfortunately with his flashlight, it disappeared immediately. Mrs. Philbin felt extremely uncomfortable on that occasion and had no desire to return to the house.

By now I knew that the house had at least three ghosts: a man, a woman and a baby—and a spotted dog. The scene observed in one of the rooms sounded more like a psychic impression of a past event to me than a bona fide ghost.

I later discovered that still another part-time guide at the house, William H. Richardson, of 470 Silvery Lane, El Cajon, had not only experienced something out of the ordinary at the house, but had taken part in a kind of seance with interesting results. Here is his statement, given to me in September of 1965, several months *after* our own trance session had taken place.

"In the summer of 1963 I worked in Whaley House as a guide.

"One morning before the house was open to the public, several of us employees were seated in the music room downstairs, and the sound of someone in heavy boots walking across the upstairs was heard by us all. When we went to investigate the noise, we found all the windows locked and shuttered, and the only door to the outside from upstairs was locked. This experience first sparked my interest in ghosts.

"I asked June Reading, the director, to allow several of my friends from Starlight Opera, a local summer musical theatre, to spend the night in the house.

"At midnight, on Friday, August 13, we met at the house. Carolyn Whyte, a member of the parapsychology group in San Diego and a member of the Starlight Chorus, gave an introductory talk on what to expect, and we all went into the parlor to wait for something to happen.

"The first experience was that of a cool breeze blowing through the room, which was felt by several of us despite the fact that all doors and windows were locked and shuttered.

"The next thing that happened was that a light appeared over a boy's head. This traveled from his head across the wall, where it disappeared. Upon later investigation it was found to have disappeared at the portrait of Thomas Whaley, the original owner of the house. Footsteps were also heard several times in the room upstairs.

"At this point we broke into groups and dispersed to different parts of the house. One group went into the study which is adjacent to the parlor, and there witnessed a shadow on the wall surrounded by a pale light which moved up and down the wall and changed shape as it did so. There was no source of light into the room and one could pass in front of the shadow without disturbing it.

"Another group was upstairs when their attention was directed simultaneously to the chandelier which began to swing around as if someone were holding the bottom and twisting the sides. One boy was tapped on the leg several times by some unseen force while seated there.

"Meanwhile, downstairs in the parlor, an old-fashioned lamp with prisms hanging on the edges began to act strangely.

As we watched, several prisms began to swing by themselves. These would stop and others would start, but they never swung simultaneously. There was no breeze in the room.

"At this time we all met in the courtroom. Carolyn then suggested that we try to lift the large table in the room.

"We sat around the table and placed our fingertips on it. A short while later it began to creak and then slid across the floor approximately eight inches, and finally lifted completely off the floor on the corner where I was seated.

"Later on we brought a small table from the music room into the courtroom and tried to get it to tip, which it did. With just our fingertips on it, it tilted until it was approximately one inch from the floor, then fell. We righted the table and put our fingertips back on it, and almost immediately it began to rock. Since we knew the code for yes, no, and doubtful, we began to converse with the table. Incidentally, while this was going on, a chain across the doorway in the courtroom was almost continually swinging back and forth and then up and down.

"Through the system of knocking, we discovered that the ghost was that of a little girl, seven years old. She did not tell us her name, but she did tell us that she had red hair, freckles, and hazel eyes. She also related that there were four other ghosts in the house besides herself, including that of a baby boy. We conversed with her spirit for nearly an hour.

"At one time the table stopped rocking and started moving across the floor of the courtroom, into the dining room, through the pantry, and into the kitchen. This led us to believe that the kitchen was her usual abode. The table then stopped and several antique kitchen utensils on the wall began to swing violently. Incidentally, the kitchen utensils swung for the rest of the evening at different intervals.

"The table then retraced its path back to the courtroom and answered more questions.

"At 5:00 A.M. we decided to call it a night—a most interesting night. When we arrived our group of 15 had had in it a couple of real believers, several who half believed, and quite a few who didn't believe at all. After the phenomena we had experienced, there was not one among us who was even very doubtful in the belief of some form of existence after life."

It was Friday evening, and time to meet the ghosts. Sybil Leek knew nothing whatever about the house, and when Regis Philbin picked us up the conversation remained polite and non-ghostly.

When we arrived at the house, word of mouth had preceded us despite the fact that our plans had not been announced publicly; certainly it had not been advertised that we would attempt a séance that evening. Nevertheless, a sizable crowd had assembled at the house and only Regis' polite insistence that their presence might harm whatever results we could obtain made them move on.

It was quite dark now, and I followed Sybil into the house, allowing her to get her clairvoyant bearings first, prior to the trance session we were to do with the cameras rolling. My wife Catherine trailed right behind me carrying the tape equipment. Mrs. Reading received us cordially. The witnesses had assembled but were temporarily out of reach, so that Sybil could not gather any sensory impressions from them. They patiently waited through our clairvoyant tour. All in all, about a dozen people awaited us. The house was lit throughout and the excitement in the atmosphere was bound to stir up any ghost present!

And so it was that on June 25, 1965, the Ghost Hunter came to close quarters with the specters at Whaley House, San Diego. While Sybil meandered about the house by herself, I quickly went over to the Court House part of the house and went over their experiences with the witnesses. Although I already had their statements, I wanted to make sure no detail had escaped me.

From June Reading I learned, for instance, that the Court House section of the building, erected around 1855, had originally served as a granary, later becoming a town hall and Court House in turn. It was the only two-story brick house in the entire area at the time.

Not only did Mrs. Reading hear what sounded to her like human voices, but on one occasion, when she was tape recording some music in this room, the tape also contained some human voices—sounds she had not herself heard while playing the music!

"When was the last time you yourself heard anything unusual?" I asked Mrs. Reading.

"As recently as a week ago," the curator replied, "during the day I heard the definite sound of someone opening the front door. Because we have had many visitors here recently, we are very much alerted to this. I happened to be in the Court Room with one of the people from the Historical Society engaged in research in the Whaley papers, and we both heard it. I went to check to see who had come in, and there was no one there, nor was there any sound of footsteps on the porch outside. The woman who works here also heard it and was just as puzzled about it as I was."

I discovered that the Mrs. Allen in the curator's report to me of uncanny experiences at the house was Lillian Allen, her own mother, a lively lady who remembered her brush with the uncanny only too vividly.

"I've heard the noises overhead," she recalled. "Someone in heavy boots seemed to be walking across, turning to come down the stairway—and when I first came out here they would tell me these things and I would not believe them—but I was sitting at the desk one night, downstairs, waiting for my daughter to lock up in the back. I heard this noise overhead and I was rushing to see if we were locking someone in the house, and as I got to almost the top, a big rush of wind blew over my head and made my hair stand up. I thought the windows had blown open but I looked all around and everything was secured."

"Just how did this wind feel?" I asked. Tales of cold winds are standard with traditional hauntings, but here we had a precise witness to testify.

"It was cold and I was chilly all over. And another thing, when I lock the shutters upstairs at night, I feel like someone is breathing down the back of my neck, like they're going to touch me—at the shoulder—that happened often. Why, only a month ago."

A Mrs. Frederick Bear now stepped forward. I could not find her name in Mrs. Reading's brief report. Evidently she was an additional witness to the uncanny goings-on at this house.

"One evening I came here—it was after five o'clock; another lady was here also—and June Reading was coming down the stairs, and we were talking. I distinctly heard something move upstairs, as if someone were moving a table. There was no one there—we checked. That only happened a month ago."

Grace Bourquin, another volunteer worker at the house, had been touched upon in Mrs. Reading's report. She emphasized that the sounds were those of a heavy man wearing boots—no mistake about it. When I questioned her about the apparition of a man she had seen, about six weeks ago, wearing a frock coat, she insisted that he had looked like a real person to her, standing at the top of the stairs one moment, and completely gone the next.

"He did not move. I saw him clearly, then turned my head for a second to call out to Mrs. Reading, and when I looked again, he had disappeared."

I had been fascinated by Mrs. Suzanne Pere's account of her experiences, which seemed to indicate a large degree of mediumship in her makeup. I questioned her about anything she had not yet told us.

"On one occasion June Reading and I were in on the study and working with the table. We had our hands on the table to see if we could get any reaction."

"You mean you were trying to do some table-tipping."

"Yes. At this point I had only had some feeling in the house, and smelled some cologne. This was about a year ago, and we were working with some papers concerning the Native American uprising in San Diego, and all of a sudden the table started to rock violently! All of the pulses in my body became throbbing, and in my mind's eye the room was filled with men, all of them extremely excited, and though I could not hear any sound, I knew they were talking, and one gentleman was striding up and down the center of the room, puffing on his cigar, and from my description of him June Reading later identified him as Sheriff McCoy, who was here in the 1850s. When it was finished I could not talk for a few minutes. I was completely disturbed for a moment."

McCoy, I learned, was the leader of one of the factions during the "battle" between Old Town and New Town San Diego for the county seat.

Evidently, Mrs. Bourquin had psychically relived that emotion-laden event which did indeed transpire in the very room she saw it in!

"Was the Court House ever used to execute anyone?" I interjected.

Mrs. Reading was not sure; the records were all there but the Historical Society had not gone over them as yet for lack of staff. The Court functioned in this house for two years, however, and sentences certainly were meted out in it. The prison itself was a bit farther up the street.

A lady in a red coat caught my attention. She identified herself as Bernice Kennedy.

"I'm a guide here on Sundays," the lady began, "and one

Sunday recently, I was alone in the house and sitting in the dining room reading, and I heard the front door open and close. There was no one there. I went back to continue my reading. Then I heard it the second time. Again I checked, and there was absolutely no one there. I heard it a third time and this time I took my book and sat outside at the desk. From then onward, people started to come in and I had no further unusual experience. But one other Sunday, there was a young woman upstairs who came down suddenly very pale, and she said the little rocking chair upstairs was rocking. I followed the visitor up and I could not see the chair move, but there was a clicking sound, very rhythmic, and I haven't heard it before or since."

The chair, it came out, once belonged to a family related to the Whaleys.

"I'm Charles Keller, father of Milton Keller," a booming voice said behind me, and an imposing gentleman in his middle years stepped forward.

"I once conducted a tour through the Whaley House. I noticed a lady who had never been here act as if she were being pushed out of one of the bedrooms!"

"Did you see it?" I said, somewhat taken aback.

"Yes," Mr. Keller nodded, "I saw her move, as if someone were pushing her out of the room."

"Did you interrogate her about it?"

"Yes, I did. It was only in the first bedroom, where we started the tour, that it happened. Not in any of the other rooms. We went back to that room and again I saw her being pushed out of it!"

Mrs. Keller then spoke to me about the ice-cold draft she felt, and just before that, three knocks at the back door! Her son, whose testimony Mrs. Reading had already obtained for me, then went to the back door and found no one there who could have knocked. This had happened only six months before our visit.

I then turned to James Reading, the head of the Association responsible for the upkeep of the museum and house, and asked for his own encounters with the ghosts. Mr. Reading, in a cautious tone, explained that he did not really cotton to ghosts, but—

"The house was opened to the public in April 1960. In the fall of that year, October or November, the police called me at two o'clock in the morning, and asked me to please go down and shut off the burglar alarm, because they were being flooded with complaints, it was waking up everybody in the neighborhood. I came down and found two officers waiting for me. I shut off the alarm. They had meantime checked the house and every door and shutter was tight."

"How could the alarm have gone off by itself then?"

"I don't know. I unlocked the door, and we searched the entire house. When we finally got upstairs, we found one of the upstairs front bedroom windows open. We closed and bolted the window, and came down and tested the alarm. It was in order again. No one could have gotten in or out. The shutters outside that window were closed and hooked on the inside. The opening of the window had set off the alarm, but it would have been impossible for anyone to open that window and get either into or out of the house. Impossible. This happened *four times.* The second time, about four months later, again at two in the morning, again that same window was standing open. The other two times it was always that same window."

"What did you finally do about it?"

"After the fourth incident we added a second bolt at right angles to the first one, and that seemed to help. There were no further calls."

Was the ghost getting tired of pushing *two* bolts out of the way?

I had been so fascinated with all this additional testimony

that I had let my attention wander away from my favorite medium, Sybil Leek. But now I started to look for her and found to my amazement that she had seated herself in one of the old chairs in what used to be the kitchen, downstairs in back of the living room. When I entered the room she seemed deep in thought, although not in trance by any means, and yet it took me a while to make her realize where we were.

Had anything unusual transpired while I was in the Court Room interviewing?

"I was standing in the entrance hall, looking at the post-cards," Sybil recollected, "when I felt I just had to go to the kitchen, but I didn't go there at first, but went halfway up the stairs, and a child came down the stairs and into the kitchen and I followed her."

"A child?" I asked. I was quite sure there were no children among our party.

"I thought it was Regis' little girl and the next thing I recall I was in the rocking chair and you were saying something to me."

Needless to say, Regis Philbin's daughter had *not* been on the stairs. I asked for a detailed description of the child.

"It was a long-haired girl," Sybil said. "She was very quick, you know, in a longish dress. She went to the table in this room and I went to the chair. That's all I remember."

I decided to continue to question Sybil about any psychic impressions she might now gather in the house.

"There is a great deal of confusion in this house," she began. "Some of it is associated with another room upstairs, which has been structurally altered. There are two centers of activity."

Sybil, of course, could not have known that the house consisted of two separate units.

"Any ghosts in the house?"

"Several," Sybil assured me. "At least four!"

Had not William Richardson's group made contact with a little girl ghost who had claimed that she knew of four other ghosts in the house? The report of that séance did not reach me until September, several months after our visit, so Sybil could not possibly have "read our minds" about it, since our minds had no such knowledge at that time.

"This room where you found me sitting," Sybil continued, "I found myself drawn to it; the impressions are very strong here. Especially that child—she died young."

We went about the house now, seeking further contacts.

"I have a date now," Sybil suddenly said, "1872."

The Readings exchanged significant glances. It was just after the greatest bitterness of the struggle between Old Town and New Town, when the removal of the Court records from Whaley House by force occurred.

"There are two sides to the house," Sybil continued. "One side I like, but not the other."

Rather than have Sybil use up her energies in clairvoyance, I felt it best to try for a trance in the Court Room itself. This was arranged for quickly, with candles taking the place of electric lights except for what light was necessary for the motion picture cameras in the rear of the large room.

Regis Philbin and I sat at Sybil's sides as she slumped forward in a chair that may well have held a merciless judge in bygone years.

But the first communicator was neither the little girl nor the man in the frock coat. A feeble, plaintive voice was suddenly heard from Sybil's lips, quite unlike her own, a voice evidently parched with thirst.

"Bad...fever...everybody had the fever..."

"What year is this?"

"Forty-six."

I suggested that the fever had passed, and generally calmed the personality who did not respond to my request for identification.

"Send me...some water...." Sybil was still in trance, but herself now. Immediately she complained about there being a lot of confusion.

"This isn't the room where we're needed...the child...she is the one...."

"What is her name?"

"Anna...Bell...she died very suddenly with something, when she was thirteen...

chest...."

"Are her parents here too?"

"They come...the lady comes."

"What is this house used for?"

"Trade...selling things, buying and selling."

"Is there anyone other than the child in this house?"

"Child is the main one, because she doesn't understand anything at all. But there is something more vicious. Child would not hurt anyone. There's someone else. A man. He knows something about this house...about thirty-two, unusual name, C...Calstrop...five feet ten, wearing a green coat, darkish, mustache and side whiskers, he goes up to the bedroom on the left. He has business here. His business is with things that come from the sea. But it is the papers that worry him."

"What papers?" I demanded.

"The papers...1872. About the house. Dividing the house was wrong. Two owners, he says."

"What is the house being used for, now, in 1872?"

"To live in. Two places...I get confused for I go one place and then I have to go to another."

"Did this man you see die here?"

"He died here. Unhappy because of the place...about the other place. Two buildings. Some people quarrelled about the spot. He is laughing. He wants all this house for himself."

"Does he know he is dead?" I asked the question that often brings forth much resistance to my quest for facts from those who cannot conceive of their status as "ghosts."

Sybil listened for a moment.

"He does as he wants in this house because he is going to live here," she finally said. *"It's his house."*

"Why is he laughing?"

A laughing ghost, indeed!

"He laughs because of people coming here thinking it's *their* house! When he knows the truth."

"What is his name?" I asked again.

"Cal...Caltrop...very difficult as he does not speak very clearly...he writes and writes...he makes a noise...he says he will make even more noise unless you go away."

"Let him," I said, cheerfully hoping I could tape-record the ghost's outbursts.

"Tell him he has passed over and the matter is no longer important," I told Sybil.

"He is upstairs."

I asked that he walk upstairs so we could all hear him. There was nobody upstairs at this moment—everybody was watching the proceedings in the Court Room downstairs.

We kept our breath, waiting for the manifestations, but our ghost wouldn't play the game. I continued with my questions.

"What does he want?"

"He is just walking around, he can do as he likes," Sybil said. "He does not like new things...he does not like any noise...except when he makes it...."

"Who plays the organ in this house?"

"He says his mother plays."

"What is her name?"

"Ann Lassay...that's wrong, it's Lann—he speaks so badly...Lannay...his throat is bad or something...."

I later was able to check on this unusual name. Anna Lannay was Thomas Whaley's wife!

At the moment, however, I was not aware of this fact and pressed on with my interrogation. How did the ghost die? How long ago?

"'1889...he does not want to speak; he only wants to roam around."

Actually, Whaley died in 1890. Had the long interval confused his sense of time? So many ghosts cannot recall exact dates but will remember circumstances and emotional experiences in detail.

"He worries about the house...he wants the whole house...for himself...he says he will leave them...papers...hide the papers...he wants the other papers about the house...they're four miles from here...several people have these papers and you'll have to get them back or he'll never settle...never...and if he doesn't get the whole house back, he will be much worse...and then, the police will come...he will make the lights come and the noise...and the bell...make the police come and see him, the master...of the house, he hears bells upstairs...he doesn't know what it is...he goes upstairs and opens the windows, wooden windows...and looks out...and then he pulls the...no, it's not a bell...he'll do it again...when he wants someone to know that he really is the master of the house...people today come and say he is not, but he is!"

I was surprised. Sybil had no knowledge of the disturbances, the alarm bell, the footsteps, the open window...and yet it was all perfectly true. Surely, her communicator was our man!

"When did he do this the last time?" I inquired.

"This year...not long...."

"Has he done anything else in this house?"

"He said he moved the lights. In the parlor."

Later I thought of the Richardson séance and the lights they had observed, but of course I had no idea of this when we were at the house ourselves.

"What about the front door?"

"If people come, he goes into the garden…walks around…because he meets mother there."

"What is in the kitchen?"

"Child goes to the kitchen. I have to leave him, and he doesn't want to be left…it was an injustice, anyway, don't like it…the child is twelve…chest trouble…something from the kitchen…bad affair…."

"Anyone's fault?"

"Yes. Not chest…from the cupboard, took something…it was an acid like salt, and she ate it…she did not know…there is something strange about this child, someone had control of her, you see, she was in the way…family…one girl…those boys were not too good…the other boys who came down…she is like two people…someone controlled her…made her do strange things and then…could she do that…."

"Was she the daughter of the man?"

"Strange man, he doesn't care so much about the girl as he does about the house. He is disturbed."

"Is there a woman in this house?"

"Of course. There is a woman in the garden."

"Who is she?"

"Mother. Grandmother of the girl."

"Is he aware of the fact he has no physical body?"

"No."

"Doesn't he see all the people who come here?"

"They have to be fought off, sent away."

"Tell him it is now seventy years later."

"He says seventy years when the house was built."

"Another seventy years have gone by," I insisted.

"Only part of you is in the house."

"No, part of the house...you're making the mistake," he replied.

I tried hard to convince him of the real circumstances. Finally, I assured him that the entire house was, in effect, his. Would this help?

"He is vicious," Sybil explains. "He will have his revenge on the house."

I explained that his enemies were all dead.

"He says it was an injustice, and the Court was wrong and you have to tell everyone this is his house and land and home."

I promised to do so and intoned the usual formula for the release of earthbound people who have passed over and don't realize it. Then I recalled Sybil to her own self, and within a few moments she was indeed in full control.

I then turned to the director of the museum, Mrs. Reading, and asked for her comments on the truth of the material just heard.

"There was a litigation," she said. "The injustice could perhaps refer to the County's occupancy of this portion of the house from 1869 to 1871. Whaley's contract, which we have, shows that this portion of the house was leased to the County, and he was to supply the furniture and set it up as a Court Room. He also put in the two windows to provide light. It was a valid agreement. They adhered to the contract as long as the Court continued to function here, but when Alonzo Horton came and developed New Town, a hot contest began between the two communities for the possession of the county seat. When the records were forcefully removed from here, Whaley felt it was quite an injustice, and we have letters he addressed to the Board of Supervisors, referring to the fact that his lease had been broken. The Clerk notified him that they were no longer responsible for the use of this house—after all the work he had put in to remodel it for their use. He would bring the matter up periodically with the Board of Supervisors, but it was tabled by them each time it came up."

"In other words, this is the injustice referred to by the ghost?"

"In 1872 he was bitterly engaged in asking redress from the County over this matter, which troubled him some since he did not believe a government official would act in this manner. It was never settled, however, and Whaley was left holding the bag."

"Was there a child in the room upstairs?"

"In the nursery? There were several children there. One child died here. But this was a boy."

Again, later, I saw that the Richardson séance spoke of a boy ghost in the house.

At the very beginning of trance, before I began taping the utterances from Sybil's lips, I took some handwritten notes. The personality, I now saw, who had died of a bad fever had given the faintly pronounced name of Fedor and spoke of a mill where he worked. Was there any sense to this?

"Yes," Mrs. Reading confirmed, "this room we are in now served as a granary at one time. About 1855 to 1867."

"Were there ever any Russians in this area?"

"There was a considerable otter trade here prior to the American occupation of the area. We have found evidence that the Russians established wells in this area. They came into these waters then to trade otters."

"Amazing," I conceded. How could Sybil, even if she wanted to, have known of such an obscure fact?

"This would have been in the 1800s," Mrs. Reading continued. "Before then there were Spaniards here, of course."

"Anything else you wish to comment upon in the trance session you have just witnessed?" I asked.

Mrs. Reading expressed what we all felt.

"The references to the windows opening upstairs, and the ringing of these bells...."

How could Sybil have known all that? Nobody told her and she had not had a chance to acquaint herself with the details of the disturbances.

What remained were the puzzling statements about "the other house." They, too, were soon to be explained. We were walking through the garden now and inspected the rear portion of the Whaley house. In back of it, we discovered to our surprise still another wooden house standing in the garden. I questioned Mrs. Reading about this second house.

"The Pendington House, in order to save it, had to be moved out of the path of the freeway...it never belonged to the Whaleys although Thomas Whaley once tried to rent it. But it was always rented to someone else."

No wonder the ghost was angry about "the other house." It had been moved and put on *his* land...without his consent!

The name *Cal...trop* still did not fall into place. It was too far removed from Whaley and yet everything else that had come through Sybil clearly fitted Thomas Whaley. Then the light began to dawn, thanks to Mrs. Reading's detailed knowledge of the house.

"It was interesting to hear Mrs. Leek say there was a store here once..." she explained. "This is correct, there was a store here at one time, but it was not Mr. Whaley's."

"Whose was it?"

"It belonged to a man named Wallack...Hal Wallack...that was in the seventies."

Close enough to Sybil's tentative pronunciation of a name she caught connected with the house.

"He rented it to Wallack for six months, then Wallack sold out," Mrs. Reading explained.

I also discovered, in discussing the case with Mrs. Reading, that the disturbances really began after the second house had been placed on the grounds. Was that the straw that broke the ghost's patience?

Later, we followed Sybil to a wall adjoining the garden, a wall, I should add, where there was no visible door. But Sybil insisted there had been a French window there, and indeed there was at one time. In a straight line from this spot, we wound up at a huge tree. It was here, Sybil explained, that Whaley and his mother often met—or are meeting, as the case may be.

I was not sure that Mr. Whaley had taken my advice to heart and moved out of what was, after all, his house. Why should he? The County had not seen fit to undo an old wrong.

We left the next morning, hoping that at the very least we had let the restless one know someone cared.

A week later Regis Philbin checked with the folks at Whaley House. Everything was lively—chandelier swinging, rocker rocking; and June Reading herself brought me up to date on July 27th, 1965, with a brief report on activities—other than flesh-and-blood—at the house.

Evidently the child ghost was also still around, for utensils in the kitchen had moved that week, especially a cleaver which swings back and forth on its own. Surely that must be the playful little girl, for what would so important a man as Thomas Whaley have to do in the kitchen? Surely he was much too preoccupied with the larger aspects of his realm, the ancient wrong done him, and the many intrusions from the world of reality. For the Whaley House is a busy place, ghosts or not.

On replaying my tapes, I noticed a curious confusion between the initial appearance of a ghost who called himself Fedor in my notes, and a man who said he had a bad fever. It was just that the man with the fever did not have a foreign accent, but I distinctly recalled "fedor" as sounding odd.

Were they perhaps two separate entities?

My suspicions were confirmed when a letter written May 23, 1966—almost a year later—reached me. A Mrs. Carol

DeJuhasz wanted me to know about a ghost at Whaley House...no, not Thomas Whaley or a twelve-year-old girl with long hair. Mrs. DeJuhasz was concerned with an historical play written by a friend of hers, dealing with the unjust execution of a man who tried to steal a harbor boat in the 1800s and was caught. Make no mistake about it, nobody had observed this ghost at Whaley House. Mrs. DeJuhasz merely thought he ought to be there, having been hanged in the backyard of the house.

Many people tell me of tragic spots where men have died unhappily but rarely do I discover ghosts on such spots just because of it. I was therefore not too interested in Mrs. DeJuhasz' account of a possible ghost. But she thought that there ought to be present at Whaley House the ghost of this man, called Yankee Jim Robinson. When captured, he fought a saber duel and received a critical wound in the head. Although alive, he became delirious and was tried without representation, *sick of the fever.* Sentenced to death, he was subsequently hanged in the yard behind the Court House.

Was his the ghostly voice that spoke through Sybil, complaining of the fever and then quickly fading away? Again it was William Richardson who was able to provide a further clue or set of clues to this puzzle. In December of 1966 he contacted me again to report some further experiences at the Whaley House.

"This series of events began in March of this year. Our group was helping to restore an historic old house which had been moved onto the Whaley property to save it from destruction. During our lunch break one Saturday, several of us were in Whaley House. I was downstairs when Jim Stein, one of the group, rushed down the stairs to tell me that the cradle in the nursery was rocking by itself. I hurried upstairs but it wasn't rocking. I was just about to chide Jim for having an overactive imagination when it began again and rocked a little longer before it stopped. The cradle was at least ten feet from the doorway, and a metal barricade was across it to prevent tourists from entering the room. No amount of walking or jumping had any effect on the cradle. While it rocked, I remembered that it had made no sound. Going into the room, I rocked the cradle. I was surprised that it made quite a bit of noise. The old floorboards are somewhat uneven and this in combination with the wooden rockers on the cradle made a very audible sound.

"As a matter of fact, when the Whaleys were furnishing carpeting for the house, the entire upstairs portion was carpeted. This might explain the absence of the noise.

"In June, Whaley House became the setting for an historical play. The play concerned the trial and hanging of a local bad man named Yankee Jim Robinson. It was presented in the Court Room and on the grounds of the mansion. The actual trial and execution had taken place in August of 1852. This was five years before Whaley House was built, but the execution took place on the grounds.

"Yankee Jim was hanged from a scaffold which stood approximately between the present music room and front parlor.

"Soon after the play went into rehearsal, things began to happen. I was involved with the production as an actor and therefore had the opportunity to spend many hours in the house between June and August. The usual footsteps kept up and they were heard by most of the members of the cast at one time or another. There was a group of us within the cast who were especially interested in the phenomenon: myself, Barry Bunker, George Carroll, and his fiancée Toni Manista. As we were all dressed in period costumes most of the time, the ghosts should have felt right at home. Toni was playing the part of Anna, Thomas Whaley's wife. She said she often felt as if she were being followed around the house (as did we all).

"I was sitting in the kitchen with my back to the wall one night, when I felt a hand run through my hair. I quickly turned around but there was nothing to be seen. I have always felt that it was Anna Whaley who touched me. It was my first such experience and I felt honored that she had chosen me to touch. There is a chair in the kitchen which is made of rawhide and wood. The seat is made of thin strips of rawhide criss-crossed on the wooden frame. When someone sits on it, it sounds like the leather in a saddle. On the same night I was touched, the chair made sounds as if someone were sitting in it, not once but several times. There always seems to be a change in the temperature of a room when a presence enters. The kitchen is no exception. It really got cold in there!

"Later in the run of the show, the apparitions began to appear. The cast had purchased a chair which had belonged to Thomas Whaley and placed it in the front parlor. Soon after, a mist was occasionally seen in the chair or near it. In other parts of the house, especially upstairs, inexplicable shadows and mists began to appear. George Carroll swears that he saw a man standing at the top of the stairs. He walked up the stairs and through the man. The man was still there when George turned around but faded and disappeared almost immediately.

"During the summer, we often smelled cigar smoke when we opened the house in the morning or at times when no one was around. Whaley was very fond of cigars and was seldom without them.

"The footsteps became varied. The heavy steps of the man continued as usual, but the click-click of high heels was heard on occasion. Once, the sound of a small child running in the upstairs hall was heard. Another time, I was alone with the woman who took ticket reservations for *Yankee Jim*. We had locked the doors and decided to check the upstairs before we left. We had no sooner gotten up the stairs than we both heard footfalls in the hall below. We listened for a moment and then went back down the stairs and looked. No one. We searched the entire house, not really expecting to find anyone. We didn't. Not a living soul.

"Well, this just about brings you up to date. I've been back a number of times since September but there's nothing to report except the usual footfalls, creaks, etc.

"I think that the play had much to do with the summer's phenomena. Costumes, characters, and situations which were known to the Whaleys were reenacted nightly. Yankee Jim Robinson certainly has reason enough to haunt. Many people, myself included, think that he got a bad deal. He was wounded during his capture and was unconscious during most of the trial. To top it off, the judge was a drunk and the jury and townspeople wanted blood. Jim was just unlucky enough to bear their combined wrath.

"His crime? He had borrowed (?) a boat. Hardly a hanging offense. He was found guilty and condemned. He was unprepared to die and thought it was a joke up to the minute they pulled the wagon out from under him. The scaffold wasn't high enough and the fall didn't break his neck. Instead, he slowly strangled for more than fifteen minutes before he died. I think I'd haunt under the same circumstances myself.

"Two other points: another of the guides heard a voice directly in front of her as she walked down the hall. It said, 'Hello, hello.' There was no one else in the house at the time. A dog fitting the description of one of the Whaley dogs has been seen to run into the house, but it can never be found."

Usually, ghosts of different periods do not "run into" one another, unless they are tied together by a mutual problem or common tragedy. The executed man, the proud owner, the little girl, the lady of the house—they formed a lively ghost population even for so roomy a house as the Whaley House.

Mrs. Reading didn't mind. Except that it did get confusing now and again when you see someone walking about the house and weren't sure if he had bought an admission ticket.

Surely, Thomas Whaley wouldn't dream of buying one. And he was not likely to leave unless and until some action was taken publicly to rectify the ancient wrong. If the County were to reopen the matter and acknowledge the mistake made way back, I am sure the ghostly Mr. Whaley would be pleased and let matters rest. The little girl ghost had been told by Sybil Leek what had happened to her, and the lady goes where Mr. Whaley goes. Which brings us down to Jim, who would have to be tried again and found innocent of stealing the boat.

Of course, there is that splendid courtroom there at the house to do it in. Maybe some ghost-conscious county administration will see fit to do just that.

I'll be glad to serve as counsel for the accused, at no charge.

FOOTBALL
FAN-GHOSTS

$\mathcal{S}$usan D. of Columbia, South Carolina, was born in Texas. Her father had been in the military and after the last war her parents moved to South Carolina, where her father's family had lived for generations. Susan was the eldest of three sisters. They grew up in a small town in the upper section of the state and then moved to Columbia, where her father became the superintendent of a state boarding school for unusual students. At that point Susan was seventeen. Later she entered a local college and stayed for two years. When I met her, she was living with her husband, who was also in education, and they had a little boy. Because of a background of premonitions she had some interest in studying psychic phenomena, but this interest was rather on the vague side.

The first complete incident Susan can remember happened when she was just twelve years old. At that time she had spent the night with her grandmother, also named Susan. During the night the little girl dreamed her grandmother had died. She was awakened from her dream by her cousin Kenneth with the sad news that her grandmother had indeed died during the night.

There had always been a close relationship between her and her father, so when her father was taken to the hospital with a heart attack in 1967 she was naturally concerned. After a while the doctors allowed him to return to his home life, and by the time her little boy was a year old in March of 1968 her father seemed completely well and there was no thought of further illness on the family's mind. Two days after they had all been together for the first birthday celebration of her little boy she awoke in the middle of the night with an overpowering anxiety about her father's well-being. She became convinced that her father would leave them soon. The next morning she telephoned her sister and started to discuss her concern for her father. At that moment her father interrupted her call by asking her sister to get her mother immediately. He died on the way to the hospital that very afternoon.

Susan's father had a very close friend by the name of Joe F. with whom he had shared a great love of college football games. Joe F. had passed on a short time before. A little later, Susan and her husband attended a game at the University of South Carolina. This was in the fall of 1968. On the way to their seats Susan looked up toward the rear section of the arena and quickly turned her head back to her husband. She was so upset at what she saw that it took her a moment to calm down and take her seat. There, not more than eight feet away from her, stood her late father just as he had looked in life. Moreover, she heard him speak to her clearly and in his usual tone of voice. Her husband had not noticed anything. She decided not to tell him about it. As she slowly turned her head back to where they had come from she noticed her father again. This time Joe F., his life-long friend, was with him. The two dead men were walking down the walkway in front of the seats and she had a good opportunity to see them clearly. They seemed as much alive then as they had been when she knew them both in the flesh.

Susan D. had an aunt by the name of Mrs. V. They had frequently discussed the possibility of life after death and psychic phenomena in general, especially after the death of the aunt's husband, which had come rather unexpectedly. It was then that the two women realized that they had shared a similar extraordinary experience. Mrs. V. had also gone to a football game at the University of South Carolina, but her visit was a week later, for a different game than Susan's had been. Since the two women had not met for some time there had been no opportunity to discuss Susan's original psychic experience at the football game with her aunt. Nevertheless, Mrs. V. told her niece that something quite extraordinary had happened to her at that particular football game. She too had seen the two dead men watch the game as if they were still very much in the flesh. To Mrs. V. this was a signal that her own husband was to join them, for the three had been very good and close friends in life. As it happened she was right. He passed on soon afterwards.

Susan D. heard the voice of her father after that on several occasions, although she didn't see him again. It appears that her father interceded frequently when Susan was about to lose her temper in some matter, or take a wrong step. On such occasions she heard his voice telling her to take it easy.

JAMES DEAN,
AND LESSER
HOLLYWOOD
GHOSTS

*N*orth Beachwood Drive in Hollywood was an average street. Most of the houses on this particular block were two- or four-family houses divided up into apartments. Farther up the street was one of the major motion picture studios, but the block in question was rather quiet and not at all ghostly in appearance. The C. family moved into apartment No. 4 in one of the houses on the 1200 block in 1963. Mr. C. was an artist, and they had a four-year-old daughter at the time. The apartment was the only one at the top of a stairway, and anyone coming up those stairs would be a member of the C. family or someone paying them a visit.

Shortly after the C.'s had moved into their new apartment, they noticed some rather unusual things. After they had settled in the new place and started paying attention to the surroundings, they became aware of a strange phenomenon occurring every night between eight and nine P.M. Someone was walking up their stairs. At first only Mrs. C. paid attention to it. Clearly the steps she heard were the footsteps of a very old person having difficulty ascending the stairs. The footsteps were deliberate and loud, slowing down and then picking up speed again. After a while they stopped, but no one was ever heard coming down the stairs again. This went on for several evenings in succession.

Mrs. C. realized that there was no one actually coming up the stairs, and she wondered if she was hallucinating. She therefore did not mention it to her husband. Several days passed. One evening, again at the same hour, her husband suddenly looked at her and said, "Quiet, I hear something." Both C.'s then clearly heard the same slow footsteps coming up their stairway. This time, however, they jumped up and tore the door open. There was no one there. Mr. C. immediately ran down the stairs as quickly as he could and looked around the corner and up and down the block, but there was no one to be seen. Mrs. C. then confessed that she had heard the same noises several nights in a row.

They decided to lie in wait the following night. Sure enough, between eight and nine pm someone unseen tried to come up their stairs, but when they ran out to look, there was no one about. They were puzzling as to what to do about this phenomenon when their neighbor, Peggy V., decided to spend a night with them. Her daughter and the C.'s daughter were playmates. That night, everyone was fast asleep—Mrs. V. on the couch in the living room and the C.'s in their bedroom—when an uproar woke them between two and three A.M. What woke Mrs. C. was an incessant scream coming from Mrs. V. As soon as she could be calmed down somewhat, Mrs. V. explained that she had been awakened by the sound of someone brushing his teeth and gargling in the bathroom. Puzzled as to who it might be, Mrs. V. had sat up on the couch. To her horror she clearly heard the dining room chairs in the dark apartment being pulled from the table, people sitting down on them, glasses being used and silverware tinkling, and muffled conversation. Since she knew very well that there was no one in the apartment but herself and the C.'s at the time, she screamed in absolute horror, unable to understand what was happening.

In conversation the following morning, Mrs. C. discovered that her neighbor had some occult interest in the past and was apparently "mediumistic." The C.'s themselves were not hostile to the idea of ghosts. Both of them were slightly interested in the occult and had a few books on the subject in their library. Mr. C. had always felt that ghosts were indeed possible, although he had never thought of having some of his own in the place where he lived.

The next day Mrs. C. went to see the owner of the building. After some hesitation, the landlady, Mrs. S., admitted that the previous tenant of their apartment had committed suicide in it—as a matter of fact, in the very bed in which the C.'s were now sleeping. That was quite enough for the C.'s. They decided to move out of the apartment. When Mrs. S. was told of their determination to live elsewhere, she gave them an argument. "The old lady was a wonderful person," she exclaimed. "It is not a shame to commit suicide." Tactfully Mrs. C. explained about the phenomena they had witnessed.

Mrs. C. had had no ESP experiences either before or after living in the apartment on Beachwood. Nor had she any desire to again experience anything like it. One ghost was quite enough for her.

Polly Blaize was a lady in her early fifties, filled with the joy of life and spilling over with the excitement of many experiences with the world of spirits. She came from a distinguished old New England family; many of her ancestors were either passengers on the *Mayflower* or early colonial dignitaries, and she counted two American presidents, Franklin Pierce and John Tyler, among her near relatives. Of Scottish background, she left New England at an early age to come to Hollywood, where she worked briefly for Warner Brothers. An early marriage proved a failure but left her with two small children. She had a succession of various administrative jobs, and she had remarried in 1965. Her second husband was a design engineer working for NASA. Polly—or as she was more formally known, Pauline—later lived with her husband in one of the beach communities south of Los Angeles, but the experiences I am about to relate happened to her when she lived in and around Hollywood.

Not long after she had moved to California with her parents, Polly became friendly with a young boy named Billy Bennett. They were teenagers together when their families lived across from each other on Highland Avenue in Hollywood. Billy lived in an apartment that was part of a row of one-story apartments of the court type. The apartments have long since been leveled. His mother was then a famous silent screen star by the name of Belle Bennett, best known for her starring role in the 1925 version of *Stella Dallas* with male lead Ronald Colman.

Time passed, and Pauline was married. Her first marriage did not last very long, and she found herself at age twenty with the responsibility for two small children: a one-year-old daughter and a two-year-old son. One night she was in bed, fully awake, when she heard the shrieking sounds of what seemed to her like a flock of birds. The window was open and she heard the birds coming through it, hovering around her with the sound of beating wings. The sound was so loud she could barely hear the human voice in the midst of this flock of birds. There was nothing to be seen, but the voice was that of Billy Bennett. "Beware of people who can hurt you, I still love you; I am ever near to protect you," the voice said, over and over. All this time she could see absolutely nothing but the darkness of the room.

Only a few days before the incident, Billy had died suddenly at the Presbyterian Hospital in Hollywood. His warning proved to be accurate indeed. For many years Mrs. Blaize lived almost as a recluse, until she met her second husband and married again, this time with happier results.

But the incident that has etched itself most deeply into her memory took place years later when her daughter was five years old. They had just moved into a one-bedroom apartment on Cheremoya Avenue in Hollywood. It consisted of a living room and a bedroom, and between the two was a dressing room large enough to contain a chest of drawers, a counter, and a large dressing mirror. About a week after they had moved into this apartment, Polly was suddenly awakened by the sound of what seemed to her like a heavy thud. It sounded as if a human body had dropped, followed by what sounded like a body pulling itself across the living room floor, from the dressing room area halfway to the kitchen, which was located on the other side of the living room. At first Polly paid no attention to these odd sounds, but when they repeated themselves exactly in the same manner at exactly the same time night after night, she became alarmed. Much later, she learned that her little girl was just as much aware of these sounds as she was.

Polly decided to make some inquiries of the landlady. The latter, named Beatrice Scriver, listened to the account of the nightly disturbances and then turned white. Since everyone in the building, which contained eight apartments, seemed to be familiar with the story, there was nothing for Mrs. Scriver to do but to let Polly in on the secret.

Prior to Polly's moving into the apartment, the place had belonged to a woman and her nineteen-year-old son. The young man was a successful athlete and had high hopes for a professional career. Suddenly he was informed that he would have to lose one of his legs because of severe illness. After he had been given this verdict by his doctors, the young man returned home and in front of his dressing room mirror shot himself to death. He fell to the floor, his body hitting it near the dressing-room door. Not quite dead, he pulled himself into the living room, pushed himself up on one elbow, then dropped again to the floor, only to try to pull himself up again. He did this several times in an effort to reach his mother, who was then in the kitchen. Because she had the water running, she had not heard the shot through the closed door.

Polly shuddered—Mrs. Scriver had described the exact sounds she had heard night after night in her apartment. But there was still another sound she wanted an explanation for. It sounded to her as if a basket were being pulled along the floor. The landlady nodded grimly. The young man's body had been taken out of the apartment in a basket, down the back stairs and to the morgue.

But that was not the end of the story by any means. Being spiritually attuned, Polly realized she had to help release the young man from his sufferings. Quite obviously, she argued, he did not realize what had happened to him. (In the intervening time, the young man's mother had also passed away.)

Polly thanked the landlady for the information and went back to her apartment. Her eyes fixed themselves on the dark rug on her living room floor. Turning the carpet back, she noticed a large brown stain and realized that it was made by the young man's blood. That was all the proof she needed. That night she waited until the sounds started up again. Speaking in a soft voice, she then called him by name.

"Your mother has gone ahead of you and is waiting for you; do not keep her waiting any longer," she said, pleading with the unseen presence. There was only silence.

Several nights in a row she spoke the same words, and finally there was a sound in answer to her pleading. She was seated in a chair near the spot where he had died when she suddenly heard a long, drawn-out voice as if called to her from far away, saying, "Mama—help me." The voice sounded hollow, as if it were coming from some distant place, but she heard it clearly and responded. For a while the sounds continued. Polly did not give up; she kept repeating her plea, asking the young man to reach out to his mother so that he could be free from the unhappy surroundings where he had died. Ultimately the message got through to him, and just as suddenly as the phenomena had entered Polly's life, they stopped. With a sigh of relief Polly Blaize realized that she had successfully freed the ghostly young athlete.

Lise Caron and her husband Leo moved to Los Angeles in 1965. The family had originally lived in Paris, but the two older daughters, named Liliane and Nicole, had decided to strike out on their own and go to the United States. They liked it so much they induced their parents to follow them. Thus Mr. and Mrs. Caron and the third daughter joined the two young women in Los Angeles in a house at El Centro Avenue in the 1200 North block. A cluster of houses in the Spanish style was arranged around a narrow courtyard, open on one side toward the street. The landlord occupied the house at the bottom of this cluster of houses, and the apartment that was to be the home of the Carons was the first one on the right.

Liliane had been married a short time before her parents' arrival in Los Angeles and had moved out, leaving Nicole the sole occupant of the apartment. Nicole had decided that the place was too small for three additional people and had therefore rented a single apartment close by, intending to leave her former apartment to her parents and their youngest daughter.

When Lise Caron arrived at the house, she had a good impression of it. The street was quiet, the house, though old, seemed in good condition, and she felt that they would be happy in it. The apartment itself consisted of a good-sized living room separated from the dining room by a folding door.

At the time of their arrival, the dining room had been transformed into a bedroom for Martine, the youngest daughter. Between the dining room and a short hallway stood a chest of drawers. On top of the chest a candle was burning. Surprised, Mrs. Caron turned to her daughters, asking why they were burning a candle. The answer was an evasive one, but Lise was too tired from the long journey to pay much attention to it. Thus, when Nicole implored her mother to leave the candle in its place, she nodded and went on to other things. To the right side of the hallway was a bedroom in which stood two beds separated by a night table with a lamp on it. To the left of the hallway was the bathroom, and in front of the dining room door was the kitchen door. This kitchen door would swing with a particular noise as it went from one side to the other. In every room there were flowers and green plants helping to create a happy impression. The Carons were so happy to be together again after the long separation that they lingered over their dinner. It was quite late when they decided to go to bed.

Mr. and Mrs. Caron went to their bedroom, while Martine closed the folding door between the bedroom and the living room. She then went to bed in her makeshift bedroom in the living room.

Almost as soon as Mr. Caron lay down he was asleep. Mrs. Caron was still in the bathroom when she suddenly received the impression that there was someone observing her. Turning around, she saw no one. She continued with her chores, but again received the distinct impression that someone was standing at the bathroom door staring at her. Turning around again, she said, "Is that you, Leo?" But a look into the bedroom convinced her that her husband was fast asleep. She decided to see whether Martine might have gotten up and come in to see her.

Martine was still up, and when her mother came over to her she seemed to have a strange look on her face. "What is wrong?" Mrs. Caron asked her daughter.

"I don't feel comfortable here," the girl said, and explained that she had a strange feeling of a presence. Mrs. Caron did not wish to upset her youngest daughter, so she made light of this, at the same time opening the folding door to change the atmosphere of the room. The only light came now from the flickering candle, and that too helped to create somewhat spooky impression. But since everyone was tired, she did not want to make an issue of it and decided to find out about the candle later. Then she returned to bed. As soon as she had lain down, she again had the feeling of another presence.

But the next few days were too exciting to leave room for worry about the impressions of that first night, and in the end she ascribed her strange feelings to the need for adjustment to new surroundings.

Unfortunately, the impressions continued night after night. A few days after their arrival she woke up to the noise of the kitchen door swinging. She thought that her husband had gone to the kitchen to get a drink. But a glance at his bed showed her he had not. A little later, she awoke again to see someone standing between their two beds. She thought her husband had gotten up, but to her surprise saw that he was fast asleep. In fact, she could see right through the strange person standing between the two beds. She sat bolt upright, her heart pounding, looking straight ahead at the apparition. At that moment, the stranger vanished into thin air.

She awakened her husband and told him what had happened. Quickly he put on his coat and ran around to the outside of the house, thinking an intruder had somehow gotten into the apartment. But there was no one about.

The next morning she decided to talk about this with her older daughters. It was then that she received an explanation for the strange goings-on and the flickering candle on the dresser. When the two girls had first rented the apartment, they too had the feeling of a presence with them. At first they had been rather scared by it, but after some time they ignored the unusual impressions, preferring to live with whatever it was that was disturbing in the atmosphere rather than to look for a new apartment. This had gone on for some time, when one night they were aroused by the noise of the kitchen door opening. Both women woke up simultaneously fastening their eyes upon the darkness of their bedroom. There between the two beds stood a man. Their first thought was that a burglar had gotten into the house. But, as they jumped from their beds the apparition vanished. A quick check of doors and windows disclosed that none of them was open, nor was there anyone outside.

Several days later Liliane heard the same noise again. Bravely she opened her eyes and saw a white apparition close to Nicole's bed. Again she sat up in bed, and the apparition vanished. She was not sure, but the second apparition might have been that of a woman. After that the two women decided they needed the help of a medium and went to see famed clairvoyant Brenda Crenshaw. Mrs. Crenshaw, wife of newspaper writer James Crenshaw, had been a practicing medium in the Hollywood area for many years and had an impeccable reputation for honesty and accuracy. After a few minutes the two women were told that the medium saw the problem surrounding them quite clearly.

It appeared that a young couple had committed suicide in the apartment some time before. On checking this they found the information to be correct. From that moment on they decided to place a candle in the apartment and to pray for the unfortunate ones every day, in the hope that they might find peace. With their daily prayer becoming part of the routine, they managed to continue living in the haunted apartment.

Mrs. Caron wasn't exactly ecstatic about the idea of continuing to live with the ghostly couple. On the other hand, she thought that perhaps she might release them. She promised herself to stay calm should anything further occur. Her opportunity came a few nights after her conversation with her daughters. She woke up again to the sound of the kitchen door opening by itself. Slowly Mrs. Caron looked up and saw a young man standing between the two beds, close enough to be touched. He was standing near her husband's feet. Mrs. Caron could see him very clearly. He was a short man, with curly hair, but since his back was turned toward her she could not see his face. She estimated that he was between thirty and thirty-five years old. He stood there without moving, as if transfixed. Mrs. Caron hoped that he would turn around so she could see his face, but he did not. After a while the apparition started slowly to vanish, until it was completely gone. He never returned to the apartment visually, but his influence could still be felt for a long time after this incident.

Continuing their prayers for the release of the unhappy couple, the Carons nevertheless felt that their apartment was not exactly a happy one and decided to move just as soon as they could find another place.

I spoke to Mrs. Caron in 1970 and found that all was well in their new place. She had no idea as to what had happened to the apartment on El Centro Avenue but readily supplied me with additional information about the landlord. In October of 1972 I drove to the house on El Centro Avenue in the company of Paula Davidson and her brother.

Walking about in front of the apartment, Paula felt nothing in particular. As for me, I felt rather depressed at the sight of this cluster of houses, which somehow reminded me of something out of Hollywood's past, but that may have been due to my knowledge of the incidents just described. Bravely I rang the doorbell. A dark-haired middle-aged lady opened the door, peering out at me, wondering what I wanted. I explained that I was writing a book about Hollywood; not saying that I meant *Haunted Hollywood.* I asked the lady whether she knew anything about the background of her apartment.

"I am sorry I can't help you," she replied politely. "I have been living here only two years."

"Is there anything special that you might have observed during those years?" I asked.

The lady shook her head and smiled rather wryly. "Nothing really. Except that I've been very unhappy here. I've had nothing but bad luck ever since I moved into this apartment. I haven't the vaguest idea why."

Anyone who thinks that such experiences are rare and happen only to the imaginative or perhaps those who are "believers" just doesn't know his or her facts. I have hundreds upon hundreds of parallel cases in my files, all of them reported by sane, sensible and rational people from every social and economic level. These incidents occur in new houses as well as in old ones. Take the case of Mrs. Barbara McDuffa, a lady who later moved to West Los Angeles. She had gone through a harrowing and, to her, inexplicable experience which preyed on her mind until she could find some sort of explanation for it. She needed a "rational" explanation, because otherwise there was the suggestion that she had perhaps imagined the whole thing or that there was something wrong with her powers of perception. Eventually she heard of my work and telephoned me while I was on the Gil Henry radio program in the area. We talked about the matter, and I assured Mrs. McDuffa that there was nothing wrong with her mind, her eyes or her hearing. It just happened that she had moved into a haunted apartment.

In the late 1960s, Mrs. McDuffa, her mother, and her son David moved into a brand-new, never before-lived-in apartment on Roscoe Boulevard in Panorama City, a community at the end of Van Nuys, which in turn bordered on North Hollywood. At that time Mrs. McDuffa scoffed at the supernatural or the notion that there might be ghosts or haunted apartments. If anyone had mentioned such possibilities to her, she would have thought him insane or jesting.

The first night after they had moved into the new apartment, they went to bed fairly early, because there remained much work to be done in the morning. It was a warm night and Mrs. McDuffa couldn't sleep. She decided to get up and open the bedroom window. As she started for the window, she suddenly perceived a tall figure of a man, wearing an overcoat and hat, standing in the closet doorway at the foot of the bed. Mrs. McDuffa had left the closet door open, but there wasn't anything in it as yet since they hadn't unpacked their things. When she saw the figure she rushed for the light switch. As soon as the light went on the figure disappeared. For a moment Mrs. McDuffa was stunned, but then she assumed that she had had an hallucination and went back to bed.

The following night she was awakened from a deep sleep by the sound of footsteps on the carpet. As she was trying to get her bearings, she noticed that her mother had been awakened by the same noises. It sounded as if someone were walking on the carpet, shuffling his feet, yet there was no one to be seen. The two women exchanged experiences but eventually put them out of their minds, since there was a great deal of work to be done in the apartment, and no one had much time to think about such matters as the supernatural.

The footsteps, however, continued for several nights. They were now joined by a tapping sound on the window of the bedroom. Since there weren't any shutters or trees or bushes or anything else near the window that could have caused this noise, they were puzzled. Worried that the unseen phenomena might upset the little boy, the ladies then put the boy's bed into their room and shut the door of the other room at night. Still thinking that it might be a prowler or some other physical force, they pulled a dresser up in front of the door so that no one could enter. The door of the bedroom opened into a little corridor. There was no direct access to either the windows or the entrance door of the apartment. That night, as if in response to their new security measures, the closed bedroom door started to rattle. The door-knob moved as if someone were trying to get in. The force rattling the door was so strong that only a wind of hurricane force could have caused it. Nevertheless, it was totally quiet outside the house; none of the windows were open, and there was no natural explanation for the rattling sound or the movement of the door-knob. The women had to conclude that they had been "blessed" by a ghost.

One day Mrs. McDuffa was combing her hair in her bedroom. Suddenly she felt a pressure on her shoulder and then felt something brushing her cheek as if an unseen person had passed very close by her. She turned around, but again there was no one to be seen. Shortly after this experience she heard the noise of a glass being put down as if someone had taken a drink of water in the kitchen. There was no one in the kitchen at the time. Several days after this experience, Mrs. McDuffa, now fully aware that there was something strange going on in their apartment, went to bed, turning on the bedside lamp in order to read. The moment she had turned it on, the lamp went out by itself. Three times Mrs. McDuffa turned it on, only to see it go out of its own volition. She checked the bulb, but it worked perfectly in other lamps. The next day she called in an electrician and had the switch examined as well as the lamp. He could find nothing wrong with either. That night she turned the lamp on again and nothing went wrong with it. Apparently her unseen visitor had decided to leave things well enough alone for that night.

Several days after this experience, Mrs. McDuffa was getting ready to go to work. It was a dark, rainy morning, and as she shut the door she looked back toward the apartment. A bright light shone across the living room as if the sun were shining in. Both her mother and her son saw the same thing and looked at her in amazement. There was no way such a light could have appeared in her living room.

One evening everyone had gone to bed; the hall light was left on and the door between the two bedrooms stood open. Mrs. McDuffa was looking toward the open bedroom door when she suddenly became aware of two roundish shapes made of a white, cloud-like substance. It seemed to her to resemble in a vague way the outlines of a human figure, but no details could be seen. As she observed this apparition in a state of shock mingled with fascination, the whitish shape slowly drifted into the second bedroom and disappeared.

But that was the end of the trail as far as Mrs. McDuffa was concerned. The following day she made arrangements to move. They had lived at the apartment for less than three months. Since she had lived in many places before without encountering anything unusual, Mrs. McDuffa became convinced that she had somehow stumbled upon a very haunted apartment. She has no idea who the apparition might be, nor did she make any inquiries with the landlord. All she wanted was to get out of the place, and fast.

John K. was twenty-six years old, lived in Hollywood and worked as a freight cashier at a steamship company. "I don't quite know where to begin," he said when he contacted me in May of 1971. He explained that he felt he was being harassed by reincarnation memories or by someone he thought was in some mysterious way connected with his personality. Since I was always on the lookout for "evidential" reincarnation cases, I was naturally interested. In October of the same year we met at the Continental Hotel in Hollywood. Mr. K. turned out to be a slight, quiet-spoken young man far from hysterical and not particularly involved with the occult. Gradually I pieced his amazing story together and discovered what lay at the base of his strange and terrifying experiences.

John K. was born in a small town in the Ozarks with a

population of only forty-two people. The house he was born and raised in was quite old, built before the Civil War. His family lived there until he reached the age of twelve, when they moved to another small town in southwestern Arizona. There his father was employed by the government on a nearby Army base. At the age of twenty, Mr. K. dropped out of college after his junior year and headed straight for Los Angeles, where he had lived ever since.

His first twelve years in the Ozarks were spent on a farm with five brothers and two sisters. The family lived a very primitive life. There was no indoor plumbing; heat was provided by a coal stove, and each Saturday night the entire family would take turns bathing in the same tub of water. At first there was no electricity in the house. For the first three grades, Mr. K. went to a one-room schoolhouse. "Our teacher was very young and had not yet finished her college education but was permitted to teach us anyway."

Mr. K. explained, "The reason I am relating all of my earlier surroundings to you is to point out the fact that the first twelve years of my life I lived a very isolated existence." Until he reached the age of ten, Mr. K. had not seen a television set; entertainment in his family consisted mainly of playing cards and talking. He attended the local Southern Baptist Church, into which he was duly baptized; however, after the family left the farm they dropped out of organized religion.

From an early age John K. received the impression of a presence that no one else could see. None of his immediate family had ever been out of the country, yet he was aware of the presence of a French lady whose name, he came to know, as Jacqueline. When he mentioned the presence of this woman to his family he was laughed at and told he had a fantastic imagination, so he stopped talking about it. At an early age he also developed the ability to dream of events that later happened exactly as seen in his dreams. These prophetic dreams did not forecast great events but concerned themselves with everyday matters. Nevertheless, they were upsetting to the boy. He never remembered his dreams, but when the event became objective reality he started to shiver and realized he had seen it all before. This, of course, is called *déjà vu* and is a fairly common ESP phenomenon. He could not discuss his dreams with his family, since psychic experiences were not the kind of thing one could talk about in the Ozarks in the early fifties. But he hated to stay in the house alone; he had a terrible fear of darkness and of the house itself.

One afternoon when he was ten years old, he happened to be in the house alone, upstairs in the back bedroom. All of a sudden he knew there was a presence there, and the most horrifying fear swept through him, as if he were being chocked to death. The walls seemed to vibrate, and he heard a loud sound for which there did not seem to be any natural explanation. Eventually he was able to break out of his terror and flee down the stairs.

There was something else that seemed strange to John K. from an early age on. He could never relate to men and felt completely at ease only with women—his grandmother, his mother, and his older sister. When he was very young, he began playing with his older sister, six years his senior, and enjoyed playing girls' games tremendously. He would never join his brothers in boys' games. He loved wearing long flowing dresses, fashions of an earlier time that he had found in the attic. Whenever he wore these dresses, he felt completely at ease and seemed to have a rather sophisticated air about him. The strange thing was that he insisted on wearing only those dresses of an earlier period of history; the shorter dresses of the current era interested him not at all. At those times he felt as though he were another person.

It was during those early childhood days that he first became aware of Jacqueline. Especially when he played with his sister, he felt that he was sexually just like her. He continued to wear dresses around the house until the time he started to school. Often when he came home from school he would go upstairs and put on his dresses. Finally, his father became aware of the boy's tendency and threatened to send him to school wearing a dress if he didn't stop, so John stopped. However, the impression of a female life inside him and the desire to wear long dresses persisted.

"Needless to say," he explained in complete frankness, "I was not the average run-of-the-mill boy, and I turned out to be very effeminate and was teased constantly by my schoolmates." Rejected by the other boys, he began to turn within himself and did not bother to explain his ideas to others. Although he had never traveled outside the four southern states surrounding his native village, he began to feel very emotional about France, particularly Paris. "I somehow seemed to have fond memories of a life of many human pleasures, a life of a woman who was very aware and felt a need to express herself totally," John K. explained, adding that he knew by that time that Jacqueline, whoever she might have been, had led the life of a prostitute. He thus had a sense of heavy religious condemnation, of being a wicked sinner with the threat of hell hanging over him.

When the family finally moved to Arizona, he thought that perhaps some of his agonies would subside. But the conflict between his present surroundings and the world of Jacqueline increased almost daily. At the age of fourteen he felt that since he could not belong to this world he might as well kill himself and return to where he really belonged. He wrote a farewell note to his mother, the only one to whom he could relate at the time, his sister having married and his grandmother having grown old and feeble. In the note he told his mother that he was going to return to where he belonged, that he felt he had come from another planet and it was time for him to go back. He then ran a rope over one of the rafters in his room, put a chair under it, and placed the noose around his neck, ready to jump. Then fate intervened in the person of one of his mother's friends who had stopped by unexpectedly. Since his mother was asleep, John had to answer the door. The visit lasted a long time, and by the time the lady had left he was no longer in the mood to take his own life.

From then on he did rather well in school, although most people thought him too shy and introverted. He never dated girls, since he felt himself female. But he did make friends with one particular boy and remained close friends with him for ten years. Later, the boy moved to Los Angeles. When John K. dropped out of school in his junior year of college, he came to Los Angeles and moved in with his friend. At the time he was twenty years old. He still felt like a female and was still continually aware of Jacqueline.

It was then that John became involved in the homosexual world and had the first sexual experience of his life. Whenever he had sexual relations, he felt strongly that he was fulfilling the part of the woman.

About six months after he came to Los Angeles, he started to have terrible dreams. One night when he was totally awake he suddenly saw a woman standing at the foot of his bed. She was wearing a long nightgown and had long hair and was smiling at him. She seemed to float just above the floor. At first John thought that it was his imagination and passed it off as a silly dream. The next night the same thing happened. He realized the apparition wanted to tell him something. Strangely enough, he wasn't particularly frightened. The third night the apparition returned, and her smile had turned into a frown of deep sorrow. She returned the following night, and this time her face showed utter terror. Deep veins stood out on her face, her eyes were bloodshot, and her mouth grinned hideously.

She returned once again the following night, and this time

her entire head had been torn off, and blood was spilled all over her beautiful flowing gown. John was fully aware of the utter torment of her soul. That same night something grabbed hold of his arm and forcibly yanked him out of bed and onto the floor. He screamed for help from his roommate, who was in the next room, but the young man had no compassion for his condition and yelled out for John to shut up or he would have him committed. After this incident John thought he was going mad and wondered to whom he could turn for advice.

A few months passed. He was still living in Hollywood with the same roommate but by this time was a prostitute himself. He had gone to college and found himself a good job, but he had had a strong urge to become a prostitute, and so followed it. Whenever he engaged in these activities he felt a very deep satisfaction. Also at this time he resumed wearing female clothes, and since his roommate was a make-up artist by profession, he would do the make-up for him. John would never go into the streets in this array; he would wear these clothes only at home. His friends began to call him Jackie, for Jacqueline.

Whenever he put on the clothes, John became another person. The first time he saw himself in complete make-up and female clothing he felt that Jacqueline had won at last. He now felt that she had taken total possession of him and that he was cursed for life.

"It was not a simple case of transvestitism or going in female drag," John explained, "It was a complete soul satisfaction on my part, and when Jacqueline came out she controlled me completely. She was very strong and I was very weak."

It finally reached the point that when John came home at night he would dress up in female clothing and spend the entire evening in this manner. He even slept in evening gowns. He removed all the hair from his body and delighted in taking baths and dousing himself with perfumes. This went on for two years, until John felt that something had to be done about it. He realized something was wrong with him.

About that time another friend introduced him to Buddhism. For three years he practiced the Buddhist religion, and through it was able to find many answers for himself that had eluded him before. Because of his devotion to Buddhism, Jacqueline finally left, never to return again. A new male image began to emerge slowly but surely as a result of his Buddhist practices, and once again he was able to relate to the environment around him and find a reason for living.

Through a friend, John received my address. He contacted me in the hope I might hypnotize him and regress him to an earlier life in which he might encounter Jacqueline. John was firmly convinced that his predicament had been due to an unfulfilled reincarnation problem, and that perhaps through hypnosis I might put him further on the road to recovery.

"I never felt fulfillment during my pre-Buddhist sexual contacts while portraying Jacqueline," he told me, "but it did satisfy my Jacqueline personality completely. But she is totally gone now and a new John is emerging—one who is not afraid of the dark anymore and who can live alone and stand on his own two feet, and who can have control over his life. I am very optimistic about the future."

Although neither John nor his immediate family had had any interest in or knowledge of occult practices, this was not entirely true of others in his background. An Aunt Mary had been a practicing witch, had owned many books dealing with witchcraft of the fifteenth and sixteenth centuries, and had been a sore subject in the family. Nobody dared talk about her. But she had died before John was born, and all knowledge John had of his Aunt Mary was necessarily secondhand. Nevertheless, there had been ESP talents in the family on his father's side, mainly messages from dead relatives, though John was never able to obtain any details. In his family the occult was something not suitable for family conversation.

After Jacqueline had left John, he kept having ESP experiences unrelated to his ordeal. They were not world-shaking experiences, but they did convince him that his ESP faculty had remained unimpaired by the hold Jacqueline had exercised upon him for so many years. A short time before our meeting there had been a steamship strike and he was laid off. He was wondering if he should get another job outside the steamship industry when he had a strange dream. In the dream he saw his boss at the steamship company coming out of his office and saying to someone, "Call John K. back to work." At the same time he saw the number 7 flash through the dream. Upon awakening he remembered every detail. On September 7 his boss came out of his office and told an aide, "Call John K. back to work," and, as foreseen in the dream, he returned to his former position.

I was rather interested in his continuing ESP experiences since I had begun to wonder whether Jacqueline was indeed a reincarnation memory or perhaps something else. We proceeded to begin hypnotic regression. I first took John K. down to age twenty, when he remembered every detail of his life. He even remembered the names of his best friends and what was on his desk at the time. I then took him back to age twelve and his life in Missouri. In each case he even knew his exact height at the time. He knew the names of the nearest neighbors, how many children they had and even the name of their dog. Satisfied that he was deeply in the third stage of hypnotic regression, I then took him back beyond the threshold of birth into an alleged earlier life. I worked very hard and very gradually to see whether we could locate some other personality that had been John K. in a previous lifetime, but he saw nothing. I then asked him to look specifically for Jacqueline.

"Do you know who she is?" I asked.

"She is someone who doesn't like me."

"Is she a real person?"

"Yes."

"Have you ever lived in France?"

"No."

I then took him as far back as the Middle Ages, fifty years at a time, in case there were other incarnations. When we got to the year 1350, he said he felt very strange and put his hands upon his chest in a gesture I interpreted as religious. But there was no recognition of another person. I then took him, step by step, back into the present, finally awakening him, and then inquiring how he felt. Since John was a good hypnotic subject, he remembered absolutely nothing of what he had said during hypnosis.

"Do you feel different from the way you felt fifteen minutes ago?" I inquired.

"Well, I had a headache before I came; I don't have a headache now."

He felt well-rested and satisfied with himself. Jacqueline had not put in an appearance, as she would have if she had been part of John K. I then explained to the young man that his ordeal had not been caused by reincarnation memories or an unfulfilled earlier lifetime. To the contrary, he had been victimized by an independent entity, not related to him in any way, who had somehow sought him out to serve as her medium of expression in the physical world. Jacqueline, the French prostitute, whose choice of clothes indicated that she had lived in the nineteenth century, wanted to live in this century through another body. For reasons of her own she had chosen a male body for her experiment.

If there was any reincarnation connection between the two, it remained obscure. There was, of course, the possibility that John K. had been in another life someone close to Jacqueline, in her time, and had since reincarnated while Jacqueline had not, and that the woman attached herself to John K. just as soon as she could after his birth into the present life. I myself tend to favor this theory. It is unfortunate that this earlier John K. could not be rediscovered either consciously or in hypnosis. But if this earlier incarnation had led a fully satisfactory life, the need to retain traces of memory would not be there.

In the case of Jacqueline, her inner conflict between what she was doing and the religious pressure exerted upon her must have been the compelling factor in keeping her in a time slot, or, rather, suspended in time, preventing her from reincarnating herself. In her predicament and frustration she needed to express herself through someone in the present, since she could not herself go on and be someone else. Deprived of her medium, Jacqueline perhaps will have found an avenue of escape into the next stage of existence and hopefully will not be heard from again.

When it comes to seeing the ghosts of celebrities, all sorts of people are likely to imagine they are in touch with their favorite movie star, when in fact they are merely expressing a wish fulfillment. In such cases, however, there exists a real attachment, an admiration for the personality involved. Frequently the people who have such fantasies are fans who have never met the star in question but wish they had.

Not so with attractive Doris Danielson, a Texas divorcee whom I met in Houston, after she had requested my help in clearing up the mystery of her psychic experiences. Then in her thirties, she worked as a secretary.

"Miss Danielson, have you ever had any interest in psychic phenomena since you have grown up?" I began my questioning.

"No, I haven't."

"Have you had any experiences whatever that you might classify as psychic besides the one we are about to discuss?"

"No."

"When did this phenomenon take place?"

"It was in March of 1957. I was about to be discharged from the Air Force and was staying with a friend, Roger Smith, overnight. His house was in Trenton, New Jersey. I had been a stewardess, and I was planning to leave for New York to try to get into modeling. This happened the night before I left.

"I woke up for some reason in the middle of the night and crawled to the edge of the bed on my hands and knees. I asked myself, why did I wake up? I couldn't think of any reason. Then I looked at the door—it appeared to be getting brighter! Then a circle formed in the middle of the door. It was red. The circle started coming toward me. And inside the circle was James Dean's head."

"Had you seen his face before?"

"I'd seen him in the movies, but I had no particular interest in James Dean; I simply thought he was a good actor. But I never thought about him. The only parallel in my life was that my boyfriend at the time resembled James Dean somewhat in his likes and dislikes, such as motorcycles, speed, and all that."

"Did he look like him?"

"Not really."

"How long did the image last?"

"I don't know, but I kept thinking if I stared at it long enough it might disappear. I stared, but instead it floated across the room, and only then did it disappear. It came from the door and floated toward me as I was sitting on the bed. Just a head in a circle."

"Did it speak?"

"No."

"Was there any form of movement?"

"I can't remember any form of movement. His hair was very curly. Suddenly, it was gone. I sat there and pinched myself to make sure I was awake. When it was gone I really became scared, and I prayed."

"Have you had any similar experiences before or after?"

"No. The only other experience I had was after I had moved to Houston. I was married then, and my husband had gone on guard duty and was to be away for two weeks. Two days after he was gone, this happened. I had just turned out all the lights and gone to bed. I heard somebody come down the hallway. I thought it was my husband coming back, although I wasn't expecting him. He was the only one who had a key. I said, 'Bob, is that you?' But there was no answer. Then I felt someone come right into the bedroom and stand by my bed. The springs of the bed creaked as if someone were sitting on it. I shot out of the bed on the other side and ran to the bathroom, where I turned on the lights. There was nobody in the bedroom."

"Was the house in any way connected with a tragedy?"

"No. It was a brand-new house when we moved in."

"Did the footsteps sound like a man's or a woman's?"

"I had thought it was my husband coming home, but I don't know how I could have heard footsteps, because there was a rug on the floor."

"Have you seen any James Dean movies since the first incident?"

"No."

One can only surmise that the late actor recognized Doris as a potential communicator, but somehow never got his message across the veil.

MRS. DICKEY'S
TROUBLESOME
GHOSTS

I heard about Lucy Dickey from a mutual friend in Washington. Nicole had met Lucy and heard about her disturbing experiences with ghosts. Nicole thought that perhaps I could help Mrs. Dickey either get rid of her ghosts, or at least come to terms with them. I readily agreed, and on May 11, 1968, we drove out to Vienna, Virginia.

When we arrived at the Dickey house, I was immediately impressed by the comparative grandeur of its appearance. Although not a very large house, it nevertheless gave the impression of a country manor—the way it was set back from the road amid the trees, with a view towards a somewhat wild garden in the rear. A few steps led up to the front entrance. After Nicole had parked the car, we entered the house and were immediately greeted by a lively, petite young woman with sparkling eyes and the aura of determination around her.

We entered a large living room that led to a passage into a dining room and then into the kitchen.

In the center of the ground floor was a staircase to another floor, and from the second floor, on which most of the bedrooms were located, there was a narrow staircase to a garret that contained another bedroom.

The house was beautifully furnished in late Colonial style, and antiques had been set out in the proper places with a display of taste not always met these days.

After I had inspected the house superficially from top to bottom, I asked Mrs. Dickey to sit down with me so we could go over the situation that had caused her to ask for my help. We sat in comfortable chairs in the downstairs living room, and I began to question her about the house.

"Mrs. Dickey, how long have you lived here?"

"About two and a half years. Myself and five children live here now. And we have two young foreign students living with us now; they've been here about a month."

"How many rooms are there in the house?"

"There are about twenty."

"*About* twenty? You're not sure?"

"Well, twenty. Real estate-wise we don't count the bathrooms, but I do."

"Yes, and the closets. Don't forget the large closets."

"I don't count closets."

"Did you know much about the house at the time you moved in?"

"Not much. Although we were told, before we purchased it, that it was haunted."

"By whom? I mean told by whom, not haunted by whom."

"By several people. The real estate woman mentioned it, but laughed about it, and I was intrigued. She said the house had quite a history, and there were many tales about what went on here. After we moved in, more people told us. I suspect they were trying to worry us a bit."

"What sort of tales did you hear before you moved in?"

"Just that the house was haunted."

"No details?"

"No."

"What was the first thing that made you think that there was something to these tales?"

"I was about the last member of the family to be aware that something was going on, but I had heard repeated stories from the children. I was sleeping in one of the children's rooms upstairs one night, and was awakened by heavy footsteps—not in the room but in the next room. I wondered who was up, and I heard them walking back and forth and back and forth. I finally went back to sleep, but I was kind of excited. The next morning I asked who was up during the night, and no one had been up."

"Who was in the rooms in which the footsteps were heard?"

"A six-year-old child was in one room, and my daughter, then eighteen, was in the other."

"In the room in which you thought the footsteps occurred, was there only the six-year-old child?"

"Yes, but the wall was where the old staircase went up. It's now closed off, but the staircase is still there, and I had the feeling it was either in the stairwell, or in the next room. But it felt as if it were right beside me."

"Have there been many structural changes in the house?"

"Yes."

"Did the steps sound like a man's or a woman's?"

"A man's."

"How long did it go on?"

"For at least ten minutes."

"Didn't it worry you that some burglar or a prowler might be in there?"

"No. We have dogs, and I thought it was probably a spirit."

"Do you mean you just accepted it like that without worrying about it?"

"I was a little frightened because I don't want to be touched, and I don't want to look up and see someone looking at me, but I don't care if they walk around!"

"This was the first thing you heard. What was the next thing?"

"I was sleeping in my son Douglas' room again, and I was having a very frightening dream. I don't remember what the dream was, but I was terrified. Suddenly I awoke and looked at the wall. Before I had gone off to sleep, I had noticed that the room had been sort of flooded with panels of light, and there were two shafts of light side by side, right directly at the wall. I sat right up in bed and I looked up and there was a shadow of a head. I don't know whether it was a man's or a woman's, because there were no features, but there was a neck, there was hair, it was the size of a head, and it was high up on the wall. It could have been a woman with short, bushy hair. It was so real that I thought it was Joyce, my daughter, who was about eighteen then. I said, 'Joyce' and started speaking to it. Then I realized it was waving a little bit. I became frightened. After about ten minutes of saying, 'Joyce, Joyce, who is it? Who is there?' It moved directly sideways, into the darkness and into the next panel of light, and by then I was crying out, 'Joyce, Joyce, where are you?' I wanted someone to see it with me."

"You still couldn't see any features?"

"No features at all."

"No body?"

"No body."

"Just a head?"

"Well, that's where the shaft of light ended. It was about that long, and it included the head and the neck, and nothing else showed because that was the end of the light on the wall. Then Joyce came in and I said; 'Joyce, look quickly,' and it was still there. But as I stared at this thing, it went out. It moved directly sideways and went."

"Did she see it too?"

"I don't know. You'll have to ask her when she gets here. She was quite excited. The next night we tried to get the panels of light to get back on the wall again. But we couldn't ever get the two panels of light there, and we still don't know what they were."

"Do you think these panels of light had anything to do with it? Were they from the moonlight, or were they part of this apparition?"

"That's what I don't know, but I would suspect that it had to have something to do with the thing that was there because we could never get the light back again."

"Was there any change in the atmosphere? Any chills?"

"I was extremely aware that there was something there."

"Did you feel cold?"

"Yes."

"What was the next event that happened after that?"

"In nineteen sixty-seven we decided to get a Ouija board. We had some friends who knew this house well, and said, 'You ought to work a board and find out what was there.' They owned this house for about ten or fifteen years, their names are Dean and Jean Vanderhoff."

"Have they had any experiences here?"

"Oh yes, definitely."

"When did they tell you about them?"

"After we noticed things."

"They are not here today, so can you briefly sum up what their experiences were?"

"Well, on several occasions they heard a woman talking in the kitchen when there was no other woman in the house. They heard the voice, and they also heard the heavy garage doors bang up and down at night, with great noise."

"What did the woman say to them?"

"Nothing to them. They were upstairs in bed, but they heard a woman talking. Also, very often they heard everything in the kitchen being banged, and thought all the china in the kitchen was being broken. A great clattering and banging."

"Now, you decided to tell the Vanderhoffs about your experiences?"

"Yes. We worked the Ouija board the night after I had seen

this 'thing' on the wall. We immediately got the names of people. There was a Martha and a Morgan, who communicated
with us."

"What do they tell you?"

"Martha said that it was she who was appearing on the
wall, because one child in the next room had fallen out of bed,
and Martha loves children, and tried to help. And Martha said
dear things about me—that I have a big job, and it's hard for
me to handle the children, and she's here to help."

"Does she give you any evidence of her existence as a person?"

"I think she and Morgan are brother and sister and they're
both children of Sarah. And Sarah was the first wife of Homer
Leroy Salisbury who built this house in eighteen sixty-five."

"Did you know at the time you worked the board that this
was a fact, that they had children by this name?"

"No. But we had been told that Sarah is buried here in the
yard somewhere with two children. I've searched the records
and I can't find the names of these children. I don't know for
sure whether Martha and Morgan are these two."

"But yet you do now know that there were such people
connected with this house."

"There were two children and there was Sarah. But we
don't know the names of the children."

"But you do know there was a Sarah."

"There definitely was a Sarah."

"Now, when did you find that out? That there was a Sarah?"

"Someone must have told me, and then I did find a record
about it."

"Was it before or after the first Ouija board session?"

"No, we got Sarah, the name, on the board; we didn't
know."

"You didn't know what it meant. It was afterwards, then,
that you discovered there was a Sarah connected with this

house. And she's buried on the grounds?"

"Yes."

"Still is?"

"Some people say they know where, but we don't."

"You haven't found it?"

"No. I've looked."

"What about the house now?"

"Homer Leroy Salisbury built it in eighteen sixty-five, and structural changes were made in nineteen thirty-nine, and then there has been some since then. Last summer I decided that I would enlarge the terrace because a lot of stones were here. We used all the stones that were here and did it ourselves.

"It was the night after we started tearing it all out and putting new footing down and all. It was the night after, two of my children, Lelia and Doug, had an experience that we thought was because we were making the big change. We worked the board every time we had something happen. But Martha and Morgan came and said they were not unhappy with the terrace."

"What was the next visual or auditory experience, apart from the Ouija board?"

"I have had no other, except a month ago I felt, but did not see, an apparition. That night, we had a big party here. A twenty-two-year-old woman named Nancy Camp offered to work the board. We had never met before. She and I sat at the board and started working it."

"And what happened?"

"The interesting thing was that immediately a new spirit came. His name was Adam, and he gave his last name—it began with a B, something like Bullock. He said he'd been slaughtered in the eighteen hundreds by Beatrice. Beatrice had killed both him and his daughter. He needed help. We asked, 'Would you appear?' He agreed to appear to the two of us only.

So we went to the back room, closed the door, and sat there."

"Did you actually see him?"

"I didn't, but Nancy did. I watched her as she saw him. She knocked me over backwards and the chair went in the air, then she knocked her chair down, threw the board in the air, and became absolutely terrified, and finally ran out the door."

"Who was this Adam?"

"I don't know."

"Was he connected with this house?"

"I don't know. But he appeared again, and she watched him for at least five minutes, and she described him."

"Since then, have you had any further disturbances?"

"Yes, I have. Since then it has been very difficult for me to sleep in my room at night. I'm very much aware that there's something there, in my bedroom. I definitely feel a presence."

"Is it a man or a woman?"

"Well, we worked the board and we were told it was Adam. I'd been compelled to look at the chaise lounge in the corner, and I didn't want to because I didn't want to be frightened. So I made myself not look at it, but I was terribly drawn to it, and when we worked the board the next day Sarah came and said, 'Adam was in your room, and I was in the chaise lounge, and I was there to protect you.'"

"You said earlier a lot of history happened here. You mean, on the grounds? The house is a hundred years old, but prior to that there was something here. Do you know anything about it?"

"Many people have said there was a house, the Town Hall, standing here that was occupied during the Civil War. But it was riddled with bullets, and it was burned down during the Civil War. This was a camping ground for both the Union and the Confederate armies. Slaves are buried in the yard—ten or twelve people have told me that."

"What about prior to the Civil War period?"

"I was told that there were tunnels here. This was a dairy farm and there's a tunnel from the barn, a walking tunnel. It is said that there are tunnels from the basement, but we have found nothing."

"Does this sum up your own firsthand experiences?"

"There is one more thing. This has happened to me many times in my bedroom, while I was in bed. Early in the morning I hear heavy footsteps, at least twelve of them, walking overhead. But there is no room to walk over my bedroom!"

"You mean, on the roof?"

"No, in the attic."

"Is it a male or female footstep?"

"I would think a man."

"Are these similar to the footsteps you heard when you were in your room and didn't get up?"

"Yes."

"Have you had experiences that I would call ESP experiences before you moved to this house?"

"No, but I've got one more thing to tell you. On a very hot summer night in June of nineteen sixty-seven I couldn't sleep. I woke up and went to my daughter's empty room, which is the little eleven-by-eleven top cupola. I had gone up there because I thought it would be breezy, and I tried to sleep. I was awakened by crying, whimpering, and moaning. I got up and walked around a couple of times, and it stopped. Then I went back to bed. About five times I had to get up because I heard moaning and crying. Finally I said to myself, 'Well, I've got two puppy dogs, it must be a dog.' I walked all the way down and went into the kitchen, but the dogs were sound asleep. I went back to bed in my own room. I had no sooner gotten into bed, when the phone rang. My daughter, then eighteen, had been in a very serious accident. My husband then slept with ear plugs and he would never have noticed the phone. I thought, I wouldn't have even been down here, had I not been awakened by the moaning and crying!"

"Was it your daughter's voice you heard?"

"Yes—she told me that she had been left with the most severely injured girl alone on the road, while the others went for help, and that the girl was crying and they were moaning; they were all crying and whimpering."

"Who else has had experiences in this house?"

"A friend, Pat Hughes, saw a woman here one night. Pat was here with a man named Jackson McBride, and they were talking, and at three o'clock I left and went to bed. At about four o'clock in the morning, Pat heard noises in the kitchen and thought that I had gotten up. She heard someone walking back and forth. Pat was over there, and said, 'Come on in, Lucy, stop being silly. Come in and talk to us.' And this apparition walked in, and then Pat said, 'It's not Lucy'—she realized that the ghost looked similar to me. It was tall and slim, had long dark hair, and had a red robe on and something like a shawl collar, and her hand was holding the collar. Pat was excited and said, 'My God, it's not Lucy! Who is it?' She said to this man, 'Come and look,' but he was afraid. Then Pat turned to go back and try to communicate, but it had vanished! Later, they heard a great rattle of things in the kitchen."

"How long ago did that happen?"

"About six months."

"Has anyone else seen or heard anything here?"

"One night Joe Camp, Nancy Camp's brother, saw a shadowy woman in white. On two different occasions."

"Anything else?"

"A year ago when we came home around eleven P.M. we found two of the children still up and frightened. I've never seen Douglas and Lelia so terrified."

"And what did they tell you?"

"I'd like Lelia to tell it to you herself."

I turned to Lelia, who was ten at the time, and encouraged her to speak.

"I was sleeping in bed," she began, "when I saw something go past the window. I said, 'Oh it's nothing, it's probably just the trees.' Then my brother saw it pass his window. He came out and we just started running around the house until Mother came home."

"What did it look like?"

"Sort of blurry—"

"Did you see a face?"

"No. Grayish. Sort of fuzzy. And a crinkling noise."

"And how long did it last?"

"About three to five minutes."

"We found a ring with three rubies in it, the night after this woman in red appeared," Mrs. Dickey interjected at this point. "She found it in her room. A lovely gold ring."

"Was it there before?"

"We never saw it before. Do you believe in animal ghosts?" Mrs. Dickey asked thoughtfully. "We had eleven people here once, in the living room and we were working the Ouija board one afternoon. Suddenly, and for no reason at all, we heard a big horse run across the front porch! We stared out the windows, but saw absolutely nothing. Still, we heard it; every one of us heard it!"

But Lelia had something more to tell. "A year and a half ago we had a farewell party for my sister's fiance—my other sister, Joyce—and on the side of the porch there was a coiled head."

"A head?"

"A head. Face. Coiled—like coiled—in a lot of wires. It had features, too."

"Male or female?"

"Man."

"How long did it last?"

"Fifteen minutes."

"And how did it go away?"

"It just went. Another time, my sister Joyce and I went down into the basement because we thought our father was there. We saw a coat hanging on the door, and all of a sudden this coat just moved. But our father wasn't down there."

"Is there any particular area of the house that is most involved in these activities? Or is it all over the house?" I asked Mrs. Dickey now.

"Under the staircase!" Lelia volunteered.

"If you were to draw a straight line from the basement to those upstairs rooms, what would you hit?"

"The basement, the stairwell, and the room upstairs, definitely; if you had to draw."

"To your knowledge, what was the upstairs' use? Who lived there in the old days? Were there small rooms up there?"

"There were small rooms, yes."

"Servants' quarters?"

"I doubt it. I know there were servants' houses around here—this was more or less the manor house. There were other servants quarters."

"So these were just small rooms on the top floor."

"Yes."

"What about the little room under the cupola?"

"That's where I had another experience," Mrs. Dickey exclaimed. "I was awakened at night, about three o'clock in the morning. Patty was out on a date, but I had told her to get in early. I heard heavy footsteps going up those old, tiny, narrow stairs to Patty's room. I called out, 'Patty, are you just getting in?' She didn't answer, and I got annoyed. I thought, why isn't she answering me and why is she making so much noise. So I went racing up the stairs and pulled down the covers, and she'd been sound asleep for hours. Another girl was with her, and they were both asleep, and I had frightened them. But the noise was so loud and so apparent, you could hear the leaning on the banister, every foot on the stair—"

"Was it like the other footsteps, the male footsteps that you heard?"

"Yes. Slow, methodical, steady, heavy footsteps."

"Did it sound as if somebody had trouble walking up?"

"No. Just walking up."

"As it is, we have two personalities to deal with, a woman and a man. Is there anything known about the house involving tragedy?"

"Not that I know of; I haven't been able to find it out. I had a maid about two months ago and she said, 'I haven't been in this place in years, but my uncle had been riding on a horse, and the horse reared and threw him up and hanged him in a tree.' And she pointed the tree out to me."

"Because the horse got frightened?"

"Threw him up in the air and he was hanged to death in the tree."

"What about that door in the wall? What is the history of that door?"

"A seventy-year-old woman has come here repeatedly to visit. She says she was born in this house; her name is Susan Richmond. She told me that when guests came, and the people in the house were in their aprons and wanted to get upstairs quickly and change, they would scoot up through the little door."

"This staircase was here from the beginning? Where does it lead to?"

"It's boarded over now, but it connected where the stairs are upstairs."

I finally questioned Joyce Dickey about her experiences in the house. Joyce, then twenty years of age, had been in the house with her mother from the beginning, two and a half years.

"You've had some experiences with your sister?"

"Yes. It was in the basement."

"Have you had any spontaneous experiences?"

"I would sit in the dining room, and all of a sudden it

would get really cold. I could feel a presence. One night we were listening to the record player when there was a sound like a huge waterfall—right by the back entrance. First, it sounded like water dripping down, and then it became like a big waterfall."

"You mean it sounded like it."

"Yes, sounded like it."

"Was there anything there?"

"No."

"Your sister said something about a coat in the basement."

"When we had first moved in here, I had to go down to the basement. My father's coat was hanging on the door, and it was kind of swinging. I opened the door and started to go down. There was this figure, supposedly my father, in front of me; I could just barely see a man's figure, walking down in front of me. I got down and turned on the light and looked around. My father wasn't there."

"But you saw a man?"

"Well—very faint."

"Did you see his face?"

"No—it was just the back, going down in front of me."

"Anything else that I ought to know?"

"I thought the last séance we had stirred things up."

"In which way?"

"The dogs were in the basement and they started to get upset, so I took them outside. One of them I couldn't get—she ran away, and I couldn't get her. into the kennel. But I got the other two in, and came back into the house. There was a noise in the kitchen, like somebody clinking against the pots and pans, and banging around. In the basement there was the sound of a man walking. Then the sounds stopped, and then they started up again, and it was dragging something along the basement floor—sounded like a big sack of potatoes. And then the dogs started barking really furiously. This was last winter."

"Did you hear the horse out front here?"

"Yes, I did. We were working with the Ouija board, when a huge horse just went clomping across the porch."

"On the wood, you mean?"

"On the wood! He just went clomping—! Like he was trotting. On the porch."

"And did you look to see if there was a horse?"

"Yes. It wasn't one of our horses."

"Where are your horses kept?"

"In the back."

"There wasn't any chance of one of them having gotten loose?"

"No. It was a big horse, and our little pony couldn't have made that much noise."

I thought of the man who had been "hanged" by his horse, and then turned my attention to Patty Dickey. Patty was almost eighteen.

"I haven't really had any experiences," she explained and smiled somewhat embarrassed. "Only one time, when my mother saw a figure in my little brother's room. That same night I woke up from a sound sleep and I felt something was in my room."

Despite their employing the Ouija board to make contact with the spirits or alleged spirits in the house, I felt that the Dickey family had indeed undergone some genuine psychic experiences. I was more convinced of this as I realized that the apparition and the auditory phenomena preceded any attempt to make contact with what was in the house by means of a Ouija board. I have never held boards of this kind in high esteem, and have on occasion warned against their use by children or by those likely to be mediums and not aware of it. Then, too, the information gleamed from the use of these boards is not very reliable on the whole. If anything tangible comes from their usage, it generally can also be obtained by other means, such as meditation, genuine mediumship, or automatic writing. But at the time when I had arrived at the Dickey homestead, the use of the Ouija board was already a matter of record, and there was nothing I could have done about it.

"It is quite clear you have a ghost, or possibly two ghosts, in this house," I said to Mrs. Dickey as I prepared to leave. "I'll arrange to come back with a competent medium sometime in the not-so-distant future, and we'll have a go at it."

Mrs. Dickey nodded enthusiastically. Her enthusiasm was such that I tried to come back immediately, but failed due to the fact that summer had come and I was off to Europe, as I did every year in those days.

It was therefore not until April 10, 1969 that I was able to arrange for a return visit to Mrs. Dickey's house. The house, by the way, was called Windover and stood on Walnut Lane, appropriately named that because there were tall old walnut trees on both sides of the street. We agreed that I would come down in the company of Mrs. Ethel Johnson Meyers, and on May 11, 1969, we arrived fully prepared to encounter whatever ghosts in the house wished to be talked to.

This time the living room downstairs was filled with several other people. I had never seen them before, of course, and I was later told that they were in some way connected with the house and the hauntings in it; but I suspect that they were more friends or curious neighbors who wanted to be in on something special. At any rate, they kept in the background and allowed Mrs. Meyers and me to roam around freely so that the medium could get her psychic bearings.

Ethel ascended the front steps like a bloodhound heading for prey. Once inside, she casually greeted everyone without wishing to be introduced any further. Apparently she was already picking up something in the atmosphere. Somewhat as an afterthought I started to instruct her in the usual manner as to my desires.

"What I would like you to do is—if in walking about freely, any impressions come to your mind, or if at any point you feel like sitting on a chair, do so, and we will follow you. And—if you have any feelings about the house—this is an old house. It will be a little difficult to differentiate between what is naturally here and these fine antiques, all of which may have some emanations. Apart from that, let me know if you get any response or vibrations."

"Well, there are a lot of things here, all right. But presently there is a tremendous amount of peace. Vitality and peace at the same time. But I'll have to get down lower in order to pick up other things. There is a catalyst around here, and I want to find that catalyst."

Ethel had now entered the living room and stood in the center.

"There's a woman coming close to me. There is also a man—I don't think he's old—he has all his hair. The woman is looking at me and smiling."

At this point, I had to change tapes. While I busied myself with the recorder, Ethel kept right on talking about the spectral man she felt in the atmosphere. As soon as my tape was in place, I asked her to repeat the last few impressions so I could record them.

"Is this name of 'Lewis' that you get connected with the man standing by the fireplace? Would you repeat that description again: gold-buckled shoes, and he had his elbow on the wooden mantlepiece?"

"Well, he has these tan trousers on, tight-fitting; definitely gold-colored or mustard-colored, cummerbund around here about so wide…"

"What period would he belong to?"

"Oh, I think he has his hair tied in a queue back here. It's grayish or he's got a wig on."

"Anything else?"

"He has got a blue jacket on that seems to come down in the back."

"Are there any buttons on that jacket?"

"Yes."

"What color are they?"

"Silver. "

"Why is he here?"

"He looks contemplative, and yet I feel as if he wants to grit his teeth."

"Is this a presence, or is this an imprint?"

"I think it's a presence."

"He comes with the house?"

"I would say so."

"Is there anything that is unfinished about his life?"

Ethel turned to the unseen man at the fireplace. "Tell me what's bothering you, friend. You have your eyes half-closed and I can't see the color of your eyes. Will you look around at me?"

I reinforced her offer with one of my own. "You may use this instrument to communicate if you wish. We come as friends."

Ethel reported some reaction now. "Oh! He's looking around at me. His eyes are a sort of green-hazel."

"Any idea why he is there?"

"He just disappeared. Like, went through here."

"Where did he go towards?"

"Went through here." She pointed towards the old stair-case in back of the room, where most of the manifestations had occurred.

"Follow the way he went!"

"I can't go through that wall!" She started walking around it, however, and I followed her. "This room was not there.

Something is different," she said suddenly and halted.

"Different in which way?"

"Is this part later?"

"I am told that it is later. What is different about that end of the house?"

Evidently she felt nothing in the more modern portion of the house.

"All right, we're going back to the older part of the house."

"You see, I can't hear anything there. Here is a man, with a lot of hair, sort of hangs down; has a drooping mustache and a beard"

"What period does he belong to?"

"Oh, this is much later, I would say."

I pointed towards the wall where so much had occurred: "Would you go to that wall over there. Just that general area, which is the oldest part of the house. I believe. I would like you to see whether this impresses you in any way."

"This man I was seeing is not around any of the people here, like those I saw a moment ago; not that late."

"Nothing contemporary?"

"No—there's nothing contemporary about the man I just saw there."

"Another period from the first one?"

"That is right."

"Two levels, in other words."

"There is a woman's voice, very penetrating; as I am getting her, she is very slim."

"What period does she belong to?"

"Around the same as the first man I saw. Do you notice a coldness in here? A difference in temperature? Something has happened right in here."

"You mean the corridor to the next room? It leads us back to the entrance door. What do you suppose has happened there?"

"There's been an acc—I don't want to say acc—I don't want to say anything but accident. There's been an accident, and a woman is screaming about it."

"You are grabbing your neck. Why?"

"She went out of her body here."

"Is she still here?"

"I would say she is. She's the thin woman I spoke of."

"Who is the person that is most dominant in this house at the moment?"

"I know that voice is terribly dominant, but the man in there was very dominant also." Ethel pointed towards the front hall again. "Can I go further in here?"

I nodded and followed.

"She cannot come through here. It is blocked. This was an opening, but there is something hanging there."

"What is hanging there?"

"I'm afraid it's the man I saw at the fireplace, in there."

"How did he die?"

"By the neck."

"Is this the man you called Lewis?"

"I think it could be. It is strange—while I am in this terribly depressed mood I can hear laughter and carrying-on about something of great honor that has happened, and it is being celebrated here. Somebody comes into this house with the greatest feeling of triumph, as it were; that they've conquered something. At the same time I'm pulled down like mad over here."

"When you say 'conquered,' are you speaking of a military victory?"

"I don't know yet, what it is. These are all impressions. I have to get much lower."

"I would suggest you find your way to a comfortable chair, and let whatever might be here find you."

But Ethel was not quite ready for trance. She kept on getting clairvoyant impressions galore.

"So many people are trying to come in. A heavy set man, kind of bald, here. Now there's another one. Now a girl, hair caught across and down in curls. She doesn't look more than ten or twelve."

"Is she connected with either the man or woman?"

"I would say around the earlier time, because she has a long dress on, down to here. Laced shoes, with ribbons tied here; you might call them ballet slippers. She has a very pointed little chin, and the eyes are sort of wide, as if they were seeing things. Then there is an older woman, with her dark hair coming down and then as if it were drawn up very high."

"Does she give you any names?"

"Anne or Annette. I get a peaceful feeling around this individual, with the exception that I seem to be communing with someone that I can't really touch."

"Would you mind explaining that?"

"Perhaps with a ghost I can't touch."

"Do you feel that they have something they wish to tell us?"

"We're not on speaking terms yet!"

"Well, perhaps Albert can catch them and tell us what they are about. If Albert would like to be present—"

But Ethel ignored my hint to let her control come in through trance. Not just yet. She was still rattling off her psychic impressions of this apparently very overcrowded house— spiritually speaking.

"Funny—there's a strange little dog, also, yonder. It looks something like a Scotty, but isn't. It has stiff hair."

"Does it come with any of these three characters you mentioned?"

"I think he belongs to the woman I just described. I have a feeling that I am seeing her for the first time, and that I heard her in the other room."

"The voices you heard before?"

"I think so. She looks terribly sad here. I know someone runs out that way."

"Why are they running out of the house?"

"I'm so reluctant to say that someone is hanging there...."

We sat down, and Ethel dosed her eyes. Patiently I waited for her spirit control, Albert to take over the conversation. Finally, after two or three minutes of silence, a familiar, male voice greeted me from Ethel's lips.

"Hello."

"Albert, are you in control?"

"There's strain, but I seem to be doing it."

"Do you have any information about this house, Albert?" I asked as soon as I was sure he was in firm control.

"You have come on a day very close to an anniversary of something."

"Can you enlighten me as to details?"

"The one who relives this is Emma."

"This Emma—what is her problem?"

"She is quiet, but he is tight-lipped. In advertent deception led to destruction of moral character. One person made a quick decision, 'I would be myself if you would let me free.' Details cannot be brought into the light, even though it was inadvertent. The attitude leading up to this situation was, if you die, your secret dies with you."

"But the other one can talk?"

"I will try to see if the other one will talk too, because it is within him the secret lies. If he will talk, so much the better. Because the other one knows not the secret of the woman."

"Can you give us the names?"

"There are two L's. Leon is one. I cannot tell you which it is now. There are two individuals, one who comes to visit the other. One who has sat in this vicinity and made his declaration. A declaration against an L, another L."

"What sort of declaration?"

"Opening up and giving publicly accounts that this one living here would keep a secret."

"What did the account deal with?"

"When one holds them quietly to themselves and desires not to give it, it is a law Over Here—you know this—so I would like to have him speak, rather than the woman, Emma, who is not completely aware of what was going on between the two L's."

"Is he willing to speak to us?"

"We are trying to get them to speak. However, he made the decision to do away with the whole business by destroying himself and taking it with him. He was alone when he did it. The other L has departed. He will not divulge his name."

"Do you know his name?"

"I do not. When it is held a secret, and it is here, I am not allowed to penetrate it until he will divulge it himself."

"Is he connected with this house as an owner?"

"I would say so."

"A long time ago?"

"It looks to me, turn of century."

'Which century?"

"Into eighteen hundred."

'Did he build the house?"

"I believe so."

"Then would he be the one that first lived here?"

"I believe this to be true. I'm looking as hard as I can, to see. There may have been transactions of another builder and his taking it over before too long. Somehow, there is some unsavory business, in the past. He is a reputable individual and cannot afford to allow some past things to come into the light."

"What was the disreputable business he was worried about?"

"Oh, I want Emma. She must never know—"

"There is only one way to do this. And you've got to do it the way I suggest."

"I will not go forever! I have lived, and I am living."

"Is this your house?"

"Go and seek Emma to stay away."

"All right. I will do that."

"She comes always to cry."

"Why is she crying?"

"Oh—I cannot stop her. Do not let me look on her."

"What have you done that you feel so ashamed of?"

"What is my own secret in my soul of souls. Must I look upon it forever."

"Or be reborn into a free and happy world."

"Beyond the life lies the deep dark pool in which oblivion covers you forever. That is what I seek."

"But you are still alive..."

"I am going there, friend. They won't let us live in silence."

"You have passed over. You are now speaking to us through an instrument..."

"I am living always."

"In spirit—but not in body."

"In body, too. I am in a body."

"Not yours."

"Mine."

"No. Lent to you temporarily, so you may speak to me. So we can help you."

"No one lends me anything. Not even a good name. The merciful God hates me..."

"Are these your hands? Touch them."

"My hands?"

"That's a watch you have on your hand—a woman's watch. "

"A woman?"

"You are in the body of a woman, speaking to me, through one of the great miracles made possible for you."

"Body. My body."

"Not your body. Temporarily…"

"Mine! How can you say, when the rope is still here?"

"There's no rope. It is a memory—an unhappy memory."

"Hang."

"You're quite free now."

"I can't get free from this!"

"Because you don't wish to. If you wished, you could."

"I live! How can I get to that Beyond?"

"If you leave your memories behind."

"The silence of the pool, of the blackness."

"I've helped you so far. Touch your left ear gently and I will prove it to you. You feel that there is an earring? Women wear earrings; you did not."

"Who did this to me?"

"Nobody did it to you. It isn't you."

"Makes talk so radical."

"There are things you don't understand about yourself, and I am here to teach you. You are free to go if you wish."

"Free, free! May I go then—into the blackness where it is no longer memory?"

"Yes, I will send you there if you wish. But you've got to be calm and listen to me. It's no use being angry and desperate."

"Who shackles me so?"

"Nobody shackles you. This is a woman's body, and you are speaking through her voice."

"Woman!"

"A lady who has been kind enough to help you."

'Who does it to me—these outrageous things?"

"You have passed into another dimension, another world, from which you are now speaking to us, by means that you do not understand. We are here to help you, not to make you unhappy. Would you like me to help you out of here? It is up to you."

"Out of here?"

"Into a better world, if you wish."

"Better world? This is oblivion?"

"You've got to ask for it. It cannot be done without your approval."

"I ask for it. I ask for that. Give it to me, give it to me."

"Then do you obey the laws to lead you there? There are certain laws. You have to follow them."

"Take my Emma. Take her into the happy land."

"All right. But in order for you to go, there is something you must do. Are you listening to me?"

"I hear. I hear."

"You must leave behind your unhappy memories."

"I can't leave them. They are part of me."

"You will give them to me, and I will take them out."

"But Leon—he will not leave me in peace."

"Leon is dead. He cannot touch you."

"Dead?"

"He's gone."

"Like that? Gone?"

"Yes. Many years have passed."

"Dead?"

"Dead. You're safe. Free."

"She will not know."

"No."

"I can see light again, and happiness, forgetful that he is gone?"

"He's gone."

"Then it will not be divulged."

"You cannot be free of it until you divulge it to me—only to me, and to no one else."

"When I go into oblivion, I can give nothing to anyone.

Let me live my life."

"Who is Leon? Who is he to you?"

"I must seal my lips. I must go my unhappy way."

"Then you will never be free."

"I must go into oblivion. You promised. You take away."

"I don't take away, but you promised to obey the law. The law is you must tell the story and then forget it."

"I tell it to my own soul. You are not God. And I have no obligation to anyone but my own God!"

I decided to find another approach. Evidently the discarnate spirit was a tough nut to crack.

"What year is this?"

There was only silence to the question.

"Who rules the country?"

"Thomas Jefferson."

"No, Jefferson is dead. This isn't Jefferson's day."

"Then I am dead."

"You are!"

"Let me go in peace. Good day!"

"You're dead, and yet you're alive. They are all alive, too, over there."

"Good day, my good friend. I can no longer speak. We do not exist on the same plane."

"No, we speak to each other through this lady. A hundred and seventy years have gone by, my friend, a hundred and seventy years. Do you understand? It is a hundred seventy years later. It's very difficult for you to understand this. You have been staying in this house for a long time for no reason, except to suffer. What happened to you, happened a long time ago. and it is all in the past. You are completely free. You needn't go into oblivion. You need needn't go anyplace if you don't wish. You're a free person."

"Ahh—and Emma?"

"She's just as free as you are. You have nothing to fear."

"My hands are free. My mind is free. Let me go with my own."

"Not until you tell me who you are. This is part of our deal, remember? If you're a man of honor you must obey the law."

"Until I find myself a man of honor—"

"You are."

"If there is a heaven above, if there is a golden light, and I am alive—these hundred and seventy years—man, are you mad? You do not speak the truth. I cannot trust you."

"It is the truth. You'll find out for yourself."

"Let me go. I have been always free."

"Very well then, tell the one who has brought you what you want to be kept a secret, that he may take you away from here."

"Emma—where is she?"

"She's over there waiting for you. They're all over there. Leon is over there, too."

"God no! Then I can't go! He will talk!"

"Then why don't you tell me? I can arrange it."

"No, you cannot. If I go into my grave with the secret, and my soul—"

"You are in your grave. You've been through the grave. You're out of it now. The secret is known."

"Then it is on my soul and it remains there."

"You can't be free with it. You must get rid of it."

"I have been told by those who have spoken to me from pulpits that if I take my great burden to Him beyond, I will never—"

"You will not succeed unless you wish to."

Again, I changed my approach, since the personality seemed unyielding.

"Is you name Lewis?"

"I will take that with me, too. I have pride, have soul, and a sense of being, and it is coming back to me. I am free. I feel it."

"Then go. Go in peace."

"Emma—I can look on you now."

"Albert, help him across."

"I can go with you now, Emma. I give you thanks, my friend. But I still maintain my freedom of soul."

"Albert, take him. Albert, please."

Immediately, Albert's crisp voice returned. "Yes, yes."

"Have you learned anything further?"

"I think he's right, my good friend. Confessions are not the best fate, and this is true."

"How did he die, and why?"

"He did it himself."

"It was suicide?"

"Yes it was."

"Why?"

"To keep from revealing the truth."

"What was so terrible about the truth?"

"That is his secret."

"What period was this?"

"It was the turn of the century I believe."

"Did he do anything wrong?"

"He has a guilt complex, that is quite certain."

"Did he tie his own arms and hang himself?"

"He put a rope around his neck—he put a rope around his hands in back of himself…"

"Who is this Leon he keeps yelling about?"

"An individual, I believe, he harmed. I would say that it was a ghost that taunted him."

"You mean the man died before him?"

"That is right."

"And Emma!"

"Emma saw the swaying body."

337

"Emma was his wife."

"That is right. There were three offspring."

"Is the girl one of them—the teen-age girl that the instrument saw?"

"I believe the granddaughter."

"Are any of them still here?"

"I do not see them. Emma is also listening, she has gone with him."

"Is anything buried in the garden?"

"Leon."

"Did he kill Leon?"

"I would say so."

"Oh, he killed him. For some reason?"

"Yes."

"You haven't got any idea what this is?"

"That would not divulge what had happened in their youth."

"What was this man's background?"

"I think he was a man of considerable wealth."

"He built this house?"

"That is right. Earlier. It could have belonged to Leon— that is, the property."

"Was he in any official position or just a businessman?"

"Man of fortune; let's put it this way. A gentleman."

"He's a bit insane, isn't he?"

"Well—when one lives for a hundred and seventy years with a memory of guilt, plus your throat being crushed by ropes and your arms being torn by the ropes that are on the hands…"

"Yes, it must be uncomfortable. Well, be sure the instrument is protected, and I suggest we bring her back."

"I will release the instrument."

"Thank you for coming."

A moment later, Ethel was back as "herself," remembering

nothing of the previous hour. I handed her the ring that so mysteriously appeared in the house and asked her to psychometrize it.

"I would say this belongs to an older woman. It would be mother to the younger woman."

"Do you get any additional information about this?"

"I would say an E. She's the mother of a younger woman, also with an E."

"That younger woman—what about her? How does she fit in?"

"The younger woman I think is the one I hear screaming. I feel this woman may even be seen sometimes. I want to rock, I want to rock. She says nothing, or does nothing, but just rocks. The younger woman, the thin woman, they seem concerned about each other."

I turned to Mrs. Dickey to check out some of the material.

"Mrs. Dickey, to refresh my memory, who built the house?"

"This structure was built in eighteen sixty-five by Homer Leroy Salisbury."

"But before that?"

"The records for those years are destroyed; the books are not in existence. But the basement foundation is much older. Revolutionary, perhaps. There are windows down there, and doorways. It may have been originally the first place that people lived in."

"Is there any record of the owner of the land before the turn of the eighteenth century?"

"Not that I know of."

"Have you ever seen a person in the area in which Mrs. Meyers felt the main disturbance?"

"I have not, but a friend has."

"Who was the friend?"

"Pat Hughes."

"What did she see or feel in that area?"

"She heard noises and footsteps, and saw a woman walking into this room, right by this wall. Walked right in and stood in the room."

"What did the woman look like?"

"She had dark hair, fairly young, tall and slender, with a red robe or long red dress on, and she had her hand up at her throat."

"What about the man Mrs. Meyers described?"

"Adam comes here, and we think he's harmful. He frightens us. Since I've seen you last, we've had something happen that we never had before. Joyce and Patty and I walked in here. It was a quiet day and we sat down on these two couches. It was evening. We were just talking quietly and had our mind's on Joyce's forthcoming wedding when we heard the most enormous noise—just like the whole house was crashing down. This wall over here almost vibrated. We all jumped up and we couldn't figure it out."

"There was nothing to cause it?"

"No. Again, during the night, a shattering noise woke up everybody."

Mrs. Jean Vanderhoff, who had formerly owned the house, was among those present. Long after she had left the house, she found herself working a Ouija board. To her surprise, a personality contacted her through the board—and not too gently, either.

"He said he had been hunting for me," Mrs. Vanderhoff began.

"Now this is a character that came through your Ouija board?"

"That came through the Ouija board."

"Long after you moved out of here."

"Yes, several months ago; this year. He said he had been

hunting for me for a long time because I had to take him back—to bring him back to this house—and that I was the only one that could do it."

"What was his name?"

"Nat. And he said he was the master's servant, and that he and his daughter were buried out behind the barn. I asked him various and sundry questions, but mainly he wanted to come back because his daughter was still here, and I said, 'Well, why are you causing these people all of this trouble? You never caused us any.' He replied, 'Well, you have never lain at the top and tasted the unhappiness.' I said, 'Are you telling me your room was in the tower?' He said, 'yes,' and he had to get back, because his daughter was still there. I said, 'I wouldn't consider taking you back as long as you misbehave.' He replied, 'I will misbehave because I will drive them out.'"

"While you were living here, did you have any experiences?"

"Only when we remodeled. We put in this bay window across here."

"What happened when you remodeled?"

"At night there were the most tremendous noises, and it sounded as though they were throwing furniture around, and every morning at two o'clock the garage doors banged up and down. We had a friend sleeping in the back room, and one morning I said, 'What were you doing with a girl in your room?' And he said, 'I had no girl in my room.'"

"Do you remember who it was that slept in that room, this friend?"

"Colonel Powell."

"Did he know anything unusual about the house beforehand?"

"No, he said he had no one in his room. Then the next night we heard all this racket out there and rushed out to catch whatever it was, and the table had been moved in the kitchen. He fell over this table and hurt his leg."

"Interestingly," commented Mrs. Dickey now, "we got a communicator named Emma, that came through on the board."

"When? This is important."

"Since you were here the last time. We never had Emma before, but we don't play with the board much anymore because you said to leave it alone."

"When was the first time the name Emma came to you?"

"After your first visit. But we got no messages, we just kept getting this name."

"Prior to our visit today, has anybody discussed with you the name Emma?"

"No."

"Therefore, the Emma you got on the Ouija board is separate from what we got here today."

There was a moment of silence, then Mrs. Dickey resumed talking about the past of the house. "Indians were around here along time ago as this was part of the Indian trail. Also, the foundations of the older house are underneath the fireplace."

"I see a door, where the man was," Ethel said and scowled. "He was standing about here, when I first saw him, and he went through right about there. I think there were two rooms here."

"Is this correct?" I asked Mrs. Dickey.

"Correct," she replied. "It was divided."

Ethel suddenly seemed to be listening to something or someone. "I don't think you'll get this disturbance, but I keep hearing a sound like moaning, high moaning—ooh—ooh."

With Ethel leading us, we ascended the narrow stairs to the top room.

"What do you think of this room?" I asked the medium.

"I get a different person up here altogether. Male. High forehead, hair parted, longish face, fairly good-sized nose. Looks like an Irishman. Seems to have a beard on, and then takes it off."

"Is he connected with the other situation?"

"No, he's dressed differently. I get the name Pat. I think he went out with a heart condition."

Ethel stopped at the desk in the corner.

"Somebody sat here and wrote."

"Is a writer connected with this house?" I asked Mrs. Dickey.

"I think you're talking about Salisbury, the man who built this house. He was tall, and lean, and very erudite. He wrote a diary of his Civil War experiences."

"The noise that came when you changed things about the house, I think came from the Irishman, Pat."

It was getting late in the day and I wanted to get Ethel Meyers home in time for dinner, so we said good-bye and just caught the New York flight. Once in the air, I had a chance to think over some of the things that had happened this eventful afternoon. For one thing, a whole array of characters from the past had been identified, more or less, by my medium. Most outstanding, in an evidential sense, was the fact that the name Emma had been received by those in the house prior to Ethel's coming and the trance session with her in which the name Emma was disclosed. Despite my misgivings about the use of the Ouija board, I have always held that on occasion true psychic material can come in this manner. Later, I was to learn that Lucy Dickey was indeed a budding medium, and that it was her presence in the house that made the Ouija board work. It is possible that the young people living with her might have added some psychic power to it, but the essential catalyst was Mrs. Dickey herself.

It is not remarkable but rather pleasing in a scientific way that Ethel Meyers pinpointed immediately upon arrival the area of the main disturbances. The staircase and the door leading to an area that had been rearranged structurally was indeed where the figure of the man had appeared and where most of the noises had originated. We had inspected the premises from the cellar to the top, especially around the area of the chimney, which roughly took up the center of the house. There had been no rational explanation for any loud noises in the area. Nothing was loose, nothing could have caused a loud noise, rattling, movements of objects, or anything of the kind, so eloquently and distinctively described by several witnesses.

The following day, Mrs. Dickey wrote me a note thanking us for coming out. She promised to look into the background of the house somewhat more thoroughly at the Library of Congress.

"I believe I have exhausted the usefulness of the Fairfax County Courthouse records. If I can help you in any way, let me know. I will be happy to pick you up and chauffeur you if Nicole is busy. I believe fully in your work, and I like your approach. You leave behind a string of grateful admirers. Your friend, Lucy."

I thanked Lucy Dickey and instructed her to be alert to any further manifestations, should they occur. With so large a cast of spectral characters in the house, it was possible that we had not dislodged all of them. As a matter of fact, it was highly likely that we might have overlooked one or the other.

When I returned from Europe I received another letter from her, dated September 25, 1969. Mrs. Dickey wrote: "I have noticed in the past few months a growing sensitivity and psychic development in myself. Things are happening to me I do not quite understand. Nothing further has happened with our 'friends' in the house. No news from them at all. The house remains for sale."

Mrs. Dickey had previously mentioned her intent to sell the house.

But we had not heard the last of ghostly Adam. On

December 9, 1969, I had an urgent report from Lucy Dickey. There had been a party at the house for young college-age friends of her daughter. One of the young men had gone upstairs to one of the bathrooms. As he was going about his business, he turned to find a man staring at him from behind. Terrified, he rushed downstairs. He had, of course, never been told about the ghost or any details about the specter's appearance. Nevertheless, he described Adam in every detail, from the white, full-sleeved shirt and baggy black knicker-type pants on to the expression in his eyes. But despite this frightening encounter, there was nothing further to disturb Lucy's peace in the house: no more uncanny noises, no spectral appearances. Only one thing—she had difficulty selling the house. The more she tried, the less it worked. It was almost as if someone, unseen perhaps, prevented the house from being sold—perhaps because they had come to like Lucy and considered her a channel of expression. To make things worse, her husband was still in part of the house despite the fact that they had obtained a divorce. Lucy was extremely unhappy about the situation, and desired nothing more than to sell the house, although she loved every inch of it.

Time went on, and finally a buyer for the house showed up. Overjoyed, Lucy Dickey advised me of the fact that ownership was soon to pass into other hands. She had already taken an apartment in Washington and was ready to move. Naturally, she had told the new owner, a Ms. Mary Jane Lightner, all about the ghosts in the house and what the Dickeys and their predecessors had gone through with them. Ms. Lightner was not a believer in such things as ghostly phenomena, but her curiosity was aroused since, after all, this was now going to be her home. Together the two ladies asked me to send them a good psychic to see whether there was indeed anything left in the house or whether perhaps all was quiet.

I advised that a medium might very well relive past

impressions without this proving the continued presence of a ghost or ghosts. It is sometimes very difficult to distinguish between an imprint from the past and actual living spirit entities.

I sent them John Reeves, a teacher turned medium, with whom I had been much impressed. On May 10, 1970, John Reeves went to Washington and over to see the two ladies at the house in Vienna. He knew nothing whatsoever about the circumstances or about the ladies, merely that he was to look at an old house and give his impressions.

Immediately upon entering the downstairs of the house, he went to the fireplace and disclosed that there had been a murder and much violence in that area. He then described a woman, thin, with straight hair in back, wearing a long dark grey dress. He felt this was in the 1860s, and that the woman was not the only spirit on the premises. "A man killed his wife's lover in this passageway," John Reeves intoned, "and then he hanged himself." While the two ladies shuddered, the medium continued describing what he felt had happened in the house. "I can see blood drop from his mouth, on both sides of his mouth."

"How was the man killed?" Lucy wanted to know.

John Reeves pointed at a set of heavy black andirons. "One of the andirons was used to kill," he explained. "Somehow these events put a curse on this house. There may also be another separate murder in one of the rooms," he added cheerfully.

Ms. Lightner had heard quite enough. "Mrs. Dickey must have told you," she said to the medium. It seemed impossible for John Reeves to come up with the same story Ethel Johnson Meyers had come up with a year earlier, without some sort of collusion, she thought. Lucy Dickey assured her that there was no such thing. John Reeves knew nothing of either the house or Mrs. Meyers' and my work in the house. While the ladies shook their heads, Reeves left and went back to New York.

Were Adam and Lewis one and the same person? We know that Leon was the name of the other man, whose bones still presumably rot in the garden behind the barn. The woman's name was Emma. Adam—or Lewis, whichever he was—no longer can claim that the secret is all his. Thanks to John Reeves, and of course Ethel Meyers, we know that his problem was one of the oldest problems in the world. Cherchez la femme. A debt of honor had apparently been paid and all was not quiet at Windover down in Vienna, Virginia.

A short time later I wanted to visit the White House and made one more attempt to get into the Lincoln Bedroom. There was some indication that I might get permission, and I called upon Lucy Dickey to come along and serve as my medium for the occasion since she lived in Washington.

"Me? A medium?" she replied, taken aback. "Why, I never thought of myself in that manner!"

I sensed a disturbed feeling in the way she put it. Had I frightened her? Patiently I explained that her psychic experiences at Windover made it plain that she had mediumistic abilities. She didn't have to be a professional medium to be classified as psychic.

She breathed easier after that, but I couldn't get her to go with me to the Lincoln Bedroom. Even if I had gotten permission, I am sure Lucy Dickey would have avoided meeting Mr. Lincoln. And who is to blame her? After all she had had quite enough with Adam, Leon, Emma, Martha, and Morgan.

A CRIME OF PASSION IN NEW ORLEANS

ean Hatton came from a family in which the psychic had been in evidence for several generations—things such as pre-cognitive dreams and clairvoyance. Foreknowledge of events or places had been rampant on her mother's side of the family, and as a pre-teen Jean had some ESP experiences. Around forty years of age at the time the events related here occurred, she and her husband lived in the heart of New Orleans. She was a professional musician for a while and had taught music in high school for five years. Her mother's family was Irish, Dutch, and Native American, while her father's side of the family cane from Wales, England, and Ireland. Thus a predominance of Celtic elements in her background might have been responsible for her readiness to accept the realty of psychic phenomena. At any rate when she moved from her childhood home in San Antonio to New Orleans she made friends with a married couple who lived on Decatur Street in the French Quarter. The very first time she tried to enter their apartment she almost tripped. She felt a kind of elastic force trying to keep her out as if she were not welcome. The house in which the couple's apartment was in was a very old house. The house and some of the adjoining ones were among the few that hadn't been destroyed in the fires so common in this part of town. At least two hundred years old, the house in question was one of the finest examples of colonial architecture.

Forcing her way through the invisible curtain, Jean then entered the apartment. She saw an old fireplace against one wall facing a bedroom door. The entrance was to the right. To the left were the living room and a long narrow room probably used as a pantry or wardrobe. The owner of the apartment tried to tell her that something very tragic had occurred there, but before he could do so Jean herself told him the story. How she could have known this was as much a mystery to her as it was to her host. But she pointed at a clock and insisted that it would always stop at three o'clock in the morning because it was then that "something had happened." Before she knew what she was doing, Jean found herself standing by the fireplace looking at the clock. Then she turned toward the door, resting her hands on the mantelpiece. She seemed to be wearing a white gown with full sleeves, probably a nightgown. At this moment she clearly heard steps. A door was opened and through it came the "wrong man." The man she saw now clairvoyantly was tall, with unruly gray hair and a deepset-type face. He wore a silk hat and a black cape. She knew then that the woman was trying to express herself through her; she knew that she had been stabbed where she stood and had fallen in front of the fireplace.

At this moment Jean came out of her semi-trance. It was all she could get, but her host assured her that this impression was not a fantasy. He explained that he had seen such a woman walk at night, her bloody hands crossed at her breasts. Both he and is wife had frequently heard the footsteps of someone coming up the stairs to their third-floor apartment. One night his wife, Sheri, was home alone and playing old folk songs on her guitar, when she looked up and saw the two entities standing there in the door. She was not afraid so she kept on looking at them before they faded away.

It became clear to the owner of the apartment that something very drastic had occurred at a previous time. But they could not figure it out and learned to live with their spectral visitors. One day the husband was up in the attic, above their apartment, clearing up some flooring. To his horror he discovered two human skeletons underneath. Hastily closing the door to the attic behind him, he took the two skeletons and quietly buried them. He decided not to report the matter to the police after all since it might have been something that had occurred a long time ago and calling attention to it now might draw unfavorable attention to him and the house. From that moment the psychic phenomena stopped abruptly. But the owner of the apartment was not satisfied until he knew what had caused the two skeletons to be buried in so unusual a place as the attic of the apartment.

He started to dig into the place of the house and asked questions around the area. As far as he could determine, the woman in the nightgown had lived in the apartment, and once while she was waiting for her lover the door had opened and, instead of her lover, her husband came through it. He had discovered the relationship and had come to kill her. After he murdered her, he waited until her lover arrived and killed him, too. Then he hid the bodies in the attic.

Silently the host handed Jean a knife to touch and psychometrize, that is to say, read from it what could be gleaned of its past. As if she had been handed a glowing piece of coal she dropped it immediately. She could not touch it no matter how often she tried. The knife was an old knife of nondescript appearance, with a discolored blade and of no particular merit. Almost hysterical and sobbing, Jean assured her host that it was the knife that had been used to murder the woman. He nodded. He himself had found the blade among the bricks of the fireplace.

A HOUSE FULL OF SPECTERS

*T*oni S. was a young woman of good educational background, a psychologist by profession, working for a large business concern, and not given to daydreaming or fantasizing. She was the daughter of Mrs. Elizabeth K., or rather the daughter of Mrs. K.'s second marriage. The thrice-married Mrs. K. was a North Carolina lady, a socially prominent woman who had traveled extensively. Neither of these ladies was the kind of person who pulls out a Ouija board to while away the time, or to imagine that every shadow cast upon the wall was necessarily a ghost. Far from it; but both ladies were taken aback by what transpired in their old house at the town of East La Porte, built on very old ground.

Originally built about fifty years earlier, it was to be a home for Mrs. K.'s father, who then owned a large lumber company, and the tract of timber surrounding the house extended all the way across the Blue Ridge Parkway. Undoubtedly, an older dwelling had stood on the same spot, for Mrs. K. unearthed what appeared to be the remains of a much older structure. The house was renovated and a second story built on, about thirty-five years before. At that time her father had lost one leg as the result of an automobile accident, and retired from his lumber mill activities to East La Porte, where he intended to spend his remaining years in peace and quiet. He had liked the climate to begin with, and then there was a sawmill nearby, which he could oversee at the same time. The house was a double-boxed frame house, perhaps fifty-by-fifty square, containing around fifteen rooms.

Mrs. K.'s family referred to it as "the summer cottage," even though it was a full-sized house; but they had other houses that they visited from time to time, and the house at East La Porte was merely one of their lesser properties. Downstairs there was a thirty-by-fifteen foot reception room, richly covered with chestnut from Furnace Creek, one of the sawmills owned by the family. It was in this room that Mrs. K.'s father eventually passed on.

The house itself was built entirely from lumber originating in one of the family's sawmills. There was a center hall downstairs and two thirty-foot rooms, then three smaller rooms: a bath, a card room, and what the family referred to as a sleeping porch. On the other side of the center hall was a lounge, a kitchen and a laundry porch. Running alongside the south and east walls of the house was a veranda. Upstairs was reached by a very gentle climb, with the stairs in the middle, and as one climbs the steps there was a bedroom at the head of the stairs, and in back of the stairs two more bedrooms, then a bathroom, and finally a storage room; to the left of the stairs were three bedrooms.

The attic was merely a structure to hold up the roof, but it did not contain any rooms. There was a cellar, but it contained only a furnace. Although the acreage surrounding the house ran to about sixty acres, only three acres belonged to the house proper. All around the house, there was nothing but wilderness and to get to the nearest town, one needed a car!

Mrs. K. enjoyed traveling, and didn't mind living in so many residences; in fact, she considered the house at East La Porte merely a way station in her life. She was born in Alaska, where the family also had a sawmill. Her early years were spent traveling from one sawmill to another, accompanying her parents on business trips.

Under the circumstances, they were never very long in residence at the house in East La Porte. Any attempt to find out about the background of the land on which the house stood proved fruitless. This was Cherokee territory, but there was little written history concerning the time before the Cherokees. Anything remotely connected with psychic phenomena was simply not discussed in the circles in which Mr. K. grew up.

The first time Mrs. K. noticed anything peculiar about the house was after her father had passed away. She and her father had been particularly close, since her mother had died when she was a small child. That particular day she was sitting at her late father's desk in the part of the house where her father had died. The furniture had been rearranged in the room, and the desk stood where her father's bed had previously stood. Her father was on her mind, and so she thought it was all her imagination when she became aware of a distinctive sound as if someone were walking on crutches, coming down the hall.

Since Mrs. K. knew for a fact that she was the only person in the house at the time, she realized that something out of the ordinary was happening. As the footsteps came closer she recognized her father's tread. And then she heard her father's familiar voice say, "Baby" coming from the direction of the door. It gave her a feeling of great peace, for she had been troubled by emotional turmoil in her life. She felt that her late father was trying to console her, and give her spiritual strength.

Nothing happened until about a year later. It was August, and she had been in New York for awhile. As she was coming down the stairs of the house, she found herself completely enveloped with the fragrance of lilacs. She had not put any perfume on, and there were no lilacs blooming in August. No one was seen, and yet Mrs. K. felt a presence, although she was sure it was benign, and loving.

A short time later she was sitting at a desk in what used to be her father's study upstairs, thinking about nothing in particular. Again she was startled by the sound of footsteps, but this time they were light steps, certainly not her father's. Without thinking, she called out to her daughter, "Oh, Toni, is that you?" telling her daughter that she was upstairs.

But then the steps stopped, and no one came. Puzzled, Mrs. K. went to the head of the stairs, called out again, but when she saw no one she realized it was not a person of flesh and blood that had walked upon the stairs.

During the same month, Mrs. K.'s daughter Toni was also at the house. Her first experience with the unseen happened that month, in an upstairs bedroom.

She was asleep one night when someone shook her hard and said, "Hey you!" Frightened, she did not open her eyes, yet with her inner eyes, she "saw" a man of about fifty years of age, but she was much too frightened to actually look. Instead she dove underneath the covers and lay there with her eyes shut. There was nothing further that night.

In the fall of the same year, 1962, Toni decided to have a pajama party and spend the night with a group of friends. Her mother had gone to bed because of a cold. Toni and her friends returned to the house around eleven-thirty from bowling. They were downstairs, talking about various things, when all of a sudden one of Toni's girlfriends said, "Toni, your mother is calling you."

Toni went out into the hallway, turning on the lights as she approached the stairs. Footsteps were coming down the stairs, audible not only to her but to her two girlfriends, who had followed her into the house. And then they heard a voice out of the clear blue sky, calling out, "Toni, it is time to go to bed." It was a voice Toni had never heard before. She went up the stairs and into her mother's room. But her mother was fast asleep, and had not been out of bed. The voice had been a woman's voice, but it had sounded strangely empty, as if someone had been speaking to her from far away.

The following year, Toni was married and left the house. Under the circumstances, Mrs. K. decided to sublease part of the house to a tenant. This turned out to be a pleasant woman by the name of Alice H., and her husband. The lady had been injured and was unable to go far up the mountain where she and her husband were building a summer home at the time. Although Mrs. K. and her new tenants were not associated in any way except that they were sharing the same house, she and Alice H. became friendly after a while. One afternoon Alice H. came to Mrs. K.'s apartment in order to invite her to have supper with her and her husband that night. She knew that Mrs. K. was in her apartment at the time because she heard her light footsteps inside the apartment. When there was no reply from inside the apartment, Alice was puzzled so she descended to the ground floor, thinking that perhaps Mrs. K. was downstairs.

Sure enough, as she arrived downstairs, she saw a shadow of what she assumed to be Mrs. K.'s figure walking along the hallway. She followed this shadowy woman all the way from the ground floor guest room through the bath into Mrs. K.'s bedroom and then through another hallway and back to the bedroom. All the time she saw the shadowy figure, she also heard light footsteps. But when she came to the bedroom again, it suddenly got very cold and she felt all the blood rush to her head. She ran back to her husband in their own apartment and informed him that there was a stranger in Mrs. K.'s rooms.

But there was no one in the house at the time, except themselves, for Mrs. K. had gone off to Ashville for the day. The experience shook Alice H. to the point where she could no longer stand being in the house, and shortly afterward she and her husband left for another cottage.

In August of the same year, Toni S. returned to her mother's house. By now she was a married lady, and she was coming only for a visit. Her husband was a car dealer, in business with his father. At the time of the incident he was not in the house. It was raining outside, and Toni was cleaning the woodwork in the house.

Suddenly her Pekinese dog came running down the stairs, nearly out of her mind with terror, barking at the top of her lungs. Toni thought a mouse had frightened the dog, so she picked her up and proceeded up the stairs. But the dog broke away from her and ran behind the door. All of a sudden, Toni felt very cold. She kept walking down the hall and into the room where there was a desk standing near the window. Someone was going through papers on her desk, as if looking for a certain piece of paper, putting papers aside and continuing to move them! But there was no one there. No one, that is, to be seen. Yet the papers were moving as if someone were actually shuffling them. It was two o'clock in the afternoon; the light was fairly bright.

Suddenly, one letter was pulled out of the piles of papers on the desk, as if to catch her attention. Toni picked it up and read it. It was a letter her father had sent her in February, at the time she got married, warning her that the marriage would not work out, after all, and to make sure and call him if anything went wrong. Things had gone wrong since, and Toni understood the significance of what she had just witnessed. At that very moment, the room got warm again, and everything returned to normal. But who was it standing at her desk, pulling out her father's letter for her? The one person, who had been close to her while he was in the flesh, was her grandfather.

During Toni's visit at the house, her husband, who was to be her ex-husband, also had some uncanny experiences. Somebody would wake him in the middle of the night by calling out, "Wake up!" or "Hey you!" This went on night after night; one night both Toni and her husband awoke around two in the morning because of the sound of loud laughing, as if a big party were going on downstairs.

Toni thought that the neighbors were having a party, and decided to go down and tell them to shut up. She looked out the window and realized that the neighbors were also fast asleep. So she picked up her dog and went downstairs, and as she arrived at the bottom of the stairs she saw a strange light, while the laughing kept going on and on. There were voices, as if many people were talking all at once, having a social. In anger, Toni called out to them to shut up, she wanted to go to sleep, and all of a sudden, the house was quiet, quiet as the grave. Evidently Southern ghosts have good manners!

After her daughter left, Mrs. K. decided to sublease part of the house to a group of young men from a national fraternity, students at a nearby university. One of the students, Mitchell, was sleeping in a double bed, and he was all alone in the house. Because the heat wasn't turned up, it being rather costly, he decided to sleep in a sleeping bag, keeping warm in this manner. He went to sleep with his head at the head of the bed, which meant due east, and his feet going due west. When he awoke, he found himself facing in the opposite direction, with his head where his feet had been, and vice versa. It didn't surprise the young man, though, because from the very first when his fraternity brothers had moved into the house, they had heard the sounds of an unseen person walking up and down the stairs.

One of their teachers, a pilot who had been a colonel in the Korean War, also had an experience at the house. One day while he was staying there, he was walking up the stairs and when he reached about the halfway mark, someone picked him up by the scruff of his neck and pushed him up the rest of the way to the landing.

But the night to remember was Halloween Eve, 1963. Mrs. K. was in the house, and the night was living up to its reputation: it sounded as if someone with manacles on were moving about. Mrs. K. was downstairs, sleeping in one of the bunk beds, and a noise came from an upstairs hall. This went on for about two hours straight. It sounded as if someone with a limp were pulling himself along, dragging a heavy chain. Mrs. K. was puzzled about this, since the noise did not sound anything like her father. She looked into the background of the area and discovered that in the pre-colonial period there had been some Spanish settlers in the area, most of whom kept slaves.

Toni S. took her involvement with hauntings in stride. She had had psychic experiences ever since she could remember; nothing frightening, you understand, only such things as events before they actually happen—if someone was going to be sick in the family, for instance, or who might be calling. Entering old houses was always a risky business for her. She picked up vibrations from the past and sometimes she simply couldn't stand what she felt and had to leave at once.

But she thought she had left the more uncanny aspects of the hauntings behind when she went to New York to work. Somehow she wound up residing in a house that was 110 years old. After a while, she became aware of an old man who liked sitting down on her bed. She couldn't actually see him, but he appeared to her more like a shadow. So she asked some questions, but nobody ever died in the apartment and it was difficult for Toni to accept the reality of the phenomena under the circumstances. As a trained psychologist, she had to approach all this on a skeptical level and yet there did not seem to be any logical answers.

Soon afterward she became aware of footsteps where no one was walking, and of doors closing by themselves, which were accompanied by the definite feeling of another personality present in the rooms. On checking with neighbors upstairs who had lived in the house for seventeen years, Toni discovered that they too had heard the steps and doors closing by themselves, but they had put no faith in ghosts and dismissed the matter as simply an old structure settling. Toni tried her innate psychic powers and hoped that the resident ghost would communicate with her. She began to sense that it was a woman with a very strong personality. By a process of elimination Toni came to the conclusion that the last of the original owners of the house, a Mrs. A., who had been a student of the occult, was the only person who could be the presence she was feeling in the rooms.

Toni didn't mind sharing her rooms with a ghost, except for the fact that appliances in the house had a way of breaking down without reason. Then, too, she had a problem with some of her friends; they complain of feeling extremely uncomfortable and cold, and of being watched by someone they cannot see. What was she to do? But then Toni recalled how she had lived through the frightening experiences at East La Porte, North Carolina, and somehow come to terms with the haunts there. No ordinary Long Island ghost was going to dispossess her! With that resolved, Toni decided to ignore the presence as much as she could and go about her business—the business of the living.